Ngaio Marsh

A Life

EX LIBRIS

VIRTUS NOBILITAT

MARSH

Ngaio Marsh

A Life

By
Margaret Lewis

Poisoned Pen Press
May 1998

ISBN 1-890208-05-1

Manufactured in the United States of America

Poisoned Pen Press
Publisher, Susan Malling
6962 E. First Avenue, Suite 103
Scottsdale, AZ 85251

TABLE OF CONTENTS

LIST OF ILLUSTRATIONS

33 Holding her award as Grand Master of the Mystery Writers of America. *(Estate of Ngaio Marsh / Bruce Harding)*
34 The writer at work in her armchair. *(Condé Nast Publications)*

In text
p.80 Sketch for 'Over the Edge of the Earth'. *(Miss Pamela Mann)*
p.142-3 The director's production script for *Julius Caesar*. *(Alexander Turnbull* Library)
p.196 A sketch from the ms of *Death at the Dolphin*. *(Mugar Memorial Library)*

On Cover
1 Ngaio as a young child with doll.
2 Ngaio visited Japan on her world tour in 1960. By now she was an internationally celebrated writer. *(Estate of Ngaio Marsh)*

Half Title Page
1 Ngaio's personal bookplate.

FOREWORD

'It's always fun to think of Ngaio,' said one of her oldest friends to me as I was beginning to write this biography. The friend was a 'Lamprey', a member of that much-lampooned family who appear in *Death of a Peer*. And it *was* fun to think about Dame Ngaio Marsh: her dramatic appearance, her deep voice, her sense of humour, her swashbuckling way with young actors, her vulnerability.

Living in the north of England as I do, and writing about someone who spent most of her life in New Zealand, meant that extensive travel was necessary. There were two lengthy research trips to New Zealand to work in the Ngaio Marsh archive in Wellington and to meet people who had known her, and other contacts were made in Paris, Rome and the United States. I was fortunate that the Estate had agreed to this book when they did, as some of Ngaio's closest friends were still alive and I had the opportunity to talk to them. I know that this would be a much poorer book without their insights and advice.

Many of Ngaio's theatre protégés left New Zealand to further their careers abroad, and it is very satisfying to note the success of actors like James Laurenson and Sam Neill who first trod the boards in productions by Ngaio Marsh in Christchurch. At one time I thought that nearly every citizen of New Zealand had taken part in a play produced by Ngaio Marsh, and I was very surprised to discover that in her native land she was remembered almost entirely for her work in theatre, not as a writer of 32 celebrated detective novels.

A new generation of New Zealanders is looking more widely at Ngaio's contribution to their culture, and many of them joined together in Christchurch for a symposium in 1995 to mark the centenary of her birth. At a similar celebration in England, Baroness James (P.D. James) spoke at New Zealand House about her high regard for the writing skills of Ngaio Marsh. Ngaio's home in

Christchurch opened to the public the following year, and visitors can now enjoy the peaceful house and garden that she loved so much. The recent formation of the Ngaio Marsh Society will ensure that readers who admire her approach to crime fiction can share in the stimulus of an international group.

Writing a biography of such a private person as Ngaio Marsh was a challenge, but biography is a challenge. The biographer creates something that did not exist before, making something new from fragments that did not previously coalesce. How I cherished the friends who carefully kept her letters, producing them cautiously from ring binders, boxes and cupboards. Without them I would not have been able to share with readers the flavour of Ngaio's salty wit and her comic descriptions of everyday events. But even to friends, this was still Ngaio's public face. The biographer can never claim truly to know another person, no matter how hard the effort or extensive the research. As Mark Twain wisely said, 'Biography is the clothes and buttons of the man, but the real biography of a man is lived in his head twenty-four hours a day, and *that* you can never know.'

Margaret Lewis
Hexham, Northumberland
January, 1998

PREFACE

In a small archive in St Margaret's College, Christchurch, New Zealand, can be found a worn stick of crimson greasepaint, a fountain pen and a battered wooden box of paints, with brushes and mixing dishes well used. Together, they represent the three aspects of the life of Dame Ngaio Marsh that she valued most: her work as a Shakespearean producer, her writing and her painting.

In the theatre, her exciting interpretations of Shakespeare have created a legend in the Antipodes. Her thirty-two novels continue to delight those who enjoy an elegant telling of an ingenious tale that just happens to involve violent death among an interesting group of characters. And her painting, especially her paintings of the Southern Alps of New Zealand, remained a love that never left her, even when life became filled with other activities. Through her fiction these interests often blended; the New Zealand landscape held her closely and formed the backdrop to a number of novels, and the mysteries set in a variety of theatres from the North Island to the banks of the Thames provided an opportunity to depict a world that always gave her pleasure. Her fictional detective, Roderick Alleyn, marries a painter, Agatha Troy, allowing the third strand of Ngaio Marsh's life to be woven into her books.

Ngaio Marsh is more likely to be remembered for her novels than for her contribution to New Zealand theatre or her painting, even though all her life she maintained that the theatre was her first love. She was enormously influential in encouraging the performing arts in her own land, but essentially the productions of Shakespeare that brought so much pleasure to a Christchurch audience will remain an achievement limited to time and place. As the memory of those productions fades, new directors and actors will come forward, building on the foundations she laid. The work she did has already become part of the cultural history of New Zealand, along with the contributions of many other talented men and women who shared with Ngaio a conviction that their country had to take notice of 'the things of the mind'.

Whether Ngaio herself felt that she had used her talents wisely is difficult to tell. Endowed with many artistic gifts, in a new country which in its early years placed a limited value on the creative spirit, Ngaio was entirely confident only about her work with student actors. Even as a novelist whose work spanned nearly fifty years, she was unsure of her achievement, struggling with plots, waiting anxiously to hear from her agents, grateful beyond belief for praise. Nevertheless, of the four Queens of Crime who dominated the 1930s—Margery Allingham, Agatha Christie, Ngaio Marsh and Dorothy L. Sayers—Ngaio Marsh reigns supreme for excellence of style and characterisation. She expanded the genre in a fresh and creative way, adding psychological depth and a welcome strand of humour to the basic murder investigation. Even today, when the classic Golden Age formula of detective fiction has diversified along many different paths, the novels of Ngaio Marsh continue to be republished for a new generation of crime fiction readers. Like a vintage car, or her own cherished Jaguar XK150, they have ceased to be old-fashioned and have the timeless qualities that always go with sound craftsmanship and good style.

Writing to friends just before she died, about her last novel, *Light Thickens,* and the profound uncertainties that she felt about the manuscript, she concluded characteristically, 'I'm glad I tried'. What better epitaph could anyone request? Except, perhaps, the words of the late Sir Anthony Quayle, actor, director and a friend for many years, who wrote about Ngaio, 'She was a generous, intelligent, warm-hearted spirit and made the world a richer place'.

CHAPTER 1

A Pioneer Heritage: 1895–1909

The city of Christchurch, on the South Island of New Zealand, lies on a flat plain, backed by the Cashmere Hills. To the south-west stretches the long spine of the Southern Alps, whose dramatic peaks thrust abruptly from the Canterbury Plains like a row of mountains propelled into a toy theatre. The tiny safe harbour of Lyttelton lies south-east of the city and it was to this anchorage, ringed with hills, that the first four ships bearing settlers to an almost empty coast arrived in 1850. On 16 December the *Charlotte Jane* (620 tons) and the *Randolph* (761 tons) anchored in the sheltered bay, followed by the *Sir George Seymour* (850 tons) on 17 December, and the *Cressy* (720 tons) ten days later. These tiny ships (the *Charlotte Jane* was only 131 feet long and 32 feet wide) had carried 782 men, women and children from England and had been at sea for between 99 and 110 days. The image of these people, cramped and tired after long weeks at sea, climbing up the steep hills above the harbour and looking out across the Canterbury Plains is one that Ngaio Marsh referred to many times. This was her cultural heritage; born on 23 April 1895, she was only forty-five years removed from these early pioneers.

The establishment of Christchurch, under the control of the Canterbury Association, is a fascinating example of nineteenth-century social engineering. The settlers were all members of the Church of England, and were chosen to represent a cross-section of British life. The aim of the Anglican gentry who established the Association was to 'alleviate the misery of the British industrial poor, but order migration with the proper balance between squire, merchant, artisan and labourer in a re-creation of the provincial and agricultural ideal'.[1] The assumption of the worthy gentlemen who sponsored the venture was that men and women who were farmhands and servants in the old world would transplant happily to a similar situation in the new, with no aspirations to rise above their station. Unfortunately the hard-working settlers who arrived on the Canterbury Plains did not all feel completely satisfied with the social stratifications envisaged for them. Servants became so much in demand that they could command high wages, and soon many of them were able to buy property and achieve a degree of independence that would have been impossible in Britain. Lady Barker, writing in *Station Life in New Zealand* in 1866, found that in Christchurch:

> The look and bearing of the immigrants appear to alter soon after they reach the colony. Wages of all sorts are high, and employment a certainty. Some people object to the independence of their manner, but I do not; on the contrary, I like to see the upright gait, the well-fed, healthy look, the decent clothes (even if no one touches his hat to you), instead of the half-starved, depressed appearance, and too often cringing servility of the mass of our English population.[2]

Meanwhile, ambitious squatters were leasing vast tracts of land for sheep farming in areas outside the control of the Canterbury Association, and ultimately they created the only industry that was to provide economic prosperity for the city of Christchurch. These powerful land barons built themselves antipodean mansions, dressed for dinner and held on to their thousands of acres in the face of all attempts to reform the holding of land. Not until the last decade of the nineteenth century was legislation passed to break up large estates and make state loans available for the purchase of small farms.

Ngaio Marsh's grandfather, Edward William Seager, was not one of those who became wealthy through land speculation, farming or mercantile endeavour. He arrived in Lyttelton Harbour aboard the *Cornwall* (580 tons) on 8 December 1851, after a voyage of three months from England. The son of a porter at the Inner Temple at the Inns of Court in London, Edward Seager had met James Fitzgerald, the emigration agent for the Canterbury Association, and with the help of the Rector of St Anne's Church, Soho, managed to persuade him that he was a fit and proper person to join the new colony. In fact, Edward was Nonconformist in religion, not Church of England, but he was an energetic and resourceful man who evidently had no difficulty in securing appropriate backing for his request. Although registered as a blind-maker on the ship's list, Seager was soon appointed as the ship's schoolmaster, with an improvement in his rations and the promise of £25 on arrival in New Zealand.

At the age of twenty-three, with no family ties behind him, Edward Seager had many opportunities from which to choose. The ship bearing his future wife Esther Coster with her parents, seven sisters and one brother had arrived three months earlier. The Costers were farmers from Gloucestershire and took up land outside Christchurch on their arrival in the new colony. When Edward married Esther in June 1854 he was already a dashing and romantic figure in the Colonial Police Force. Having enlisted as a constable, his famous escapade in tracking down the sheep stealer Mackenzie, who had removed 1,000 sheep from the pioneer settlement established by the Rhodes brothers on the Levels south of Christchurch, had made him a popular and well-known figure. His integrity led to the award of additional government appointments, such as Prosecutor under the Arms Act, Inspector of Slaughterhouses and Deputy Immigration Officer. Finally, on promotion to Sergeant-Major in 1858, he was also put in charge of Lyttelton Gaol. As proof of his superior status he was provided with a horse, but the careful colonial authorities recovered the cost by monthly deductions from his salary. He must have felt that it was important for the police to present a dignified and impressive appearance, because in 1860 he designed a new dress uniform for the force consisting of navy-blue fine cloth and gold and silver embroidery, with an impressive cap for senior ranks.

While in charge of the prison at Lyttelton, and later also at Christ-church, Seager was ahead of his time in advocating a regime of fresh air, cleanliness and constructive work. He became increasingly concerned about the number of lunatics who were housed in the jail simply because there was nowhere else for them to go, and his advice led to the construction of a new asylum at Sunnyside, on the outskirts of Christchurch in 1863. With the rank of sub-Inspector in the Armed Constabulary, Edward Seager took up the post of Supervisor of the Asylum, and he moved into his new house with his wife and four children. Shortly after the move, on 27 July 1864, Rose Elizabeth Seager, Ngaio Marsh's mother, was born, giving credence to the joking remark often made by Ngaio that some of her ancestors were born in a lunatic asylum and some in a jail. Six more children were born to Esther at Sunnyside, although two boys died in infancy and the eldest daughter, Julia, died at the age of 23.

Edward Seager is himself the subject of a biography, and his work as the Supervisor of Sunnyside is of considerable interest. Contrary to most nineteenth-century institutions dealing with the mentally ill, Sunnyside placed unusual emphasis on beneficial mental and physical activity, and Seager set up a programme of picnics, amateur dramatics, cricket matches, musical activities and sea bathing. A study of the reasons Seager records for the admission of patients indicates that for many people this kind of social and educational programme, with good food, clean quarters and an orderly regime, was exactly what might be prescribed today by a forward-looking health authority. Many people at Sunnyside had gone mad after long periods of isolation in the bush, and several women are noted as suffering from milk fever, and mental and physical distress at the loss of a child. (Katherine Mansfield's abrasive short story 'The Woman at the Store' vividly evokes the ordeal of a woman whose loneliness borders on insanity after she has been abandoned at an isolated farm with her daughter—a not uncommon situation if the reasons given for admission to Sunnyside during Seager's time as Supervisor are true.) Inevitably, drink was the cause of many a downfall. Very few people failed to respond in some measure to Seager's enlightened management, and the curative rate was high. With the support of his practical and firmly Christian wife who acted as matron and deputy when Seager was away, Sunnyside thrived and became an example to other institutions throughout New Zealand and Australia. An 1873 report on all New Zealand asylums made for the British Government by Dr E. Paley, Inspector of Asylums in Victoria, Australia, found that at Sunnyside the patients were neat and clean, and the food good in quality and cooked with care. Paley 'was much struck with the varied means of amusement provided for the patients'.[3]

Edward Seager was lively and good company, and for a few years he was a friend of the English novelist and painter, Samuel Butler, who emigrated to New Zealand in 1859. Butler's stern, clerical father had insisted that his son prove himself a man before abandoning himself to his alarming artistic tendencies. Butler energetically carved out a sheep station which he called Mesopotamia, located near the head-waters of the Rakaia River in the Southern Alps. Soon he was running a very successful enterprise, and doubled his investment in four years. He returned to England in 1864 with sufficient income to support himself as a student of painting, independent of his father, for several years. But there was more than financial gain to his stay in New Zealand. The landscape of Mesopotamia was the inspiration for his visionary novel *Erewhon* (1872), and he admitted in a letter to his aunt dated 19 September 1861, that 'I felt an immense intellectual growth shortly after leaving England—a growth which has left me a much happier and more liberal-minded man'.[4] Self-knowledge, too, came from a perception of the effects of isolation on the human spirit; he occasionally experienced 'that dreadful doubt as to my own identity—as to the continuity of my past and present existence—which is the first sign of that distraction which comes on those who have lost themselves in the bush . . . and I felt that my power of collecting myself was beginning to be impaired'.[5] But once the sheep station was established, Butler was occasionally able to ride down to Christchurch to seek out congenial company, where he joined the Christchurch Club and wrote some pieces for the Christchurch newspaper *The Press*. He was well aware, however, that in a new colony 'it does not do to speak about John Sebastian Bach's "Fugues" or pre-Raphaelite pictures'.[6] Edward Seager was one of the friends that he invited back to Mesopotamia, and in her autobiography, *Black Beech and Honeydew*, published in 1966, Ngaio tells of her grandfather's visit, and how Butler churlishly dealt with an unwelcome guest by failing to notice that he had fallen from a cart while being bounced across a river on the way to the settlement: 'they met the guest, wet and bruised and plodding desperately towards the Southern Alps. Butler abused him like a pickpocket and could scarcely wait for him to climb back on his perch'.[7]

Seager himself was sociable and loved to entertain. He was a good singer and active in local choirs. He eagerly supported any local theatre initiatives, and early in his career as Supervisor he had a well-equipped theatre installed in one of the buildings at the asylum. Here he organised pantomimes, plays and his favourite conjuring displays, at which he was an expert. The patients acted, made props and generally contributed what they could, as did his daughters, Ngaio's aunts and her mother. An organ valued at £800, the largest in Christchurch, was bought for the recreation hall. Always open to new ideas, Seager became fascinated by the magic lantern and, using private subscriptions, purchased a 'dissolving view apparatus' for £200, which enthralled his patients with projected slides. During 1874 Seager recorded 55 outings or entertainments for his patients.

It was on the stage at Sunnyside that Rose Elizabeth Seager first trod the boards with her father. At the age of twelve she took the part of Susan in Douglas Jerrold's play *Black-Eyed Susan*. The Christchurch *Press* reported that she was slightly nervous but altogether it was a 'capital performance' and Seager seized the opportunity to repeat it as soon as possible in aid of his organ fund.

Given the ingenious and capable way in which Seager and his wife ran Sunnyside, it is difficult to find much support for the medical authorities who insisted in 1888 that he be replaced by a qualified medical practitioner. Both Edward and Esther were compulsorily retired and had to fight hard for compensation. An additional blow was the loss of their home: they had always lived 'on the job' and had never bought a house of their own. Esther, practical and resourceful as always, rented a large house in Sydenham, an industrial suburb of Christchurch, and took in lodgers while Edward eventually obtained the post of Usher at the Supreme Court. In a curious way a cycle had repeated itself, since his post was similar to that of his father in the Inner Temple, London. Later they were able to move into a small house near the Court with spacious gardens bordering the Avon River that flows through Christchurch. Seager ended his days writing his recollections for the local newspapers, taking part in amateur dramatics and giving the occasional magic lantern show. He died in 1922 at the age of ninety-five, having survived his wife by eleven years. The Edward Seager School at Sunnyside bears his name.

Ngaio Marsh wrote of her grandfather in *Black Beech and Honeydew* with great affection. At the same time there is a suspicion that the vague story of her grandfather as an heir in Chancery, with lost ancestral estates in Scotland, meant more to her than the man's real achievements as one of New Zealand's pioneers. Similarly, Ngaio's father, Henry Edmund Marsh, who was sent to New Zealand to seek his fortune, was equipped by Ngaio with trails of aristocratic background that had little substance, involving descent from the piratical de Marisco family of Lundy and from Esquire Marsh who served King Charles II. This sense of family became sufficiently important to her in later life for her to have a Marsh crest imposed on her silver and bookplates.

Born on 9 May 1863, Henry Marsh was the eldest of ten children of a London tea broker, and while the family lived in Streatham, south London, Henry and his younger brother Edward attended Dulwich College as day boys. This grammar school had been founded by the Elizabethan actor Edward Alleyn in 1613. Although Henry was there for only four years, the stories he told his daughter about the school made a considerable impression, and ultimately led to the surname of her fictional detective, Roderick Alleyn. Unfortunately the Marsh family business began to decline in the 1870s, and the children were brought up by their widowed mother in what Ngaio chose to call 'reduced circumstances' in a house in Epping.

Ngaio's father was impractical, absent-minded and, in his later years, bad-tempered, but his daughter was devoted to him. His absent-mindedness led to Ngaio's date of birth initially being given as the day on which he registered her in 1899, when she was already four years old, a confusion that Ngaio seems to have done little to correct in her later years. Henry's intended banking career in England was adversely affected by ill-health as a young man, and he was sent out to South Africa to recover. Shortly after his return to England, his influential uncle William Marsh, then a Vice-Admiral and Administrator of the British colony of Hong Kong, arranged for him to take up a position in the Colonial Bank in New Zealand, and in 1888 he left England for the Antipodes. When this enterprise collapsed, Henry Marsh became a bank clerk in the Bank of New Zealand in Christchurch, and he remained there, in that position, all his life. 'I can imagine nobody less naturally suited to his employment', said Ngaio. But she esteemed him highly:

His rectitude was enormous: I have never known a man with higher principles. He was thrifty. He was devastatingly truthful. In many ways he was wise and he had a kind heart, and a nice sense of humour. He was never unhappy for long: perhaps, in his absent-mindedness, he forgot to be so. I liked him very much. [8]

Henry Marsh's most valuable and tangible achievement was probably the construction of their family home in the Cashmere Hills outside Christchurch, away from the mists and epidemics which arose from the unhealthy drained land where the city was built. When Rose and Henry were married in 1894 they rented a modest house in the genteel suburb of Fendalton, and Ngaio was born there. At that time Henry's income as a bank clerk could just stretch to a maid, May, and a nursemaid, Alice, who looked after Ngaio when she was young. Although the house was small, the garden was extensive, and Ngaio played there with her cat Susie and her spaniel, Tip. Grandfather and Grandmother Seager lived nearby and there were large family gatherings in the house beside the river, and parties where 'Gramps', as she called him, performed conjuring tricks and played the piano for the polka. The move up to the Cashmere Hills, to an unfinished house in an area which had only a few scattered dwellings, was a dramatic one. They lurched across the plain for hours with their belongings piled up on a horse and wagon and then were faced with several months living in bell-tents until the house was completed. The sight of Ngaio, already tall for her age, leaving her tent early in the morning dressed in a smart school uniform of blue serge sailor suit and nautical hat, to be joined by her father in dark suit and wing collar, bound for the bank, must have been bizarre, although she apparently accepted it quite happily. Rose, who had inherited the Seager ability to cope in all circumstances, coped.

Ngaio was still a small child when the move into their new house took place, and she found the wild country that surrounded them tremendously exciting. An early photograph shows a simple, square, wooden house, with an open veranda, half-way up a steep, bare hillside that had been newly planted with tiny trees. The veranda was always Ngaio's preferred bedroom in summer and remained so until she was over fifty. The house was designed by Samuel Hurst Seager, Rose's cousin, whose architectural work in Christchurch is now carefully preserved. In later years the three-quarter-acre garden was painstakingly developed by Ngaio who, as soon as she could afford it, always had a paid gardener. The garden now stretches below the house in a series of elaborate terraces with flowerbeds full of roses and English shrubs, as well as native trees and plants. Ngaio looked on this house, then called 'Marton Cottage', as 'the fourth member of our family' and, although it was much altered throughout the century, its personality remained the same. The family never moved from here, and Ngaio died there on 18 February 1982, at the age of 86. It is still owned by her family and is furnished much as she left it.

There seems little doubt that Rose and Henry Marsh were very contented in their life together: 'I married as fine a woman as any man could deserve, and although poor we were very happy',[9] wrote Henry just before he died. They married when Henry was thirty and Rose twenty-nine, and an important bond was their shared interest in amateur theatricals; indeed, they first met while acting together in a production in Christchurch. Their only child, Edith Ngaio Marsh, was born a year after their marriage. It was not uncommon at that time for children to be given a Maori name among their other names, and Rose gave her daughter the name of a native shrub with a small white flower which grows prolifically near the coast. Ngaio quickly became the favoured name and there is no evidence of her ever having been called Edith.

Ngaio's earliest memories involved watching and hearing her mother rehearsing in the house: 'there was almost always a play toward in our small family'. Rose Marsh had obtained plenty of experience in acting and organising theatrical events from her father at Sunnyside, and had undoubtedly become a talented performer. In 1890, before her marriage, she had been invited by a professional company led by George Milne to join them in the role of Lady Macbeth:

Dear Madam

I have heard of your fine abilities as an amateur actress, both here and in Dunedin, and write to inquire whether you would so favour me as to appear one night with me? Have you ever tried Lady Macbeth? If so, would you undertake that role? It would excite much interest, and I should be very much obliged. It needs something in this city to galvanize the public into interest in Shakespeare. [10]

Fifty years later, Rose Seager's daughter was also to attempt to galvanise Christchurch with Shakespeare, and devoted a great deal of her life to doing so. The Christchurch weekly *Press* gave high praise to Milne's production and singled out Miss Seager for special commendation:

> Macbeth was fortunate in his Lady, on this occasion. . . . Miss Seager showed very high qualities; she looked the gracious spouse, and was in speech the tempting devil, both to perfection. The scathing taunts by which Macbeth is spurred to his first crime, were delivered with intense naturalness and power, one felt that that was how such a woman would have spoken, and was not surprised to see Macbeth moved in consequence. As for the sleep-walking scene it was deeply impressive. Lady Macbeth, entering, wore a true face of tragedy, drawn, gaunt, frozen with horror . . .[11]

Rose Seager declined another offer to join a professional company which was to go to England, but she was sufficiently self-confident to travel with them to Australia and to sample the life of a company of actors on tour. The itinerant life did not appeal to her, however, and on returning to New Zealand she married the gentle-faced Henry Marsh and used her very considerable acting talent as an amateur. Ngaio felt embarrassed and rather frightened at hearing her mother rehearsing her lines in the house, yet she 'loved to hear all the theatre-talk, the long discussions on visiting actors, on plays and on the great ones of the past. When I was big enough to be taken occasionally to the play my joy was almost unendurable'. [12]

Although Ngaio's mother was demonstrative in her acting, her attitude towards her daughter was often austere. Both parents placed great stress on correct behaviour and this did not include spontaneous displays of affection. Nevertheless, they were sympathetic and understanding when nightmares tormented her as a small child and a recurrent dream in which 'everything became Too Big' invariably ended in her mother's arms. The reticence and reserve that their daughter was expected to cultivate as she grew up shaped her relationships emphatically for the rest of her life. As an adolescent, Ngaio accepted her mother's views on men, that 'anything remotely provocative on my part or physically demonstrative on theirs was, in the most economical manner possible, condemned as second-rate behaviour'. Yet there is a tinge of regret when she wonders 'why such demonstrations of physical attraction as came my way should have the bad taste to be agreeable'. [13]

Henry Marsh clearly adored his daughter and wrote about her fondly:

> Ngaio was brightness itself—a most intelligent child, a keen sense of humour, and always drawing or writing stories as soon as she could do anything and of course we thought the world of her. She was lucky in having such a wise and capable mother who established a firm authority over her from the first. [14]

When it was time for Ngaio to leave her mother's careful nurture and go to school, she was sent to a select dame school run by Miss Sybilla E. Ross (called 'Tib's' by her ex-pupils). Her early years at school were unhappy. For the first time she was made to suffer because of her height, her shyness and her surprisingly deep voice. She was terrified at being made to stand up in class, towering above the other girls, and her hands began to shake uncontrollably, a nervous condition that still occasionally afflicted her as an art student many years later. Her mother, conscious that starting school is often particularly difficult for an only child, left her daughter to fight her own battles. Ngaio remembers this as a toughening but not improving experience:

> Fear is the most damaging emotion that can be inflicted on the character of any child and on one already morbidly prone to inexplicable terrors as I was, the early torments I underwent at Tib's were pretty deadly. [15]

But she survived, learned how to cope with other children and make friends with fellow pupils; her mother, ever watchful, in the background.

By the age of twelve, when she had left this school, she meticulously kept a daily journal.[16] It reveals a number of clashes with her mother and it is clear that Rose had a very rigidly defined idea of how Ngaio should and should not behave. None of the entries is more poignant than the following:

April 23 1907
Hip hooray it is my birthday & I have got lots & lots of things but the best is a watch that Daddy and Mother gave me. We had great fun in the afternoon for all of us dressed up.

April 24 1907
Oh dear I almost wish that I had not had a birth-day for Mother seems hurt that I did not take the fancy dress down in to the workshop. She will not speak or if she does it is only to be angry with me. Perhaps I will be able to do something to please her.

But most of the journal is full of happier accounts of her relationships with her parents and her friends: playing with dolls with her friend Hazel Evans ('This afternoon we taught dolls school for a long time and getting sick of it we whopped them all and expelled them'), riding her pony, Frisk, on the hills, or sketching out of doors with her mother. Already Rose was encouraging Ngaio's artistic tendencies. In summer, sketching and water-colours were considered an essential part of daily life. Holiday activities for Ngaio and her friends from school involved pro-ducing notebooks full of stories and drawings which Rose would mark and comment on, and then award prizes of books. Ngaio was taken to plays and concerts at an age when many children would have been left at home. Her journal reveals a mixture of adult perceptions and childhood responses, such as her conclusion that a celebrated pianist she had been taken to hear played 'beautifully but with no heart'. There was much visiting with friends and Seager relatives who lived nearby, and frequent excursions to the Exhibition. The New Zealand International Exhibition of Arts and Industries, which was held in Christchurch in 1906 and 1907, led to the construction of the largest building in the country at that time. The Exhibition included machinery, an art gallery, a concert hall, a fernery and a 375-foot cyclorama of the Battle of Gettysburg. Outside there was a large funfair, and often there were fireworks at night: 'they were like all the beautifullest stars together O they were heaven' wrote Ngaio with satisfaction.

But it was trips to the theatre that received the most ecstatic entries, such as this one, for 15 February 1907:

We went to the theatre Oh it was lovely it was an oporor I don't know how to spell it though.

Or later, on 17 August:

> We went to the play called Bluebell today so you may guess how excited we were before we started. It was glorious I never enjoyed myself so much in all my life.

Ngaio's companion at 'Bluebell in Fairyland' was her friend Ned Bristed ('Ned and I were in perfect accord') who was a year older than her, and remained a devoted friend until his death in action in the First World War.

Ngaio's struggles with her piano lessons, the dreaded music theory and her party piece 'Elfin Dance' clearly kept her busy, as well as lessons every morning with her mother. Miss Ffitch, the governess who educated Ngaio before she attended secondary school, and who introduced her to the study of Shakespeare, had not yet been engaged. It is hardly surprising that the authoritarian presence of her mother permeates the journal so strongly, and that her father's more forgiving attitudes are recorded with appreciation.

The pain of parting from people that she loved also emerges from these childhood confidences. Ngaio was to feel this many times during a long life of meetings and farewells as she travelled between New Zealand and Europe. In her journal she writes bitterly about the departure of her mother's friend Miv Nixon to her home in Dunedin:

> Oh it is dreadful horrible awful to think that what I must put down for today is true. Miv has gone. I feel as if every other second I would howl. I can not think it is so. What shall we do without her . . . Oh why must she go.

The journal depicts a blend of happiness and anguish that is already being shaped expressively in prose. She was conscious of why she was making a record of her life as a twelve-year-old, noting seriously that:

> I am writing this Diary because I want it for my little girl if I ever have one. I think it would be nice for her to see what her mother did when she was a little girl. I am afraid I have not room to tell all the little knick knacks so you must try to understand the life of a girl who lives on the free hills goes without stockings in summer and runs about all day—Ngaio Marsh.

Whether Ngaio's childhood was as idyllic as this suggests is debatable. In interviews later in life she talked about the loneliness of the only child, and the fantasies and phobias so often experienced by children who live intensely in the world of the imagination. She admitted to inventing imaginary friends, and certainly for the first few years after it was built, the new house at Cashmere stood a long way from any neighbours. Again, not unusually for an only child, she responded more to adults than to other children. As a small girl most of her local playmates were boys, and she joined in their rough-and-tumble games, learning how to fire a rifle and smoke a pipe. Photographs of her at the time, however, book in hand or cuddling Tip the spaniel, reveal the sensitive, vulnerable eyes that many later portraits of the mature woman were also to catch.

Seager family gatherings were always treasured, especially the celebration of Christmas with aunts and uncles who were all experts in impromptu theatricals and charades. At this time Ngaio began to create a romantic view of Christmas that was to have lifelong significance. One of her earliest published stories, 'Moonshine', is about Christmas, and a child's discovery that Santa Claus was not a real person. The story movingly describes how the knowledge affects the child as she watches her father lay out her presents. She also learned to reconcile the literature of a European Christmas with the reality of her own experience: 'home-made toboggans that shot like greased lightning down glossy, mid-summer tussock: hot, still evenings, the lovely smell of cabbage-tree blossom, open doors and windows and the sound, far away, down on the flat, of boys letting off crackers'.[17] The ceremony of presents became important, with Ngaio carefully accumulating small gifts (pink sugar pigs, wooden dolls and small fairytale books were popular choices for her friends) and placing them on labelled shelves in a black japanned cabinet in her bedroom. During the last thirty years of her life 'The Christmas Tree' was to become a cherished annual event at her home, where friends and their children joined her for a party just before Christmas Day, and received gifts parcelled up in huge, decorated boxes. The care with which Ngaio prepared her childhood offerings was replicated in later years to create a kind of legend among two generations of friends. It was, they felt, a touch of the magic that transformed so much of what she did.

CHAPTER 2

Branching Out: 1910–20

There is usually a point in every child's consciousness when suddenly life is much more interesting outside the home than within it, no matter how happy and fulfilled the relationship with one's parents. Enrolling at St Margaret's College represented such a moment for Ngaio Marsh. Having attended a small dame school and then spent a lonely time as a solitary pupil first with her mother and with a governess, Miss Ffitch, she now found herself in the company of other girls who devoured books, wrote poetry, and revelled in the theatre. The school was a new foundation when Edith Ngaio Marsh registered in February 1910, having opened only the previous year. A strict High Anglican school for girls, the fees, and the cost of the uniform, ensured that only the Christchurch elite could attend. Ngaio reflects in her autobiography that 'it must have been a great sacrifice to send me to St Margaret's', and recognised that her mother bore many of the economies, including walking an extra stop from the tram.

There is no doubt that the Marsh family was living frugally at that time. Henry's salary as a bank clerk was small and there is no mention of any domestic help for Rose once they moved out into the country. A major financial blow struck when money was stolen from Henry's desk at the bank, and he was required to replace it. Only a small but providential legacy from an uncle eventually allowed the theft to be repaid. Until this predicament had been resolved the economies borne by the whole family were acute, but the decision was still taken to try to provide the best possible education for Ngaio, no matter how difficult this might be financially.

Apart from the expense, the Anglo-Catholic atmosphere of St

Margaret's might also make the choice of this school appear unusual. Neither parent was in tune with the religious attitudes expected of girls who attended the school; Ngaio always referred to her father as a 'truculent rationalist' and her mother was elusive and vague about her own beliefs. But later she concluded that, 'perhaps they considered that the, as it were, personified focus given by a Church school to pure ethics, would be salutary. If so, I think they were right. The fervour, the extremes and the uncertainties of adolescence must find some sort of channel. I took mine out in Anglo-Catholic observance'.[1] After leaving school Ngaio reacted strongly against what she called 'the brick wall of dogma', although she recognised that it 'may be merely a kind of blind use of symbolism for something felt but not comprehended'.

Although the search for meaningful beliefs was to stay with her until the end of her life, her hunger for friendship was happily met at St Margaret's. Here Ngaio became close to other young girls who were to change her life dramatically: 'it was superb to be one of a crowd'. Her 'dame school' friend Sylvia Fox, a few years her junior, followed Ngaio to St Margaret's in 1912, and joined the literary and dramatic set. Others who remained her friends for life were the Burton girls, daughters of an English clergyman, who were already experienced actresses, and Maire Rhodes, later Hutton, who with her husband was to run one of the most attractive sheep stations on the Canterbury Plains, at Bangor. Maire and her brother Tahu Rhodes had lived across the road from the Marsh family in Fendalton, before they moved up to the hills, and they had played together as small children. Ngaio never lost these early friends.

At school, her ability with words was quickly noticed. The Canterbury *Times* of 26 October 1910 reports on the results of the Navy League's school essay competitions, which gave a credit to Ngaio Marsh of St Margaret's College. The anonymous examiner, having complained about 'evidence of a good deal of help having been given by teachers previous to the writing of the essays', went on to say with great percipience that 'the most brightly-written essay was that of Ngaio Marsh, but it lacked substance'. Ngaio admits that the essay had thirty-one spelling mistakes, so it must indeed have had an engaging style to gain her a prize. Spelling was never one of her strong points, although she was a scrupulous grammarian. What she recognised as the greatest gift the school offered her was the appreciation of Shakespeare's plays and sonnets, under the guidance of an excellent English teacher, Miss Hughes.

By Easter 1912, when the first issue of the St Margaret's College magazine, edited by Ngaio Marsh and W.G. Hughes, was published it was clear that she had already developed a sophisticated writing style. Her article on the school's social life deftly defines the atmosphere, with its Literary Club, its fancy dress dances and its bazaars in aid of good causes. She writes a vivid description of a school excursion to Tai Tapu, one of the sheep stations owned by the wealthy Rhodes family. But by far the most evocative piece in the magazine is her description of a camping holiday at Glentui, in the Southern Alps. Here is the deeply felt response to the mountains and the bush that she was to remember over fifty years later when she wrote her autobiography. The portrayal of the scents and sounds of the mountain valley, the note of the bellbirds and the tui, represented 'the voice and spirit of the bush' that has ensnared many Europeans in this primeval land. Yet she also had a sense of humour, and the same edition contains a comic poem addressed to a school pudding which begins 'O thou, to whose fair form I do address', and ends:

Come back to us, fair pudding lest we die,
Forgive our cold repulse of thee, and come!

In the second issue of the school magazine, published at the end of 1912, Ngaio had two articles, one a mock-serious piece about the Lower School Baby Show and the other a description of a debate between their school and the Girl's High School. A note appended to this report stated that in the opinion of the judges, the best speech of the afternoon was made by Ngaio Marsh. At the age of seventeen, her abilities were recognised at home and at school, but her strengths were in literature and the visual arts, not strictly academic. Photographs of her as a prefect in typically English school uniform of blazer and boater reveal a round-faced, well-developed young girl of above-average height. She looks confident and happy, the group solidarity of St Margaret's giving her security and helping her to cope with the shyness that always remained with her, no matter how effective the exterior polish was to be.

Supported at school by teachers she admired (for whom she had the normal schoolgirl crushes) and by her friends—'for the first time I found myself among contemporaries who shared my own enthusiasms and from whom I could learn'—Ngaio's relationship with her mother seemed to become less intense. Christmas holidays were spent camping in the bush, usually with her parents and a group of friends. Then, as now, in New Zealand, the wilderness exerted a strong pull for those who find refreshment in wild places, and Ngaio's father, in particular, enjoyed being released from the confines of what must have been totally uncongenial employment. These mountain camps gave to Ngaio a profound love for the Southern Alps which was to tug at her always like the tug of a billy-can in a stream. The restrictions of Edwardian society were relaxed:

> We dammed the river with turf and boulders and made a swimming pool. We had a private glade downstream where the girls could rid themselves of their neck-to-knee bathing clothes and receive exultantly the sun and the springing pleasure of young grass. One day we climbed the mountain to Blowhard and looked across a great valley into the backcountry: range after naked range with a glitter of snow on the big tops.
> 'My country', I thought.[2]

If the Christmas camps helped Ngaio to understand her father, active participation in drama at school undoubtedly brought her closer to her mother. Ngaio had parts in several plays (she was usually cast in a male role because of her height and her deep voice). But a much more ambitious project was her own play, 'The Moon Princess', which she wrote and helped to produce at St Michael's Parish Hall, Christchurch in September 1913. Her classmates Friede and Helen Burton were acting and producing, and Ngaio's mother invested her considerable dramatic talents in the part of the witch: 'Her big scene was with Helen Burton, the director and star of the production, and they both let fly with everything they had, lifting my dialogue into a distinction that it certainly did not possess'. Ngaio is characteristically modest in her assessment of the play, which is a crude compendium of a fairy tale by George Macdonald, *A Midsummer Night's Dream* and her own vaguely expressed, adolescent longings for escape to a world of magic and romance. Nevertheless, the achievement of writing a full-length piece, mainly in blank verse, with music and songs, which she saw through to fully costumed production, is still fairly remarkable for an eighteen-year-old. Her grandfather Seager was in the audience, and it was on this occasion that he presented her with two treasured items of theatre history: a coat that had supposedly belonged to Edmund Kean, the famous actor, and a book called *Actors of the Century*, thoroughly annotated by Seager himself. He must have realised even then that his granddaughter was the worthy inheritor of these precious possessions.

The Christchurch *Press* called it 'a clever little play'. The manuscript of 'The Moon Princess' still survives, complete with coloured illustrations of the scenery and costumes. In illustrating the manuscript, Ngaio began a tradition that was to carry on throughout her theatrical career.

Ngaio's fascination with the theatre was now firmly established. In working on 'The Moon Princess' she fell in love with the complex process involved in creating an imaginary world from words on a page: 'it was the whole ambience of backstage that I found so immensely satisfying: the forming and growth of a play and its precipitation into its final shape . . . I don't know when I first realised that I wanted to direct rather than to perform: at this early stage I was equally happy painting scenery, mustering props, prompting or going on for a speaking part. I was at home'.[3] But she became a student of painting, not of drama, when she left school at the end of 1913, enrolling for lessons at the nearby Canterbury College School of Art in Christchurch.

Ngaio Marsh is vividly remembered striding through the door of the studio at art college wearing a dreadful hat with a droopy feather. ('How could her mother have sent her out in it?' wondered fellow student Evelyn Polson, many years later.) Looking around from her full height of 5' 10", she paused and then announced in her resonant voice, 'All right you chaps, let's get cracking!' The hat may be explained by sparseness of income; certainly the Marsh family had little money to spare for clothes. Evelyn's father managed a small factory and was considerably better off than Henry Marsh.

Evelyn Polson, later to become Evelyn Page and one of New

Zealand's finest painters, did not enter Canterbury College School of Art until February 1915, but Ngaio had been attending afternoon classes for several years while a schoolgirl at St Margaret's. By 1915 she was a serious student, and won a number of prizes and scholarships before leaving the School in 1919. These scholarships were essential sources of finance, enabling her to buy necessary artist's materials and probably some better clothes. Although Ngaio won two prizes in her final year for figure compositions, Evelyn Polson won the highest award of the school, the College Medal.

What kind of institution was the Canterbury School of Art in those early days of the twentieth century? The answer has to be: a very distinguished one indeed. Founded in 1882, the School was affiliated to the Science and Art Department of South Kensington, London, and modelled on the Royal College of Art. Robert Herdman-Smith, a musician who had trained at the Manchester College of Art, was Director, with a staff of twelve, most of whom had trained overseas. The life class was taught by Richard Wallwork (1882–1955), who, with his wife Elizabeth, became a great source of encouragement to Ngaio, and invited her to accompany them on painting expeditions to the West Coast. Richard Wallwork painted her portrait at that time, and Elizabeth did a pastel study some years later. Wallwork was a highly disciplined, formal painter who imposed rigorous and restrictive standards on his pupils. The whole approach of the School was highly academic, and in retrospect it was obvious that, in the words of art historian Neil Roberts, 'the rather rigid, almost closed attitudes meant that there was limited stimulation at Canterbury for the more experimental and creative artist'.[4]

Nevertheless, the high standards ensured that work exhibited there was taken seriously by those who considered themselves the guardians of artistic taste in New Zealand; the fact that His Excellency the Governor-General gave out the prizes is evidence of the standing of the College at that time. A review of the 1916 Exhibition took up several columns in the Christchurch *Press* and gave warm praise to Miss Ngaio Marsh for her Time Studies, finding there 'evidence of the possession of a dramatic sense of power and suggestion'. She was also commended for her Studies in the Antique, along with Miss Macmillan Brown, Miss A. Polson,

Miss E. Polson and Miss V. Large. Certainly Ngaio was one of an unusually talented group of people, most of them women. The accident of war had removed most young men to the Front, leaving behind only the unfit and the middle-aged.

There is little evidence that Ngaio, who was nineteen when the First World War broke out, thought deeply about the conflict in Europe, even though her father was in the Civil Defence Corps, her mother was involved in Red Cross work, she and her fellow students were busy drawing patriotic posters, and the Marsh family performed together in a number of fund-raising activities. As the *Oxford History of New Zealand* points out, 'patriotism (or jingoism) was almost obligatory for New Zealanders'. Had conscription reached Henry Marsh's age range, the closely knit Marsh family would have been dealt a severe blow, but fortunately at the age of fifty-one he was to escape the terrible national sacrifice at Gallipoli and Passchendaele. Over 16,000 New Zealanders were killed and 45,000 wounded during this war. Nearly 10 per cent of the population served overseas. Not until Ngaio's childhood friend Ned Bristed, with whom she had shared her earliest experiences of going to the theatre, was killed in Flanders did the slaughter affect her personally. Although always very reticent about this relationship, Ngaio hinted in later years that there had been an understanding with Ned, and cherished a small ruby ring all her life for sentimental reasons.

An unexpected aftermath of the war was the arrival in Christchurch of Ngaio's English cousin, Hal Baker, who had gone straight from school to the trenches and had survived. He immigrated to New Zealand and was the first member of the English branch of the Marsh family whom she had met. Hal became a regular visitor to the house and remained a friend throughout her life. He shared her interest in the garden, and even as an elderly man would visit every spring to give the rose beds a thorough going-over.

About this time, Viola Macmillan Brown, Rhona Haszard, Evelyn Polson, Edith Wall, Margaret Anderson and Ngaio Marsh rented a small room in Hereford Street to use as a studio. Later, Edith Wall found them larger premises in Cashel Street, a well-lit room that had been used as a newspaper print shop. In this studio they drew and painted from life and Evelyn recollected that 'we invited quite a number of people to it and . . . we made it a policy to invite only the newest, the most modern of our contemporaries'. By now, Ngaio was totally engrossed in her life as a painter, staying late in the studio, painting continuously, taking the tram back home late at night, paintbox slung over her shoulder. She painted wherever she went, on the West Coast with the Wallworks, or with a new friend from art college, Phyllis Bethune, whose home on the fringes of the Alps she often visited. Ngaio loved these old homesteads of South Canterbury, with their antique furniture shipped out from family homes in Britain and often hauled mile after mile, over excruciating roads, to create a kind of feudal settlement in New Zealand. Like many born New Zealanders at that time she still longed for tradition and responded to attempts to impose European standards.

Ngaio spent several holidays at Mount Peel, the Acland family sheep station in the foothills of the Southern Alps. She had got to know the Aclands after leaving school, while briefly acting as tutor to Colin Acland, son of the famous New Zealand surgeon Sir Hugh Acland. Colin had been ill, and Ngaio was asked to give him lessons every morning to help him catch up on his school work. This was convenient because in 1914 the Aclands were staying in Christchurch, near the Marsh family on the Dyers Pass Road. Later Ngaio was invited to Mount Peel as a guest, and here she spent many weeks 'struggling to get down in paint the strange ambiguities presented by English trees mingled with native bush against the might of those fierce hills'. One of her paintings still hangs in the dining room of Mount Peel.

Ngaio first crossed the Southern Alps on a painting expedition organised by her tutors from art college, Richard and Elizabeth Wallwork. Ngaio's mother and a young cousin accompanied the expedition, which in those days still involved descending the Otira Gorge from the railhead at Arthur's Pass by stagecoach. It was a trip that Ngaio, who suffered from vertigo, never forgot:

> The technique in approaching the bends was to drive straight at them as if we were about to launch ourselves into Wagnerian flight. At the last second, the driver braked and swung his team. The leaders seemed, to my transfixed gaze, to wheel at right angles. Then we were around the bend and never was a colloquialism more vividly illustrated. So sharp were the turns that the coaches on the reaches

above and below us looked, when we caught sight of them through the bush, as if they drove towards us.[5]

A few years later, at Easter 1919, Ngaio and Phyllis Bethune were sufficiently enterprising to make this trip on their own, and their encounters with Saturday night revellers on the coastal train provided Ngaio with material for an article that was accepted for publication by the Christchurch *Sun* newspaper; her first professional piece. Given the restrictions of New Zealand society at that time, the two young women were able to enjoy considerable freedom of movement, with no apparent objection from parents. Plodding off into the bush with their long skirts and elaborately dressed hair, they painted the glorious scenery of Westland and explored the lakes and hills. Since no paintings can be traced from this period we will never know whether they posed for each other against a wilderness background. Evelyn Polson also tramped the same territory during the 1920s with friends from the Christchurch Group and became engrossed with a problem that she worked on intermittently for the rest of her life, the effects of dappled sunlight on the female nude. One of her best-known studies, *Summer Morn*, was painted on the West Coast in 1926; it is a light-filled painting of a statuesque nude seen from a rowing boat, against a background of sparkling water and willow leaves.

Ngaio had no doubts that her vocation was to be a serious painter: 'there was no question of looking upon art as a sort of obsessive hobby—it was everything. I knew hope and despair, hesitancy, brief certitude and very occasionally that moment when one thinks: "How did the fool, who is I, do this?" I trained myself to become so conscious of the visual element that I could scarcely look at anything without seeing it in terms of line, mass or colour'. At the same time she recognised that 'I never drew or painted in the way that was really my way: that somehow I failed to get on terms with myself'.[6] Typically, after this passage in her autobiography, Ngaio is quick to defend her tutors at the College of Art; she always found it difficult to criticise those in authority even though criticism might have been well justified.

Wherever Ngaio went she was noted for her energy and her sense of humour. Olivia Spencer-Bower, another Christchurch painter to attend Canterbury College School of Art, remembers Ngaio once cheerfully taking the place of a model who had failed to turn up for a life class: 'Mr Wallwork was pushing her around on the throne mid gales of laughter'. This experience added to her store, and was later plucked from the shelf and used in *Artists in Crime*. In this novel the victim is stabbed through the wooden framework of the throne while being forced to assume a pose as she models for a group of painters. Olivia also remembers fancy-dress parties at the Wallworks' house and elaborate games of charades: 'Once I remember Ngaio being the sea. She rolled herself in a carpet. Then unrolled herself backwards and forwards and someone attempted to dive into the midst. But what they represented I cannot remember— we were all helpless with laughter'. As well as Ngaio's sense of humour, Olivia was struck by her appearance: 'One day I met her outside a painting shop on Colombo Street. She had on an enormous camel-hair coat with high collar and great wide shoulders. I came home in rather shocked surprise and said to my mother—do you know—she's beautiful'.[7]

In fact, Ngaio's features were never classically beautiful; her nose was too long and her eyes too close together. Photographs taken in her early twenties show a tall, slim, fresh-faced girl whose expression is full of quizzical observation. She retained her long hair at her mother's insistence until the cropped styles of the 1920s could no longer be resisted; even at the age of twenty-five she was afraid to cross her mother by having it cut. A mixture of defiance and ultimate obedience characterised their relationship long beyond the years of adolescence.

When Ngaio finished her studies at the Canterbury College School of Art in 1919 she was still determined to be a painter. Family circumstances did not absolutely oblige her to find work, and although they were not wealthy, there was none of the grinding poverty that Janet Frame describes so vividly in her auto-biography *To the Is-land* (1983), or Robin Hyde (Iris Wilkinson) depicts in her novel *The Godwits Fly* (1938). Ngaio could have become a teacher, like Evelyn Polson who went to teach art in school, or a journalist like Robin Hyde. But Ngaio never seemed to question the assumption that she would continue to live at home with her parents, painting and writing, and tutoring the occasional pupil. She was already earning money from the articles, poems and stories she wrote for the Christchurch *Sun*, and was sufficiently competent to stand in for the Social Editor for a month while she was on holiday. Christchurch was particularly well served by newspapers at that time, and the Christchurch *Sun* and *Press* both had extensive literary pages and editors of considerable intellectual stature.

The possibility of a career in journalism or painting was challenged, however, by the visit of the Allan Wilkie Shakespeare Company to Christchurch. Allan Wilkie, CBE (1878–1970) was an actor-manager in the nineteenth-century mould. With his wife Frediswyde Hunter-Watts as leading lady, he first toured New Zealand in 1916 with a company of professional actors. The repertoire was mainly Shakespearean but other modern classics were performed. Between 1920 and 1930 the company became well established throughout Australia and New Zealand, giving up only with the Depression in the 1930s. Wilkie ended his career by doggedly delivering a series of solo Shakespeare recitals across the United States and Canada before his eventual retirement and return to his native Scotland. The Allan Wilkie Company rekindled all Ngaio's fascination for the theatre, and with Wilkie's bravura performance of Hamlet, her love affair with Shakespeare was under way. Ngaio described the unforgettable effect this performance had on her:

> ... since three o'clock we had waited on an iron staircase in a cold wind for the early doors to open. The play was *Hamlet*, the house was full and the Dane was Allan Wilkie. Thirty years later, when I produced the play, I remembered how, at the climax of the Mousetrap Scene, Hamlet had stood before the King and had flung his script high in the air and how the leaves had fluttered down in a crescent as the curtains fell. When, so long afterwards, I asked my young Hamlet to repeat this business, the years ebbed back on a wave of nostalgia and gratitude and there I was, on a wooden bench, clapping my palms sore, on what was perhaps the most exciting night I was ever to know in the theatre.[8]

Allan Wilkie's *Hamlet* established this play as her firm favourite. She produced it more often than any other, and it was the first major production she embarked on with the student players of the University of Canterbury. This stimulus was enough to turn Ngaio to the pen rather than the brush, and she quickly wrote a play called

'The Medallion' in mock-Regency style, 'derived without pre-
judice from Shakespeare, Sheridan, Wilde and the Baroness
Orczy'. While admitting that it 'must have been very bad in a slightly
promising way', Ngaio was sufficiently engaged with the play to
purchase an old typewriter and type it up. At the suggestion of her
mother, she left a copy at Mr Wilkie's hotel on his return visit to
Christchurch. After a brief but encouraging interview with the
Wilkies, chaperoned by Mrs Marsh, Ngaio returned to her final year
of art college in 1919 with a vague sense of restlessness that she
was unable to exorcise completely by hard work in the studio and
the successful completion of her course. It was to find an outlet in
the unexpected invitation from the Allan Wilkie Company to join
them as an actress on the next New Zealand tour in 1919–20.

When Allan Wilkie suggested that if Ngaio intended to write
for the professional theatre she needed more practical experience
of the stage, he was, of course, quite correct. She had by now
taken part in a number of amateur productions, often alongside
her parents, but professional theatre was quite another matter,
as Rose Seager knew very well from her own experiences with a
professional company thirty years earlier. Somewhat surprisingly,
given her very protective instincts, she did not object to Ngaio
joining the Wilkie Company, partly because a similar experience
had been part of her own life, and partly because she had a high
personal regard for the Wilkies.

The equilibrium of life at Marton Cottage had in recent years
been shaken by two emotional upheavals centring on Ngaio. The
first was a declaration of love from an emotionally unstable Russian
émgré 'Sacha' Tokareff who, in 1914, played opposite her mother in an
amateur production of Calderon's *The Little Stone House*. He was a
fine actor but his English was poor, so Rose invited him up to the
house for extra coaching. There he met Ngaio, who was flustered
and rather dazzled by the intensity of his sudden passion for her,
although he knew that his love was hopeless. Rose and Henry saw
what was happening and Ngaio remembers that 'I was steered past
this strange and, as I now see it, oddly lyrical encounter'. Unhappily,
after an inexplicable absence, 'Sacha' killed himself in a
Christchurch park. Ngaio wrote that 'this interlude dropped like a
meteorite into the field of my inexperience. Incongruous and
completely alien, it lay spent in the cavity it had made'. It was her

first experience of suicide and she remained appalled by the notion all her life.

A further emotional entanglement with a middle-aged Englishman also required parental rescue and although Ngaio was by now in her early twenties she still seemed to behave like a gauche teenager in relationships with the opposite sex: 'Badgered and bewildered, I shrank inside my transparent envelope and wondered if perhaps I was after all destined to marry a middle-aged Englishman simply because he so ardently desired me to do so. I became frightened and so miserable that at last, in answer to a question from my mother, I confided the whole story to her'.[9] Even Ngaio's parents appeared amazed by this predicament ('How could you be such an ass?' queried her mother in bewilderment) and, in firm Victorian tones, Henry Marsh advised the suitor to cease his attentions. The unhappy lover then took to haunting Ngaio at a distance and alarmed her by loitering outside the studio door at night. He died shortly afterwards.

After these two unsettling experiences, and the death of Ned, of whom she was genuinely fond, Ngaio may well have concluded that uncomplicated friendships were much the best way of coping with men. Rose was correct in judging that her daughter needed more experience of the world, and the offer of the Wilkie tour arrived at just the right moment.

The pages in *Black Beech and Honeydew* describing life on tour with the Wilkie Company are all too brief. There must have been a fascinating story to tell about those one-night stands in country towns and about the company with its stalwarts and stock actors such as the hard-drinking Polonius and the pork-pie-eating juvenile lead. Early in the tour, in September 1919, the company performed in the Theatre Royal, Christchurch, and Miss Ngaio Marsh was cast in *Hindle Wakes*, a play then regarded as fairly advanced in its views. The three-week run was packed out, and gave Ngaio a taste of the thrill of playing a popular play to an appreciative audience. Allan Wilkie was enormously respected and the Christchurch *Press* assured him that 'he will never fail to fill theatres throughout New Zealand'. Ngaio must have been difficult to cast within the repertoire; the role of 'sweet young thing' or *ingénue* which might normally have come her way did not fit comfortably with someone who was nearly six feet tall and crossed the stage with energetic strides: 'Only I', protested Allan Wilkie to his new recruit, 'am at liberty to take six foot strides on this stage'. To force herself to remember this lesson, Ngaio hobbled her legs above the knees with a stocking.

The company left Christchurch for the North Island, and although Ngaio refers in her autobiography to the routine of travelling about, inspecting the next theatre and preparing for a new audience, by far the most evocative description of the company on tour appears in her novel *Vintage Murder*, published in 1937 and dedicated to Allan Wilkie and his wife. Here Roderick Alleyn looks at this assembly of people travelling on a night train and thinks:

> There was something about these people that gave them a united front. Their very manner in this night train, rattling and roaring through a strange country, was different from the manner of other travellers. Dozing a little, he saw them in more antiquated trains, in stage-coaches, in wagons, afoot, wearing strange garments, carrying bundles, but always together.

Even dumped off a train in the middle of the night, 'displayed, for nobody to see, in our irreducible element', Ngaio's love for the theatre and all that it stood for was unaffected. Later she drew on these memories constantly as raw material for her novels: 'a little cellar of experiences which would one day be served up as the table wines of detective cookery'. Her painterly instincts had not deserted her, and the old wooden paintbox accompanied her on tour. She made a number of backstage sketches but none seems to have survived. The company returned to Christchurch in April 1920, where Ngaio got a good notice in the *Press* for her role in *The Temporary Gentleman*: 'Miss Ngaio Marsh made a success of the part of Eva, in fact gave a very definite reading of a small part. In her hands one felt that Eva was a very real person'. But in *The Rotters*, the same reviewer found her 'not very impressive'.

The Allan Wilkie Tour of 1920 ended but Mr and Mrs Wilkie remained friends of the Marsh family and were always invited up to the house whenever they visited Christchurch on tour. Rose often supplied Mrs Wilkie with a bouquet of carefully selected flowers if she was playing Ophelia—'the most demented flowers she ever had'. Ngaio gave Allan Wilkie the volume of theatrical notes she had inherited from Edward Seager, and in exchange he gave her the gold wishbone ring that she always wore on her forefinger: 'a trifle of some reputed antiquity'. Ngaio, meanwhile, had accepted the offer to join another tour, this time with the Rosemary Rees Comedy Company. Her mother was angry, feeling that this would lead nowhere. Now old enough to stand her ground, Ngaio said that she would find out for herself.

These theatrical tours were Ngaio Marsh's drama school. Where today young thespians struggle for acceptance at drama schools in London or New York, Ngaio learned her craft by observation and hard work:

> I went on learning about the techniques of theatre: of the differences between one performance and another, of the astonishing effects that may result from an infinitesimal change in timing, of how, in comedy, audiences are played like fish by the resourceful actor. I grew to recognise the personality of audiences: how no two are alike and how they never behave as a collection of individuals but always as a conglomerate. [10]

That these lessons were well learned can be seen from the Macmillan Brown Lectures she delivered at the University of Canterbury in 1962, which dealt in turn with the actor, the producer and the audience. By then Ngaio had a vast amount of experience behind her, but she still knew how important it was to play her audiences just as much as making play with her cast.

When the Rosemary Rees Company tour folded ('like its successors . . . to high costs and a small population') and Ngaio returned to Christchurch in 1921, she was twenty-six years old. For the next seven years she was to divide her talents between the theatre, writing and painting, making modest achievements in all three areas, but lacking complete satisfaction in any of them. In stage management she was competent and talented, and had the ability to organise people and get a show on the road. For a country which then had no drama school to train actors and producers, Ngaio was unusually well qualified to make the most of any opportunities offered to her by the flourishing amateur dramatic circles of Christchurch and district.

She was also pleased to rejoin her painting colleagues in the studio in Cashel Street, and for the next few years she exhibited regularly. In 1921 she had an oil painting in the Auckland Art Society jubilee exhibition, *On the Eastern Coast* (4 guineas), and the following year she exhibited *Evening in the Valley* (10 guineas). In 1924 she was listed as a working member of the Canterbury Society of Arts and showed an oil, *Nor-west Otira*, in the annual exhibition. But the Society of Arts was ultra-conservative and under the rigid control of its Hanging Committee which was, according to Neil Roberts of the McDougall Art Gallery in Christchurch, 'ruthless in its selection and rarely chose anything that did not fit the Royal Academy mould. In 1922 alone 250 works were rejected. The Committee was also wary of anything that might arouse controversy or did not absolutely abide by the rules of the constitution'.[11]

The women painters of the Cashel Street studio continued to paint together as a group of friends and, as they gained experience, their confidence grew. It is hard to imagine the sensation they caused in 1927 when 'The Group' mounted its own exhibition, with paintings well hung and well lit in contrast to the jumbled late-Victorian hanging style of the Canterbury Society of Arts. The expenses of the exhibition were shared; not many paintings were sold. The Christchurch 'Group' had successfully reacted against the limitations imposed by the Hanging Committee and they continued to exhibit for fifty years. The founders of this loose association of artists were seven students of the Canterbury College School of Art, of whom five, Evelyn Polson, Viola Macmillan Brown, Ngaio Marsh, Margaret Anderson and Edith Wall were women. The two men were W. H. Montgomery and W. S. Baverstock, but the presence of the women was sufficiently dominant to cause Professor James Shelley, doyen of cultural life in Christchurch for many years, to remark in his review of the 1929 Group Exhibition:

> There was a time when critics could write—as I think George Moore did—that women were incapable, by their very nature, of creative work in the arts; such a dictum would be a dangerous one to make in these days with Laura Knight dominating the walls of the Royal Academy at home [i.e. the UK] and with our own 1929 Group demanding our attention here. [12]

Ngaio Marsh denied the obviously radical connotations of The Group by commenting to Olivia Spencer-Bower that 'at no time, during my association with The Group, was there a deliberate attitude towards the Arts of Christchurch. There were no politics. We were not a bunch of rebels, or angries. We were a group of friends'.[13] Evelyn Polson was much more forthright, saying, 'we all suffered from our Victorian parents . . . I am absolutely certain that was why we started the 1927 Group. It was necessary to have somewhere to get away out of the Victorian atmosphere'.[14] And to the influential member of the Hanging Committee, Dr G. M. L. Lester, The Group was nothing if not revolutionary. He wrote in 1930 that, 'the work in this year's exhibition is representative of a definite attitude towards art of revolt and experiment. In a Conservative city like Christchurch the words revolt and experiment may not seem to be a happy omen'.[15]

CHAPTER 3

Laying Down a Cellar: 1921–30

Ngaio continued to paint in the company of other artists but her interests were changing, and she was becoming dissatisfied with her achievement. While Evelyn Polson, Rhona Haszard and Olivia Spencer-Bower were beginning to develop an individual style, Ngaio admitted 'I felt I wasn't advancing—I never felt I was doing what New Zealand was about in my painting'.[1] Increasingly she was drawn to words as the medium of expression that gave her most satisfaction, and the theatre was beginning to involve her more and more. With a friend from the Rosemary Rees Comedy Company, Kiore (Tor) King, who came to stay at Valley Road and later became the professional producer for the Canterbury Repertory Society, Ngaio started to write sketches and eventually completed a one-act play. Called 'Little Housebound' the play is obviously much more sophisticated in style than 'The Moon Princess' but it has a similar theme, expressing a desire to escape from the confines of the safe, ordinary world and seek freedom in the woods. Originally entitled 'Come out and Play', the piece is rather over-romantic, but contains some interesting ideas that relate to the author's state of restlessness at the time. The ultra-conservative society of Christchurch, and the subtle dominance of her mother—'she was over-concentrated on me'—led Ngaio to dream consistently of a world of freedom beyond the familiar limits of home.

After the theatre tours throughout New Zealand, Ngaio had returned to Christchurch still feeling part of the parental home, drawn back by affection for her father and the complex but powerful influence exerted by her mother. An only child, particularly a daughter, frequently feels the excessive burden of family expectations and control; this is especially likely if a daughter does not become independently established as a wife and mother, or make a complete break towards a destiny of her own. Ngaio was not without male admirers, but clearly feared that marriage would be the end of all her artistic ambitions. Neither of her parents was anxious for her to marry and in later years Henry actively resented her young men friends. For Rose, having shaped and moulded her towards a successful career as either a writer or a painter, marriage would have meant the risk of abandoning all the aspirations she had loaded on her daughter. Furthermore, in Ngaio's artistic set in Christchurch very few women married early; they longed for travel, for experience and independence, not for domesticity.

In 'Little Housebound' Carol is left wondering at the power the woods exert over him and his desire for freedom puzzles and unsettles him:

> . . . it is as though there were two Carols. There is the Carol that loves home and you, and the smell of wood-smoke, and all the warm house-bound things; but most of all you, my sweet. But there is another Carol and he loves the hills and the long roads stretching away into the dusk. He wants to follow them to the world's end in search of something that he can never find.[2]

Dreamy and derivative though the play may be, it provided Ngaio with the challenge she needed. She and Tor King, with another actor from the Rosemary Rees Company, took 'Little Housebound', together with some sketches and recitations, to Havelock North, a small town on the North Island with a reputation for being the haunt of artists and intellectuals. Accompanied by their mothers, which allowed them to count as a travelling company for a railway concession, Ngaio and Tor undertook a modest tour and, to their surprise, made a little money. Ngaio's initiative and ability to see a project through to completion must be recognised. Rural New Zealand at that time was hardly fertile ground for touring theatre of refined sensibility, although the major cities were receptive to well-known touring companies performing popular plays. Ngaio's instincts were leading her in the right direction, and despite her mother's views about a career on the stage, the fact that Ngaio was writing again made Rose support the venture. On returning to Christchurch Ngaio was asked to join the newly founded Wauchop School of Drama and Dancing as a tutor. 'Little Housebound' was produced in 1924 by the Wauchop School, and later, in 1931, by the Canterbury Repertory Society in a programme of plays by New Zealand authors. As a result of the tour, Ngaio was also asked to produce a number of plays for local amateur groups.

The creation of the two-sided character in 'Little Housebound' with his longing for freedom and adventure indicates a dichotomy in Ngaio's subconscious, a dichotomy that was to be worked out in later years as she repeatedly escaped to Europe, and just as repeatedly felt the longing to return to New Zealand. This desire for freedom and travel may have been one reason why romantic relationships with men did not flourish. In an interview in 1971 she admitted that once she had been engaged, but said that her fiancé had died. She went on, 'But if he'd lived and we'd married it's quite possible I wouldn't have liked it very much. I think I'm one of those solitary creatures that aren't the marrying kind'.

Solitary or not, she longed for kindred spirits, and there was a welcome widening of interests when she came into contact with a family that was to become centrally important to her world. She had become involved with a local organisation called Unlimited Charities, an amateur theatrical group specifically formed to produce large-scale musicals to raise funds for charity. Called in to replace a director who had been taken ill, Ngaio was invited to produce the show the following year. She was especially pleased with the choice of *Bluebell in Fairyland*, one of her earliest theatre-going memories:

> Some twenty years later . . . it fell to my lot to produce *Bluebell in Fairyland*. I stood in the circle and watched a dress rehearsal and was able for a moment to put into the front row the shadows of a freckled boy and a small girl: ecstatic and feverishly wolfing chocolates.[3]

Ngaio revelled in what other people might have found daunting, the orchestra, dancers, singers and crowds of actors—'it was wonderful to have crowds to manipulate as well as individual players'. And the sense of wonder that never deserted her through-out her long life in the theatre was reawakened: 'the afterglow of

Ned's and my delight seemed to reach over the years and shed an odd blessing on the venture'.

Through Unlimited Charities Ngaio was to renew acquaintance with her childhood friend, Tahu Rhodes, now a Captain in the Grenadier Guards, and to meet his wife Helen (always called Nelly), Lord Plunket's eldest daughter. Tahu had been wounded at Gallipoli, and at their wedding in England in 1916 the *Pall Mall Gazette* records the presence of 'numbers of wounded soldiers from New Zealand, having been driven up from the Anzac Hospital at Walton on Thames in two Red Cross motor wagons'. Captain Rhodes returned to the South Island where he was born and where his family maintained substantial estates. He purchased Meadowbank, a sheep station at Ellesmere, 20 miles outside Christchurch. Ngaio first visited the family, now augmented by four young children, in June 1924, after the final performance of *Bluebell in Fairyland*. The Rhodes family appear as 'the Lampreys' in her detective novel, *Surfeit of Lampreys*, published in 1940.

Social life at Meadowbank, into which Ngaio was now quickly swept, represented the kind of casual glamour that up to now she had associated only with the stage. The Rhodes family invited her into their set because she was lively, witty and fun to be with. Nelly Rhodes, almost exactly the same age as Ngaio, became her special friend. Socially their paths would not normally have crossed without the mixing bowl of amateur dramatics, since bank clerks had little in common with the powerful and wealthy Rhodes family of South Canterbury. But class barriers did not seem to prevent Ngaio from being drawn into the world of the Christchurch gentry, which even today retains a certain elegance and style, as well as aristocratic connections. Prince Charles and Princess Anne stayed at Mount Peel with the Aclands in 1970, and Prince Edward visited the same family five years later. Tahu Rhodes had attended the Prince of Wales on his New Zealand tour in 1920, and it was not surprising that the Duke of York, on his visit to New Zealand in 1926, should have visited Lord Plunket's daughter, the Honourable Mrs Rhodes. Here he endured a cabaret put together by Ngaio Marsh and members of the Rhodes family: 'I can only suppose that he, too, was unmusical or that we were bad enough to be funny; I know that we were bad'.[4]

The weekends at Meadowbank became more frequent and Ngaio's closeness to the family grew. Her name appears twelve times in their visitors' book for 1924, and so often from then on that she wrote 'in perpetua'. Her parents also visited occasionally between 1924 and 1926, probably in connection with some amateur dramatics that needed extra cast. In Rhodes family photographs of the period, Ngaio's tall figure often appears, clowning with the children or looking very much at ease with the white-flannelled, straw-hatted young men and lively young women who made up the hospitable Rhodes circle. Among them was Toppy Blundell Hawkes, a 'cadet' or trainee farmer from England who became Ngaio's frequent escort. There were camping excursions into the bush, to the magical valley of Glentui that had meant so much to Ngaio as a child, or deer-stalking expeditions in the Upper Rakaia. 'The Lampreys' fascinated Ngaio. Their impecunious adventures amused and amazed her, having grown up in a family where a little money was made to last a long time, and their zany, relaxed lifestyle, unconventional yet clearly part of the Establishment, seemed to bridge the gap between conformity and escape in a way that had so tar seemed impossible to her. A portrait of Tahu Rhodes that she painted at this time is still owned by his family.

Entertainment at Meadowbank was lavish. There were large house parties with many servants in attendance, some of whom had been brought out from England. Fancy-dress balls, a performance of J. M. Barrie's *Quality Street* and an elaborate Orphans' Queens Carnival all involved the element of theatre that Ngaio loved. But it was not all entertainment; Ngaio estimated that over £12,000 had been raised for charity by their good-humoured efforts. In describing the Rhodes family and their eccentricities Ngaio likened the household to a vehicle that was a cross between a Rolls Royce and a dodgem car, being driven by several people at the same time: 'it would travel at an uneven pace, cutting its corners, run in and out of ditches, and avoid head-on collisions by the narrowest of margins. Sometimes a vital part would fall off. Nobody would know where it was going and all the Lampreys would be very gay'.[5] For Ngaio, this interlude with the Rhodes family was like another extended season on tour as an actress. She continued to look young for her age and even at thirty could act the part of the innocent girl. It was the first of a series of roles she was to play throughout her life: responding to circumstance, providing the behaviour that was required, and moving far from her own home and background.

During these years she continued to write poetry and stories, the best of which were submitted to the annual literary competition run by the Christchurch *Sun* newspaper. This literary competition, held just before Christmas, attracted many entries and its winners were highly competent writers. The 1925 competition supplement proclaimed the growing popularity of the competition, noting that entries had grown from 187 in 1923 to 372 in 1925. Miss Ngaio Marsh won third prize of 2 guineas for her archly entitled poem to spring, 'That Crocus Feeling'. The following year, with entries up again, to 556, Ngaio won third prize for a story called 'The Gold Escort'. This is a rather florid piece about a man who falls asleep on Arthur's Pass in the Southern Alps during the Gold Rush, and dreams that a coach with a ghostly crew picks him up. It plunges faster and faster down the precipitous track, the driver lashing his horses as they hurtle to certain destruction. As with many weak ghost stories, it ends when the traveller wakes up. The *Sun* printed the story in full, with an appreciative comment on the author, 'who has distinguished herself as an artist, actress, playwright, producer, short-story writer and poet, and may claim that she is well entitled to the much abused adjective "versatile" '. Although it did not win a prize, Ngaio's poem 'Heloise' appeared in the special Christmas Supplement of 1926. It has a lyrical quality which emerges despite fairly conventional images:

Under the ban of darkness let us lie
Silently side by side, nor strive to be
Aught but quiescent in that vasty sea
Where nightly, unbefriended, we embark.
Let us lie silently, and in the dark
Turning our faces to the lampless sky
Seek out our thoughts of one another.

Then
May you alone of lovers among men
Discover in your love, tranquillity.
Let us not touch with lips nor hands nor strive
Together. Then, beloved, we may live
For one immortal breath in unity.

Yet since, untouched, you lie so far apart
I take again your head upon my heart.

Admittedly, these were 'prentice pieces', naive and derivative in many ways, but it is crucial for a writer to be recognised and taken seriously by others. *The Sun* competitions provided vital encouragement for many New Zealand writers at a time when very few possibilities for local publication existed.

At the end of 1927, the Rhodes family returned to England, and the happy times at Meadowbank came to an end. Their departure made Christchurch seem even more restrictive to Ngaio, and the lure of Europe was strong. In the Marsh family, as in many other New Zealand households of the time, England was 'home', even though Rose Marsh had been born in New Zealand and Henry lived there all his adult life. The tie with England was unbreakable, and Ngaio created a mythic picture of England that she was later to perpetuate in her fiction. In *Black Beech and Honeydew* she refers to an old silent film, *Living London*, which set up images that were to become the stuff of her dreams.

Finally, at the age of thirty-three, she was given the opportunity to see the reality behind the myth. The Rhodes family, now settled into a Georgian manor house in Buckinghamshire, wrote inviting her to stay with them. Both parents agreed that she should go, but for Rose in particular it was a severe emotional wrench. Ngaio knew that in wanting to escape she was hurting her mother ('I fell into an inward rage of compassion and love and resentment'), yet she was also aware that she had to free herself from her mother's dominance and make her own choices in life.

In seeking to return to her European roots Ngaio was following a long line of writers, painters and composers who have systematically rejected their homelands and, having shaken off the restrictive ties of their native lands, have found themselves impelled to recreate them overseas. Much of the literature of the twentieth century can be seen as a literature of exile; Katherine Mansfield's finest stories are about New Zealand, written when she was living in Europe. James Joyce carried Dublin around in a small attaché case full of tram tickets, and never needed to go back because his memories were so acute. Jean Rhys was far from Dominica when she reproduced its intensely felt landscape in *Wide Sargasso Sea* (1966). Patrick White, experiencing exile in school and university in Britain, set his first novel *Happy Valley* (1939) on the cold plains of the Monaro. He used the same hard landscape of Australia as the setting for his first artistically successful novel *The Aunt's Story* (1948), a work that was substantially completed overseas and on the ship taking him back to Sydney after the Second World War. All these writers needed the tension created by grafting the world of Europe to which they were drawn, to the world of home, which often represents a deeper spiritual and emotional reality. In 1922 Katherine Mansfield revealed in a letter to a fellow writer, the South African Sarah Gertrude Millin, that once she was cut off from literary society 'always my thoughts and feelings go back to New Zealand—rediscovering it, finding beauty in it, re-living it'. Ngaio Marsh's younger contemporary, Robin Hyde, spent much of her life longing for a Europe that, once achieved, destroyed her. In the foreword to her innovative and unusual novel *The Godwits Fly* (1938) she writes:

> Most of us here are human godwits; our north is mostly England. Our youth, our best, our intelligent, brave and beautiful, must make the long migration, under a compulsion they hardly understand; or else be dissatisfied all their lives long.[6]

The godwit is a small New Zealand bird that, defying all logic, flies each year to the northern hemisphere, travelling thousands of hazardous miles. In *Writers in Exile* (1981) Professor Andrew Gurr, himself an expatriate from New Zealand, writes perceptively about this phenomenon:

> Distance gives perspective, and for exiles it is also the prerequisite for freedom in their art. Freedom to write is a major stimulus to exile, and exile creates the kind of isolation which is the nearest thing to freedom that a twentieth century artist is likely to attain.[7]

Ngaio Marsh was able to go to England because she could pay most of her own expenses. Although her father paid for the ship's passage, she had saved some of her modest earnings from publishing stories and articles, from drama coaching and from directing plays for amateur societies. She had sold some paintings and was now well enough known to be commissioned to write a series of travel articles for New Zealand newspapers. She was beginning to be financially independent at a time when this was unusual for New Zealand women, apart from those who had inherited wealth or the few who held salaried posts. Most young New Zealanders setting out on the great adventure to England were better off than Ngaio and were not keeping themselves through their pens as she intended to do. Even Katherine Mansfield, with her claims to independence and 'power, wealth and freedom', accepted an annual income of £100 from her prosperous banker father. This sum was more than the annual earnings of a school teacher at the time, as Claire Tomalin points out in her 1987 biography of this writer.

Syndicated articles written by Ngaio Marsh under the title 'A New Canterbury Pilgrim' appeared regularly throughout 1928 and 1929. Not only did they provide an income, they also brought her name before a wide public in New Zealand and gave her a great deal of experience in writing readable prose on a variety of subjects, from mannequin parades to air shows. Her reports must also have fuelled nostalgia in the minds of recent immigrants, and encouraged even more impatient young people to find the passage money for a trip 'home'.

Many immigrants feel this unsettling pull between their adopted country and the country of their birth, but what made Ngaio unusual was that she was a born New Zealander, and her image of 'home' was entirely fictitious. Cherishing English ancestry and a notion of England as 'home' involved a number of economic as well as cultural assumptions. Goods imported from England were always considered superior, and those who could afford to buy them rather than the cheaper Australian manufactures were from the better-off sections of the community. 'Home' retained its snobbish overtones in New Zealand much longer than in Canada or Australia, with their broader cultural mix, especially after the Second World War. It could be argued that the upper-class English society that she was to become part of, with its picturesque, feudally regulated villages, its comfortable manor houses and its life of style in London, was as far from the lives of ordinary British people as was the world she had imagined as a girl in New Zealand. Certainly Ngaio's England as described in 'A New Canterbury Pilgrim' gives the impression of a life of privilege and order, where the monarchy was always respected and the fabric of society had to be preserved; the status quo was, indeed, never questioned by the commentator. How far the outsider's view was to penetrate the glossy surface of upper-class life can be interestingly teased out from a number of her books, which become increasingly critical of the hypocrisies and pretensions of English life.

There is no doubt that Ngaio left New Zealand with relief as well as a sense of anticipation, and this emotion was to be recreated many times in years to come as she caught the Inter-Island ferry from Lyttelton Harbour to Wellington to start the long sea voyage to England. Passenger liners docked in Australia, usually Sydney, and this meant that for travellers from 'the land of the long white cloud' the Tasman Sea had to be crossed before the voyage proper began. The first article sent to the Christchurch *Press* and printed in September 1928 reveals her complicated feelings as she embarked on the journey:

> I know of no experience that compares with the adventure of setting out on one's travels unless it is the far-away conviction of childhood that one lives on the borders of fairyland and that beyond every garden hedge ran the little green highways of enchantment. As one grows up and grows older these highways change their character and become railroads and ocean routes, and for me, at least, the office of Thomas Cook and Son, Christchurch, will always be the enchanted parlour whose doors open straight into Wonderland.[8]

Her attitude, even at the age of thirty-three, seems close to the hazy desires of 'The Moon Princess' and 'Little Housebound'. But all her life this traveller-enjoyed nothing better than a long sea voyage, and Sylvia Fox, the friend from her schooldays who accompanied her several times, was always surprised at the enthusiasm with which Ngaio threw herself into shipboard life. Deck games, dressing up, parties, all delighted her, even though in later years she preferred the discreet charm of small cargo boats with just a few passengers.

Ngaio had never left New Zealand before. She was immediately impressed by the bustle and sophistication of the city of Sydney; there is an interesting reference in her first article to 'the huge beginnings of the new bridge, with its promise of a colossal span across the harbour'. This was, of course, the famous Sydney Harbour Bridge, then in the process of construction. Ngaio spent ten days here, and had an unexpected pleasure when she discovered that the Allan Wilkie Company was in town, with a production of *Henry VIII*. Naturally she attended, and took the opportunity to go backstage and renew old acquaintances. The company had just suffered the loss of all its costumes, a fate that was also to befall Ngaio when she arrived in Sydney in 1949 with a group of student players.

Painting was not neglected, and she reported in her column on a visit to the National Gallery of New South' Wales, an imposing building but with disappointing contents. She liked the Australian painting but deplored the amount of space devoted to large Victorian canvases—'so many bleak square yards of dead paint'. She also took a serious interest in the Art Gallery in Melbourne, which was the next port of call, and admired a few paintings but accused the gallery of 'fetishism' in its selection of masters. Melbourne was made memorable by a performance of *Turandot* by the Melba-Williamson Grand Opera Company, where the lavishness of the costumes and the modern staging caught her eye.

In all the articles devoted to the trip to England there is a freshness of observation that evokes many scenes with particular vividness. In Sydney gangs of night-workers on the tramlines were 'like modern woodcuts' against their lighted flares, and a vista of Hobart is described as 'a landscape that would not look amiss behind a Florentine Madonna, and yet it smells of the bush and the mountain men have raw-boned fighting faces'. Already she has grasped the pleasure and the pain of being a tourist: 'this journey reminds me of nothing so much as a gazette at the moving pictures. We have flashes of places—a glimpse of this, a tantalising hint of that, and then on again to the next port of call'.

Once the *Balranald* was steaming her way across the Indian Ocean, Ngaio indulged what she called her 'vague and ill-informed interest in crowd psychology' by studying her fellow passengers. On this first voyage she was entranced by everything she encountered, despite a small and stiflingly hot cabin, deteriorating food and a dubious supply of drinking water. The drawbacks of strident fellow passengers, food poisoning and dock strikes, commonplace on future voyages, were far from her mind. She looked forward to the prospect of landing at Durban and recorded that 'the snapshot impression of two days has been the most tantalising experience I have ever had'. From a scribble on the back of an envelope she later produced an oil painting, *Native Market, Durban*, which she exhibited at the Christchurch Society of Arts in 1933 and which is now held by the Robert McDougall Art Gallery in Christchurch. Her portrait in words of the same scene is also rich in colour and evokes a sense of magic: 'It was a place of enchantment—a goblin market. Who knows, I thought to myself, what sort of fruit this is that we have bought so cheaply?' As in Sydney and Melbourne she attended the theatre, and saw Sybil Thorndike and Lewis Casson performing in Henry Arthur Jones's *The Lie*. Ngaio was overwhelmed by Thorndike's technique:

> Miss Thorndike gave what was unquestionably the most arresting performance I have ever seen. She is an amazing woman. She is not pretty, nor, perhaps, very young. Her voice is weird and she snaps her fingers—I can see her do it, waving her long boyish arms—at all theatrical traditional methods and technique.

Her delight at the vibrancy of Durban was tempered on departure by an unpleasant scene at the dockside: a small black boy was struck by one of the Afrikaaner passengers—'it was the ugliest of sights'.

Cape Town held a special significance on the voyage, because here she met Uncle Freddy, her father's favourite brother, for the first time. Another branch of the Marsh family had become established on the North Island of New Zealand when Henry's sister Amy emigrated with her husband and family in 1924, but Ngaio had not yet developed a close relationship with them. In Cape Town this was to be the only time that she would meet Uncle Freddy and his family, and the visit was a success. She admired the city with its 'tall white buildings and pleasant little fairy tale houses', and the ancient house of Koopman de Wet: 'one walks off the street into a Dutch interior as beautiful as any old master'.

The *Canterbury Pilgrim*'s fifth dispatch, bylined Las Palmas, was printed in the *Press* on 1 December 1928. After steaming up the coast of Africa the ship anchored to take on fresh water, and was immediately engulfed by small craft full of souvenir sellers. Confusion developed, with the Captain insisting that the local policeman draw his sword to disperse the importuning mob. Ngaio's eyes were drawn to the 'dusty, white, exhausted grandeur' of the harbour, which was backed 'by hills that are as sun-baked and uncompromising as our own Port Hills in mid-summer'. The detail she remembers as the ship slips away is 'a little, sad-eyed marmoset who sat in the prow of a boat gazing up at the big ship while its owners cogitated on the day's trade'.

Only after leaving the Canary Islands did Ngaio have the sudden realisation that they were now in northern seas, out of sight of the Southern Cross. Soon the ship was to pass the white cliffs of the south coast of England and make her way along the Thames to dock in London. The description of the reception given to the fictional character Roberta Grey in *Surfeit of Lampreys*, who arrives in a very similar situation and is greeted by a Maori *haka* or dance on the quayside, is not matched in Ngaio's journalism or in her autobiography, but is so bizarre that it may well have happened. The Rhodes family specialised in extraordinary receptions and practical jokes, as when Nelly's sister, Eileen Plunket, went to the local railway station dressed as a chauffeur to collect Betty Cotterill, a friend from Christchurch who had been part of the Meadowbank circle and was a good friend of Ngaio's. The driver hurtled at top speed around the lanes of Kent, refusing to answer questions and turning in at the gate, which had been passed many times, only when the hapless guest was in a state of near hysteria. The mysterious chauffeur then followed Betty into the drawing-room with the luggage and kissed her warmly, at which point Betty, not surprisingly, screamed for help. Ngaio obviously got off lightly: the only joke played on her was finding the house where she was to stay shuttered and barred, with notices stuck up advertising it for sale. She was a guest of the Rhodes family on and off for the next four years, first at Alderbourne Manor near Gerrards Cross in Buckinghamshire, and then in London, when the family moved to two large flats in Eaton Mansions, Knightsbridge. As well as her close friendship with her contemporary Nelly Rhodes (the Honourable Mrs Rhodes) Ngaio enjoyed the company of the Rhodes children, by this time five in number—in particular Eileen, who was eleven years old, Denys and Maureen. The youngest, Terence, was her godson. Eileen was to become especially close, sharing Ngaio's love of the theatre, accompanying her on many trips to Stratford and collaborating on a children's book which Eileen wrote and Ngaio illustrated. They also worked together on dramatisations of some of Ngaio's novels. Denys Rhodes was a regular correspondent and confidant for many years, and he too became a novelist while working overseas. Ngaio's letters to Denys are more honest than most about her struggles in writing fiction; they had a great deal in common including shared family jokes and nicknames (the Rhodes children called Ngaio 'Ish') and even though she was twenty-five years older than him, Ngaio delighted in his company. Maureen, first at Birling Place and then at Walnut Tree Farm in Kent, proved to be a lifelong friend and support. The Rhodes family filled Ngaio's world for several years and remained an enduring link with England for the rest of her life.

In social terms Ngaio was totally out of her class, but as an actress she was able to play a convincing part until the role became more natural. Clothes must have presented a serious problem; fortunately astute purchases and a good figure helped her to get by. As a New Zealander, a painter and a writer with theatrical experience she fell outside the normal class boundaries of English society, and her enthusiasm, style and lively good humour carried her a long way.

English life suited this energetic New Zealander perfectly, and she revelled in the theatres, galleries and night life. She wandered around London, soaking up what she many times called 'that London feeling', a sense of zestful expansiveness and enthusiasm for the new experiences that she knew would be waiting. The 'self-contained quartette' referred to in her autobiography consisted of Tahu and Nelly Rhodes, Ngaio and Toppy Blundell Hawkes, the English 'cadet' who had been working at Meadowbank when Ngaio used to visit there. She wrote that 'we were bewilderingly gay', of her days in a London before the Depression and the Second World War: 'I got the tag end of a very ravished but very wonderful 1920s in London'. The Hungaria Restaurant was the fashionable late-night rendezvous and the theatres were filled with figures who were to shape the English stage for half a century: John Gielgud was performing in *Hamlet*, and Edith Evans, Leon Quartermaine, Cicely Courtnedge, Charles Laughton, Noel Coward and Leslie Banks were all enjoying distinguished careers. The Old Vic Theatre was a particular revelation and Ngaio became a devotee of these shabby old premises on the Waterloo Road, finding it 'in the direct tradition of Elizabethan, Jacobean and Victorian audiences . . . the Old Vic, in those days, thrummed with a coarse, racy life that had no equivalent on the West End'. Always attuned to the response and quality of the audience, she found West End theatre-goers 'more alive, more full of the sense of festivity, less on the defensive, more ready to be either violently enthusiastic or actively hostile' than audiences with which she was familiar. She revelled in the whole theatre ambience and never lost her sense of anticipation before the curtain rose:

> I am not sure that this is not the very best moment in the theatre-goer's evening, and in a packed London playhouse one then snuffs up the mysterious savour of the foot-lights, looks about one at the sea of misty faces, and experiences a strange feeling of conviviality that for some reason is the chief ingredient of the overture's enchantment.

The articles she continued to send back to New Zealand often dealt with unexpected aspects of English life, such as a ride in the London Underground, going down from wet streets at the hub of the world, Piccadilly Circus. She looks at her fellow passengers and wonders about their lives: 'all the faces seemed pale and drawn, in the curious lighting of the tube; all with the exception, perhaps of the charwoman's, were sophisticated, patient, and close looking, like houses whose blinds are drawn but whose lamps shine dimly behind them. As we gathered way, all these figures moved very slightly and spasmodically, for all the world like the masked jigging puppets in Mr Noel Coward's satirical sketch, "Dance Little Lady" '. She had also found, to her surprise, that there were certain advantages to being a New Zealander in England. Another piece began:

> For some reason New Zealanders are phenomenally popular in England. I have listened to glowing tributes from a middle-aged Guardsman, from the wife of the King's Physician, from an ex-naval officer, and from my hairdresser. I had no idea, until I came to England, how hard-working, how loyal, how intelligent and

advanced we all were, or that our integrity and progress were so remarkable. Are we, indeed, such a noble people? Evidently. I know one New Zealander who prefaces all enquiries and requests with the remark, 'I've come all the way from New Zealand' because she finds it works so marvellously.

Ngaio continued to live with the Rhodes family at Alderbourne Manor throughout 1928 and 1929, but her earnings from 'A New Canterbury Pilgrim', augmented with an occasional small gift from her father, enabled her to fit in two visits to France during that time. The first was in December 1928 with Nelly Rhodes and the friend from Christchurch, Betty Cotterill, who had been so warmly welcomed by the strange chauffeur on her arrival in England. They crossed in bad weather from Dover to Calais, but Ngaio's eye for theatre brought the whole scene vividly to life in her article:

> The arrival in Calais is like stepping on the stage at an impromptu musical comedy. The porters are theatrical porters, the Customs officers might break into song at any moment, and the wharves are inhabited with marvellous creatures in a regiment of uniforms that look as if they ought to advance with that inimical march that finishes in a side drum mark time and a flamboyant salute.

She found the famous Blue Train 'a travelling palace' and enjoyed every minute of the journey as the window flashed by houses and gardens and other people's lives. In Monte Carlo, the hotel, the sea and the surrounding hills enchanted her, but what drew her most to the gambling salons was not the prospect of winning, but her desire to paint the old women who played every night in the ornate salon: 'there they sit, day after day, night after night, with lack-lustre eyes, hands that have turned into claws, skinny necks, baggy cheeks, and masses of jewels and feathers'. Ngaio was clearly fascinated by these people, all with their 'systems', all convinced that one day they would win untold wealth. Nelly, Betty and Ngaio took a much more light-hearted approach, and quickly became known as the 'ladies who laugh' as they saw all their plaques disappear. This behaviour was so uncharacteristic that the croupiers started to give them advice on how to play, and Ngaio eventually won enough to purchase an elegant suit.

On another visit to Paris the following summer, in 1929, they stayed in a small hotel in the Rue des Capucines in the Madeleine district. By now Ngaio's journalism was full of confidence, and the Paris piece is travel writing at its best. Her humorous descriptions begin with the old man at Boulogne—'evidently Father Christmas doing locum as a rouse-about on the dock' who warned them that 'il fait chaud—eet ees very 'ot'. It was indeed hot, so hot that one of the carriages on the train to Paris caught fire:

> A crowd of porters and passengers instantly gathered round, and, after much musical comedy chat, decided that it would be best to uncouple the fire and leave it behind. Meanwhile a gentleman in circular woollen trousers and a straw boater rushed into our compartment, implored us to remain calm, and fell to fanning us vigorously with the boater. Another French gentleman had got himself locked in the chambre de toilette, next door, and presently turned on all the taps, doubtless with the laudable intention of extinguishing the flames.

After this prologue, could the remainder of the performance match up? Clearly the sights, sounds and smells of Paris did not disappoint Ngaio. She describes the bookstalls and the boulevards, but also catches the unusual sights—the sleeping peasant whose horse and cart finds its own way down the street in the early morning to deliver vegetables to the market and the hairdresser whose salon is an exact replica of Marie Antoinette's boudoir. Admitting that her previous view of Paris had been entirely drawn from the literature of Guy de Maupassant, French fairy-tales and travellers' anecdotes, Ngaio finds Paris 'unbelievably and joyously true to type', and that it really is full of 'stout gentlemen with enormous beards and straw hats, of pretty milliners with bandboxes, of men in blouses, and a vague naughtiness'. It was, in fact, Toulouse Lautrec and 'Gaieté Parisien' combined.

Ngaio devoted an article to Versailles out of a sense of duty, but she was clearly not impressed, although the English guide amused her as he mopped his brow and explained in broad cockney, 'There's only one thing, reely, to remember, and that's Louis XIV. The place is fair lousy with Louis and that's a fact'. She was glad to get back to Paris, even Paris in a heat wave, and she wrote affectionately about the city, comparing it to London: 'cities have their individual voices, and the cheerful soprano of Paris has nothing in common with that endless bass roar that seems to be part of London's very breath of being'. The cities of Europe never failed to stimulate her; even as an elderly woman, walking on a stick and suffering from gout, she discovered Rome and Florence, enjoying them as much for the abundance of their humanity as well as their treasures.

In 1930 the Rhodes family decided to move to London, to the large double flat in Eaton Mansions that provides the setting for a gruesome murder in *Surfeit of Lampreys*. At the end of 1929 Ngaio and Nelly Rhodes had set up a small shop in the Brompton Road, Knightsbridge selling home-made decorative objects, and were spending more time in London. The idea had emerged after the success of a stall that they had run at a charity bazaar, and they planned 'to make any number of gift-objects, take a lock-up shop somewhere in SW3 for the Christmas quarter, make what profit we could, and stop'. The shop was called 'Touch and Go' after a theatrical review that the family had put together in New Zealand. Ngaio admitted that they were rather like Noel Coward's shopgirls, with more enthusiasm than business expertise.

Again, Ngaio turned experience into eminently readable articles, and an account of the opening of the shop duly found its way back to the Christchurch *Press*. She sets the scene on a frosty morning in autumn:

> In our window we have arranged some of the fruits of eleven months' arduous labour. Here, with frequent chilly excursions on to the pavement outside, we have set a little lonely company of painted boxes and lamp shades, of wooden powder bowls and trays. These objects have been the darlings of our hearts and the children of our brains for those eleven months; now they are on sale and we scarcely know whether they are lovely or hideous.

Soon the manageress was assessing the customers as though they were characters coming on stage from the wings, like the fluttery, terrified wife of a disagreeable old retired general who, denied a wastepaper bin by his autocratic decree, 'orders a little box in a nervous whisper and trots obediently out after her lord'. Then there is the engaged couple who buy everything because they 'look such fun', and the elderly spinsters who buy trays for their 'genteel establishment' nearby. A near-sighted old lady purchases a tray decorated all over with lips, glasses and twirls of cigarette smoke, and has to return it when her family is shocked at her choice.

The Brompton Road shop had been leased for October, November and December 1929 only, but at the end of those three months the business had made a profit, and Nelly and Ngaio agreed to take a yearly lease on superior premises round the corner, in Beauchamp Place. Again they prospered: 'we became slightly less amateurish, never got on each other's nerves, made any number of ludicrous mistakes and encounters and added to the staff largely from our circle of friends'. Their final move, to a larger shop on Beauchamp Place, saw the business now described as 'Interior Decorators', and it continued to thrive.

As well as developing her skills as both a journalist and an interior designer, Ngaio found that her unusual height and slim build could be an advantage. Her hair was, by now, cut in a fashionable bob. She was employed briefly as a mannequin (fashion model) for an exclusive shop off Bond Street run by an expatriate Russian. The unreality of the fashion show, and the contrast between the languid wealthy audience, the 'listless precision of the models' and the poorly dressed cockney assistants behind the scenes 'wearily folding up the wares' at the end of a long afternoon seems to have impressed her more than the 30-guinea dresses and the socialites sitting on gilt chairs in the salon. Another adventure was the air show at Heston, which alarmed and thrilled her with its noise and breathtaking aerial displays, including a mock dog-fight. Surprisingly, given her hatred of air travel in later years, she paid five shillings for a fifteen-minute spin in a small plane, and wrote rhapsodically:

I saw London, spread out like a plasticine model, with stray wisps of smoke and steamy clouds caught in her towers. I saw the great arteries lying like threads of silk across the countryside, and I saw how green England is, how rich in trees and fallow fields. I seemed to see anew how little, and old, and lovable she is, and how lonely in the northern seas. One dreams often of flying, and to fly in reality is rather like a dream, for during flight all values are changed and a new aspect of perspective bemuses one's senses.

50

Other pieces from the pen of the 'New Canterbury Pilgrim' featured visits to Windsor, Canterbury, and Sandwich on the Kent coast. She finds time to praise British radio and to comment on the latest exhibitions of paintings in London. These articles provide a witty and revealing commentary on English life for two years, seen with the clear eye of someone who was both part of it, and an astute observer of the scene.

All her journalism of this period was full of exuberance: 'it was wonderful to be alone and at large in London'. What did she really feel, then, when she had word that her mother was making the long journey from Christchurch to join her? Henry Marsh had now retired from the bank, and with some secretaryships adding to his pension, was able to afford a passage to England for Rose, her one and only visit. He himself was prepared to stay in Christchurch, living quietly and caring for the house and the garden.

With the arrival of Ngaio's mother in 1930 life began to take a new direction once more, this time away from the light-hearted Rhodes family whose company she so much enjoyed. Although Ngaio was pleased that her mother should also experience life in England for a time, there must also have been a very real sense of lost freedom. Rose Marsh had always exerted a strong influence on her daughter, encouraging her artistic side, both as a writer and a painter. She was undoubtedly uneasy at finding her working in a shop. Although she did not say much, she indicated to Ngaio that she had lost direction with her commercial activities.

By now the whole of the Rhodes family had transferred to Eaton Mansions with their servants, and even with two flats used as one the extra presence of Ngaio's mother would clearly be a problem. In July, she and Ngaio moved into a small basement flat nearby, which they kept until Rose went back to New Zealand in 1931. Furniture was contributed by the Rhodes family, to keep costs down. Although Ngaio claimed that the flat was in Bourne Street, members of the Rhodes family remember it being on Caroline Street, the next road along. The removal from Eaton Mansions, and the presence of her mother, meant a subtle change in Ngaio's interests.

Twenty years earlier she had been introduced to serious theatre by her mother, and now they started queuing again for cheap gallery seats, just as they had in Christchurch. A friend from New

Zealand, Dundas Walker, who had been involved with them in amateur theatricals, was also in London, as was a member of the old Allan Wilkie Company. The focus of Ngaio's life began to turn again to Shakespeare and contemporary drama instead of the more light-hearted entertainments that she saw with the Rhodes circle. An experience that was to affect her as deeply as Wilkie's *Hamlet* was her first view of Pirandello's classic play, *Six Characters in Search of an Author*. Tyrone Guthrie was directing it at the Westminster Theatre, and Ngaio went to a matinee with her mother. To Ngaio, the play represented many of her own instincts about theatre; the ephemeral, but deeply moving nature of it all, the characters emerging from nothing to be given life for a few moments on stage before they disappear again into darkness, the fusion of so many creative impulses that constitutes a theatrical performance. She wrote in her autobiography: 'If you long above everything to be a director, this is the play that nags and clamours to be done. I was broody with it, off and on, for some eighteen years before I finally got it out of my system in a burst of three separate productions in three separate countries'.

Very gently Rose Marsh was again steering her daughter towards the directions in which her true talents lay. Perhaps as a result of simply having more time to herself, now that she was not part of the turbulent world of 'the Lampreys" large household, or perhaps realising that it would please her mother, Ngaio began again to write more than journalism in the evenings. She had brought with her a novel started in about 1927 with a New Zealand setting, and worked on it from time to time while in England. It seemed to be the New Zealand landscape above all that she wanted to capture in prose, as an equivalent to her own oil paintings:

> I wrote two chapters into which I tried to put mountains and a handful of people . . . the mountains and people chose me rather than I them and I found I wanted, quite passionately, to write about them.[9]

The problems she encountered in dealing with a New Zealand setting and New Zealand characters became clearer to her several years later, when she had returned to Christchurch. Writing in the Christchurch *Press* in December 1934, she was engagingly honest in discussing her failure to develop this novel. Her essay was in response to a series of articles by novelist Jane Mander on New Zealand fiction, and Ngaio admitted in this piece that 'I have tried to write such a novel and at once found myself confronted with difficulties as great as they are hard to define'. She tries to explain the problem in terms of painting:

> When a painter in oils attempts composition he must paint his background at the same time as the figures that are to come out in front of it. Wherever the background touches the figure, both must be wet. It is quite hopeless to complete a background and then, on a dry surface, impose the figures. The result of such a method would be an uncomfortable and arid dissonance. Such, I believe, is the problem of the New Zealand novel. It is a problem of background. There can be no help at all in the construction of a *mise en scène*, overloaded with local colour, unless the characters grow out of it and live in front of it.[10]

Ngaio clearly wrestled seriously with this problem of background in the opening chapters of her novel and felt that 'for a time it seemed to me that background and figures worked well together, the one growing out of the other without too much insistence on either'. But she became dissatisfied as the work developed:

> It had lost my first intention and was steaming off busily down the well-worn rails of the colonial novel. I had merely changed the landscape and might as well have sent my characters to Canada or Jericho. Gone was the idea which was to have been the whole matter of my book. I turned, more successfully, to crime fiction.

Speaking in public about Katherine Mansfield many years later, Ngaio returned to the problem of New Zealand as a setting for literature, and praised Mansfield for not allowing scenery to overpower her characters. But the setting is doing its work, nevertheless: 'because she isn't writing her boots off to create local colour she remains one of the most successful of our writers to do precisely that thing'. A writer like Ngaio Marsh who could isolate the unique problems of writing prose fiction that was to be rooted in a new and as yet artistically undefined society, who understood the significance of a landscape that could only be felt 'through the spiritual and mental experiences of human beings', was capable of making a significant contribution to the growth of New Zealand literature. The abandonment of her New Zealand novel must be a matter of much regret. As with the challenge of landscape painting, Ngaio was unhappy with what she had achieved, and set off in a completely different direction. Her recognition of the need for such a work remained, and in *Black Beech and Honeydew* she says:

> There was, and is, room for a rattling good yarn about the Coast but I was not and am not the one to write it. A gap waited and still waits for a penetrating and aesthetically satisfying novel born of that formidable landscape. Our contemporary writers are, I think, too solemn and not grave enough to achieve it.[11]

Was this a prophecy that looked towards Keri Hulme, the writer who in *The Bone People* in 1985 brought that wild and lonely country to a universal readership? Before leaving Christchurch, Ngaio had told herself that she had two aims as a writer, to produce a serious novel about New Zealand, and to write a detective story as an exercise in style. The first of her writing aims was laid aside. The second was to prove a very flourishing enterprise indeed.

CHAPTER 4

Birth of a Sleuth: 1931–42

Chief Detective-Inspector Roderick Alleyn, CID, was born between the limp sheets of a penny exercise book on a wet afternoon in 1931. Left alone in the flat for the weekend while her mother was visiting a friend, Ngaio looked out at the rain which had poured down all day. She had been reading a detective story to pass the time, and as she made up the coal fire in the late afternoon she wondered if she could write something similar:

> I played about with this idea. I tinkered with the fire and with an emergent character who might have been engendered in its sulky entrails: a solver of crimes.
>
> The room had become quite dark when I pulled on a mackintosh, took an umbrella, plunged up the basement steps and beat my way through rain-fractured lamplight to the stationer's shop. It smelt of damp newsprint, cheap magazines, and wet people. I bought six exercise books, a pencil and a pencil sharpener and splashed back to the flat.[1]

Her disarming description in 'Birth of a Sleuth' (1977) of how she embarked upon her first crime novel, *A Man Lay Dead*, tends to obscure the fact that by this time she was already a very competent writer. From childhood her literary gifts had been encouraged, and through most of her life she had been transposing experience into prose. The travel essays she sent back to New Zealand newspapers were far more than mere descriptions of places and events; they were full of quirky observations and dramatically shaped vignettes that exactly capture the flavour of the moment. Looking back from a vantage point in the 1990s, when travel writing is a recognised genre, Ngaio's pieces rank high in any company. Their human interest makes the scene more immediate, and the novelist's essential curiosity about the hidden life behind the exterior is never absent. Ngaio was eminently qualified for her new task, and there was nothing amateur in her approach. She started as a professional and she remained one until she set down the manuscript of *Light Thickens*, her last novel, in December 1981, six weeks before her death. Having wasted ten years, as she recognised in a letter to Denys Rhodes written in the 1940s, she finally knew where she was heading.

Ngaio's fictional detective, Roderick Alleyn, was devised as a character who would be 'an attractive, civilised man with whom it would be pleasant to talk, but much less pleasant to fall out'. She tailored him to fit the country house society with which she had become familiar since arriving in England; his brother was a baronet and his mother Lady Alleyn of Danes Lodge, Bossicote, Buckinghamshire. He was tall and good-looking: 'thin with an accidental elegance ... fastidious ... compassionate ... with a cockeyed sense of humour, dependent largely upon understatement but, for all his unemphatic, rather apologetic ways, he could be a formidable person of considerable authority'.[2] He is highly professional and successful in his field; we are told in *Vintage Murder* that his book *Principles and Practice of Criminal Investigation* (published by Sable and Murgatroyd at 21 shillings) is widely read throughout the world—'we've all been trained on your book', says the local Police Inspector in Middleton, New Zealand.

Interestingly, in view of the serious novel still in her mind at this time, the author found that when she started to develop the character of Roderick Alleyn he seemed familiar: 'if I had not fallen so casually into the practice of crime-writing and had taken to a more serious form, he would still have arrived and found himself in an altogether different setting'. Was Ngaio describing here the sort of man she had been hoping to meet for many years? Did she fall in love with her creation, as Dorothy Sayers did with Lord Peter Wimsey? She denied it firmly, but admitted to liking him very much: 'I've never got tired of the old boy'. And his eventual marriage to a successful painter, Troy, must represent a certain wish fulfilment on the part of a mature writer who was still not averse to the possibilities of romance.

A Man Lay Dead was written swiftly in Ngaio's basement flat. It is very much a formula novel, set in a country house where guests are invited to take part in a 'murder game', a popular pastime with the fashionable set during the early 1930s. The puzzle is cleverly worked out, but the novel lacks the interesting characters who distinguish her more mature novels, such as The Boomer in *Black as He's Painted* (1974), or the temperamental prima donna in *Photo-Finish* (1980). She was simply following the classic advice to the tyro writer: write about what you know. As part of the Rhodes/Plunket circle, Miss Ngaio Marsh did know the social niceties of house parties and country house weekends; she had shared in this ambience since she arrived in England, and was already familiar with its transplanted variety in New Zealand. She knew that the murder game was popular at these gatherings, and she knew exactly where the drinks tray would be placed, and at what time dinner would be called. Ngaio had no fond memories of *A Man Lay Dead* in later years, and she said in a 1964 interview, 'I wish he was lying completely dead . . . the plot's quite good but there's a lot of very amateurish writing. However the book's been revived recently in paper-back and is doing quite well, blast it!'[3] (*A Man Lay Dead* was again reprinted in the Collins Crime Club's 'Famous Firsts' collection in 1981.)

On reading the exercise books Ngaio's mother had confessed that she couldn't put the novel down, but according to her daughter, 'I don't know to this day whether I only imagined an overtone of regret in her voice'.[4] It is a telling comment, because throughout her writing career she was desperately unsure about what she had achieved. Work in the theatre was not a problem; she was a confident leader and an inspiration to others. But as a prose writer she constantly denigrated her achievement and was given little encouragement by the Christchurch literary set who tended to look on crime fiction as inferior: 'We tried not to talk about Ngaio's books', said one friend recently, and Ngaio claimed in her autobiography that 'intellectual New Zealand friends tactfully avoid all mention of my published work and if they like me, do so, I cannot help but feel, in spite of it'.[5] Rose Marsh may have been the first to give this impression, or perhaps they were both thinking of the abandoned New Zealand novel that could possibly still be nurtured into life.

If we accept Julian Symons's view in his authoritative book *Bloody Murder* (1972) that crime fiction in the first part of the twentieth century falls into two Golden Ages, the first including Conan Doyle,

G. K. Chesterton, Edgar Wallace and their followers, and the second taking in the 1930s up to the Second World War, then Ngaio Marsh falls into the second era. She entered this Golden Age with a novel that followed an already well-established pattern. In these novels, as Julian Symons points out, 'the General Strike of 1926 never took place, trade unions did not exist, and when sympathy was expressed for the poor it was not for the unemployed but for those struggling along on a fixed inherited income'.[6] Raymond Chandler, who like Ngaio's father, Henry Marsh, was educated at Dulwich College, but who spent most of his life in the United States, wrote in his essay 'The Simple Art of Murder' that English detective writers knew only the conversational accent of the wealthier parts of the south of England, and used 'an arid formula which could not even satisfy its own implications'.[7] But not everyone takes this harsh view of the detective fiction of the 1930s. P. D. James sees beyond the obvious snobbery and acceptance of class prejudices to a welcome world of escape, where a settled society offers the reader a sense of confidence and security:

> The hurrying throng of 1930 wage earners, who perforce removed their own cufflinks, streaming into Baker Street station to catch the 6.30 back to mortgaged Metroland, harassed by the fear of unemployment, worried by the depression and gathering storms over Europe, must have escaped with relief into Lord Peter's opulent drawing room at 110A Piccadilly with its walls lined with first editions, its bowl of chrysanthemums on the grand piano and Bunter deferentially proffering the Cockburn '96. Wimsey's Piccadilly flat is as cosy and reassuring a refuge from the alarming world outside as is the claustrophobic sanctum at 221B Baker Street.[8]

Or, as Colin Watson declares in his essay 'Mayhem Parva and Wicked Belgravia':

> The ritual of investigation, deduction and inevitable solution, had several effects. It confirmed as desirable the rule of law and decency. The rendering harmless of the criminal at the end of each book seemed somehow to cancel out the deaths and distress that had gone before. It all made the world seem right, tight and as we were. And that, in a Golden Age of which the glister was lamentably ephemeral, was a devoutly desired delusion.[9]

How comfortably did the novels of Ngaio Marsh fit into these categories when, with Agatha Christie, Margery Allingham and Dorothy Sayers she was crowned one of the Queens of Crime? In 1934, when *A Man Lay Dead* was published, Dorothy Sayers was at her peak. *Murder Must Advertise* was published in 1933, *The Nine Tailors* in 1934, and *Gaudy Night* the following year, all of them proving that detective fiction could offer much more than a simple puzzle, investigation and solution. By 1934, Agatha Christie had published twenty-nine books (novels, plays and poems), including the two novels often regarded as her finest, *The Murder of Roger Ackroyd* (1926) and *Murder on the Orient Express* (1934). The year 1934 clearly produced a chateau-bottled crime vintage of great distinction, since it also saw the publication of Margery Allingham's *Death of a Ghost*, the first of her novels to show the development of character that was to enhance her crime fiction from then on. All four writers were expanding the genre in various ways, particularly with regard to character and the role of the detective. Readers became familiar with recurring characters, and the pleasure of opening a novel and meeting an old friend such as Miss Marple or Roderick Alleyn was, and still is, one of the aspects of crime fiction that devotees most enjoy.

None of these writers stayed rooted in the archetypal English village jokingly called Mayhem Parva; all explored fresh territory and new situations. Of the eight novels that Marsh published in the 1930s, only one, *Overture to Death* (1939), falls directly into the category of the 'English cosy', a novel set entirely in an English country village, where the highlight of the social season is a play performed by local talent in the village hall. The others deal with a variety of backgrounds—the special worlds of the theatre, in *Enter a Murderer* published in 1935, and *Vintage Murder* (1937); a hospital, *The Nursing Home Murder* (1935); a religious cult, *Death in Ecstasy* (1936); or a painting school in an artist's house, *Artists in Crime* (1938). Only *A Man Lay Dead*, her first novel, is set within the restricted confines of a country house party, although *Death in a White Tie* (1938) does deal with upper-class life in London society.

From the beginning, Ngaio was much more concerned with character than with plot, and this makes her novels very different from those of Agatha Christie, who sketched character lightly and preferred to baffle her readers with an apparently endless stream of imaginative and ingenious plots, all of which were meticulously worked out before she began. Ngaio, on the other hand, struggled hard over the intricacies of her plots, but as a proficient crossword puzzle addict she had the kind of intelligence that responded to twists and turns. The affinity between many readers and writers of crime fiction and the solution of crossword puzzles is well known. According to Colin Dexter, author of the Inspector Morse novels:

> The analogy between crosswords and whodunits is very close, I think. You've got problems, you've got clues, and you've got to find a solution. What I love about them both is the way you can wander through a maze of facts that can be interpreted in any number of ways and then suddenly come retrospectively to a blindingly obvious solution that you'd missed. I love the penny-dropping sensation of that reversal. The same kind of elegance and neatness that marks the best whodunits, Agatha Christie's *The Murder of Roger Ackroyd*, for example, is typical of a first-rate crossword clue.[10]

As Ngaio became more proficient in the genre, she also became more perceptive about her readers, dividing them into two camps, the acquiescent and the combatant. The acquiescent 'take their detective fiction in much the same way as they take their sleeping pills, their crossword puzzles or their aperitives. For them the story really is a means of escape'. The combatant is harder to please: 'his great object is to catch the writer out, and to guess who-done-it as long as possible before he is meant to do so'.[11] With the constant feeling that her formidable readers were out there waiting to pounce, Ngaio always took great care to write her novels about characters she was familiar with, in settings she knew well. She researched the ground thoroughly, and built up a good library of legal and medical books to provide authoritative detail for her violent crimes. *Taylor's Principles and Practice of Medical Jurisprudence* was invaluable, as was Simpson and Knight's *Forensic Medicine*. A chart showing the organisation and chain of command in New Scotland Yard was always pinned up on her study wall. Details of injuries, post-mortem reports, inquests, all had to be correct, and Ngaio was very proud of a comment made to her once by a senior Scotland Yard Officer that she 'had never put a foot wrong'.

Perhaps, but her later novels became increasingly outdated regarding police methods, with Alleyn and Fox inhabiting a kind of undefined time-warp vaguely associated with the 1950s.

In adopting an established literary genre and using it to write about the sorts of characters and milieu she found interesting, Ngaio was perfectly aware of what she was doing. Her rare pronouncements on the writing of crime fiction reveal a sophisticated understanding of the form. She claims that:

It is a form that can command our aesthetic approval. It is, by its nature, shapely. It must have a beginning, a middle and an end. The middle must be an extension and development of the beginning and the end must be implicit in both. The writing is as good as the author can make it; nervous, taut, balanced and economic. Descriptive passages are vivid and explicit. The author is not self-indulgent. If he commands a good style, there is every reason for maintaining it. [12]

Her concern with structure led her to compare detective fiction to metaphysical poetry, where ingenuity of style was also bounded by strict conventions. In this view she is in agreement with P. D. James, who said recently, 'I love the craft of a detective novel. You really have to construct it'. [13]

Marsh found that her novels were always character based:

I invariably start with people. With two or three or more people about whom I feel I would like to write. Because I am a maker of detective fiction I must involve one of them in a crime of violence. So I have to ask myself which of these persons is capable of such a crime, what form it would take and under what circumstances would he or she commit it. Very often I begin to write about these people in their immediate situation with no more than the scantiest framework for a plot and its denouement. This is a cockeyed method of setting about a strictly conventional form and it lands one with a great deal of rewriting. But it's the only way I can work. [14]

When in *Bloody Murder* Julian Symons wrote with disappointment that 'Marsh takes refuge from real emotional problems in the official investigation and interrogation of suspects', [15] Ngaio defended herself by saying that this was one of the 'limitations of the genre'. H. R. F. Keating said in a recent interview that Ngaio Marsh never seemed to realise how little of the procedural investigation approach was necessary in modern crime fiction. A harsher view might suggest that deeper exploration of character would have exposed more about the author than she was willing to allow. It is possible to take refuge in the firm corsetry of detective fiction, and several of Marsh's novels give the impression that she abandoned characters who were running away with her into a more revealing situation than she wished to explore. The heroine of *Opening Night* (1951), for instance, resembles Ngaio in many ways, and this novel is singled out by Symons as an example of an interesting crime novel awkwardly reined in and yoked into the heavy harness of a conventional detective investigation. This is a view shared by Jessica Mann, who finds that 'the author's reticence has diminished the life of her novels',[16] and that Marsh's work is 'pleasant and entertaining but not entirely satisfying'. [17]

Yet Ngaio was an innovator within the genre, extending it far beyond the 1920s conventions that she had inherited. Bruce Cassiday in *The Literature of Crime and Detection* (1988) sees that 'her forte was in utilising the tried-and-true elements of the country-house detective story, the English police procedural, and the psychological novel. And she did it in such a way that she strengthened the genre, rather than weakened it'. He also considers 'her ear for the spoken word, fine-tuned by her theatrical background, is one of the best elements of her work'.[18] Linked to her facility with dialogue is her gift for comedy: 'she was a comic writer of stature' states Lord Hardinge of Penshurst (who as George Hardinge was a Senior Editor at Collins for many years), pointing out that this is often overlooked when her novels are being discussed. In her thirty-two novels, written over nearly fifty years, Ngaio achieved considerable variety in approach. Instead of moving into a new form of fiction, or even attempting to write in a different form, such as drama, for which she was very well equipped, she preferred to push out the detective fiction formula in different directions.

The question of why she did not choose to write original plays is perplexing. With her adept use of dialogue in fiction, her exuberantly detailed characterisation and her abundant sense of humour, all the ingredients were present for plays that would have presented a real challenge to those of Agatha Christie. Apart from her play for children, *The Wyvern and the Unicorn* (1954), and her 1920s one-act play 'Little Housebound', Ngaio wrote nothing specifically for the stage and her adaptations of her own novels were not overly successful. But dramatic devices are often used in the novels to unmask the criminal and Alleyn proves to be adept at restaging an intricately plotted murder with all the suspects looking on.

Ngaio was skilled at charming evasions when questions came too close to the truth about her writing. The steadfast refusal to use her literary talent for anything but crime fiction is hard to understand. The excuse that her readers would be disappointed by anything but whodunits is not justified, since several crime writers, from Sir Arthur Conan Doyle onwards, have published a variety of fiction, often under pseudonyms. Under the pseudonym Mary Westmacott, Agatha Christie published six serious novels before her identity was revealed. Her first Westmacott novel, *Giant's Bread* (1930), was written when she was lonely and unhappy after the breakdown of her first marriage, and the novel reveals a great deal about her own emotions at that time. This, of course, is what Ngaio always strove to avoid. The detective novel provided exactly the right framework for a stylised view of life that would shed no light on the writer's much-valued privacy.

In the 1940s many reviewers were encouraging Ngaio to use her gift for characterisation in more diversified fiction. Were her publishers to blame with their relentless 'one a year' pressure for her novels? Or her agent, for placing so much emphasis on re-taining her position as a top crime novelist? Or did Ngaio find crime fiction a convenient way of gaining financial independence without making unsettling demands on her emotional resources? After all, she seldom spent more than nine months on a book—about the same time as a pregnancy, she used to say—and this left her considerable time to follow her great love, the theatre. Nevertheless, despite her professionalism and efficiency, Ngaio never missed a chance to point out the hard work involved in crime fiction: 'writing is a hideous trouble', she once said on New Zealand Radio. She went on to describe what in her view' was the truth about professional writers:

We worry and fumble and rehash. At two o'clock in the morning we get marvellous ideas and at eight o'clock the following evening we recognise those ideas for the nonsense they are. We have awful sessions when nothing goes right, and brief but blissful sessions when everything seems to go well. We worry ourselves sick about income tax. We have responsibilities. We do not work in a light-hearted, carefree fashion, all for fun. We do not wait for inspiration. We work because we've jolly well got to. But when all is said and done, we toil at this particular job because it's turned out to be our particular job, and in a weird sort of way I suppose we may be said to like it.[19]

But this was the seasoned professional talking, many years later. In 1932, *A Man Lay Dead* was lodged with a London agent, Edmund Cork, at the literary agency Hughes Massie. Cork was also agent to Agatha Christie, who was then well established as a writer, and he saw the development of their parallel careers from then on. The novel receded from Ngaio's immediate thoughts and personal concerns became paramount. Her mother, having stayed in London for over a year, felt that she must return to Christchurch, and Ngaio made the difficult decision not to go back with her. Ngaio wanted to extract more from her stay in London, but again the agony of the only child gripped her:

> She was wonderfully good about it. I knew she would like, above everything, for me to return with her but she didn't say so until a short time before she sailed. We looked at each other and I felt a desperate pang of guilt, an agony of compassion when I said I couldn't; that I would come before long but not yet: not now.[20]

After Rose left, Ngaio moved back into Eaton Mansions with the Rhodes family. Having made this choice, Ngaio was shocked to receive word from her father several months later that her mother was seriously ill. Nothing she could have done would have altered the situation, but she was never again to see her mother as she remembered her, lively and intelligent, sharing the special experience of the London theatre, or smiling brilliantly as her ship departed from England, leaving her daughter behind.

Ships' passages were not easy to arrange hastily in the 1930s and the journey itself could take up to two months, depending on the choice of vessel and the route. Ngaio left England in midsummer 1932 with few thoughts of the novel she had left behind. She arrived in New Zealand at the end of August. Rose Elizabeth Marsh died of cancer on 23 November, at the age of sixty-eight. The swiftness of her death no doubt intensified Ngaio's guilt at not having accompanied her back to New Zealand. It is indicative of her restricted emotional development that Ngaio should claim in her autobiography that the death of her mother marked her own coming of age. She was by then thirty-seven years old, an age when most women have had their fair share of responsibility and worry. Watching a loved one suffer and die shook her deeply, probably more so because of the gentle passage that life had afforded her so far. Ngaio's father, Henry, was to live for another sixteen years, and her care for him shaped her life emphatically during that time.

Ngaio's relationship with her mother is difficult to crystallise, and there was always a great deal that she herself could not explain:

Whatever I may write about my mother will be full of contradictions. I think that as I grew older I grew, better perhaps than anyone else, to understand her. And yet how much there was about her that still remains unaccounted for, like the odd pieces of a jigsaw puzzle. Of one thing I am sure: she had in her an element of creative art never fully realised. I think that the intensity of devotion which might have been spent upon its development was poured out upon her only child, who, though she returned this love, inevitably and however unwisely, began at last to make decisions from which she would not be deflected.[21]

In her autobiography she generally speaks more warmly of her father, and in some interviews she reveals a sense of oppression, almost of fear, in relation to her mother. Yet Ngaio seems to have been much closer to her mother's family in character and temperament, with her grandfather's love of performance and a good dose of her grandmother's practical and organisational ability, than to the Marsh family. Rose Marsh saw at an early stage that her daughter's literary and dramatic talents were unusual, and set about igniting these as best she could. Her lack of enthusiasm about the shop 'Touch and Go' was understandable: no doubt she was horrified to see Ngaio, then aged thirty-five, frittering her life away making lampshades. But without this experience, and without her extended stay in London, Ngaio could never have gone back to

New Zealand and used her store of detail to provide the background for the four more detective novels that she wrote between 1932 and 1937.

The New Zealand she returned to in 1932 could hardly have provided more of a contrast to the England she had left. The Depression was at its height, and in 1932 riots had occurred in all four major cities. In Christchurch, university students had broken up a tram-drivers' strike and many unemployed men and their families were destitute, relying on the Salvation Army or the Church to keep them from starving. Yet, as Julian Symons has pointed out, it was quite possible for a writer of classic detective fiction to keep the fictional world well separated from reality. With Ngaio's father now retired from the bank, it was not difficult to place social and political pressures firmly at a distance and to stay at a remove in the Cashmere Hills or visiting friends in the country.

During her stay in the south of England Ngaio had come to love gardens, and now she turned to creating an English country garden around her house. The trees which had been planted around the property when it was first built were now mature and provided an essential shelter-belt against cold southerly winds. The steeply sloping land meant that flowerbeds could only be created by terracing, and Ngaio designed a series of grassy paths, lawns and stone walls for her imported shrubs. Watering vulnerable plants was a constant problem in summer, and small boys visiting with their parents would be dispatched to the garden with a hose and suggestions for the most imaginative use of irrigation channels. Creating the garden took many years but as time passed it became an exuberant and colourful blend of roses, shrubs and trees. There was room for some native plants, including the little white-flowered shrub, the ngaio. The garden was featured in New Zealand *Vogue* in 1964, and Ngaio was photographed against a background of well-cared-for rose beds. There was always a paid gardener, once income from books improved, although Ngaio herself liked to do a little pottering in the garden during the afternoons. A kitchen garden supplied all the vegetables needed for the house.

One of her most flourishing trees was a mulberry. The neighbouring children, who were keeping silkworms as pets, called every day at the same time for mulberry leaves to feed them. One day Ngaio heard the bell as usual, and she crawled over to the door on hands and knees. Opening it a crack, she boomed out in a sepulchral voice from a few inches above the floor, 'Silkworms?' Standing on the doorstep, petrified and about to flee down the hill, was a total stranger.

Marton Cottage now became, as she remarked in her autobiography, 'a masculine household', where her father and his elderly friends were catered to by Ngaio, and later by her housekeeper, Mrs Crawford. Ngaio's tastes in décor did not bloom until after her father's death, when she filled the house with floral chintzes, pastel-coloured upholstery and colourful rugs. Although she claimed to be contented, friends describe the depressing experience of visiting Ngaio on dreary Sunday evenings, to find her dutifully playing Lexicon with a group of old men. She became lonely and increasingly isolated, but unquestioningly knew that she had to remain in Christchurch as long as her father was alive. Now in her forties, the girlish bloom that had always made her appear younger than she was had disappeared; she looked gaunt and anxious in the period following her mother's death, and she was smoking heavily.

Furthermore, the literary world in which she had achieved modest success overseas was in New Zealand firmly dominated by men. Drusilla Modjeska, writing in *Exiles at Home* about this decade in Australia, finds that 'it was a hostile environment for women writers. There was little to encourage them to stay in Australia then or during any of the early years of this century'.[22] Nothing in New Zealand contradicted this. Women were permitted some journalism, particularly if their contributions were restricted to the social pages of local newspapers. In 1939, E. M. Smith's *A History of New Zealand Fiction* was swift to label as propagandist women whose writing stepped beyond the boundaries of family life and scenic description. For serious prose writers there was little sympathy or support; a situation readily recognised by leading New Zealand poet Lauris Edmond, who encountered Ngaio Marsh while studying at Canterbury University, and even then, in the early 1940s, sensed her isolation as well as her talent. Only Robin Hyde, battling with the serious depression that hospitalised her for long periods in the 1930s, was writing distinctive and emotive fiction that would not be equalled until Janet Frame started publishing after the Second World War.

By setting her novels on an international stage and by using the highly refined genre of detective fiction, Ngaio managed to escape the prevailing cultural attitudes in New Zealand. She also proved she could function effectively on that international stage, although her entire literary career was marked by insecurity and lack of confidence in her work. 'I don't think I've ever known an author more humble', said Edmund Cork of Ngaio, at the end of a life dealing with many famous writers.

It soon became very clear to her that she needed periodic bursts of English life to charge the batteries and give her ideas for plots: 'I like to work against the stream'. The zest for life and intense interest in other people so apparent in her travel writing indicate how stimulating her long journeys were, and how much she gained as a writer. Above all, she must have known, whether she would admit it to herself or not, how important it was to escape from the stultifying society of Christchurch in which she was now to become an established figure. In England she felt herself come alive. To a BBC interviewer in 1960 she stressed how important these regular visits to London were for her: 'you get a certain freshness of impact each time you come. The London feeling which I get very strongly to an extraordinary extent, starts me off writing every time as soon as I come to England'. On these extended visits she adopted the privileged position of the outsider who benefited from an entree to very high society indeed, yet who kept a necessary sense of detachment. An ironic tone is often apparent in her novels, mixed with a naive admiration for certain aristocratic qualities. She was well aware of her position as observer:

> It's the difference between, say, being in a talking picture and looking at it . . . I'm in the position now where I look at the talking picture but I've also made friends with the actors in it. But I'm not yet completely part of the cast in the film, I think . . . I couldn't bear to think that I wasn't coming back every three or four years.[23]

It was to be 1937 before Ngaio would again reach out for 'that London feeling', but by then she was the author of five popular novels and had more under way. Writing and the theatre were increasingly filling her time, although she retained the friendship of the painters in the Christchurch Group. Many of them had also been to Europe in recent years and had altered their styles dramatically as a result. Ngaio was, however, becoming more and more displeased with her painting. The return to New Zealand caused her to look at the landscape of the South Island with fresh eyes, and after the death of her mother in 1932 she spent long periods with her friend, Phyllis Bethune, painting in South Canterbury. In 1933 and 1934 she exhibited a number of large oil paintings with the New Zealand Society of Arts in Auckland and with the Canterbury Society of Arts. These landscapes were typical of the style adopted by many Christchurch artists at that time, with their broad areas of colour and almost two-dimensional approach to distance. Ngaio did not only paint landscapes and the one work by her that is held in the Robert McDougall Art Gallery in Christchurch is the brightly coloured oil painting of the Native Market, Durban, first exhibited in 1933. This was the same scene vividly described by 'A New Canterbury Pilgrim' on her trip to England five years earlier.

Art historian Julie Anne Catchpole, who has made a study of the Christchurch Group, saw in these artists 'the use of line or simple masses of colour articulated by tonal gradations to define form. These qualities could be seen to a greater or lesser extent in Ngaio Marsh'.[24] The word most often used to describe her work was 'dramatic', because of her use of strong colours and hard light. This harsh New Zealand summer sunlight is well captured in an unusual painting exhibited in the Canterbury School of Art exhibition in 1935 but painted earlier, at the time when the government had instigated public construction schemes to create employment during the Depression. The painting *Relief Workers* (sometimes called *In the Quarry*) depicts a group of these men building a road just below Ngaio's house on the Cashmere Hills. Very few are actually working on what appears to be a hot and dusty afternoon, and one man is actually asleep in a wheelbarrow. When Ngaio submitted this painting with the joky title *Still Life*, a puzzled organiser telephoned to ask if the title really applied to this painting or another featuring a bowl of fruit and some dead birds. Ngaio must have capitulated; it is *Relief Workers* in the catalogue. The painting was the source of another joke that is still remembered in Christchurch. The relief workers were evidently offended at being depicted as idlers, and to answer the insult they persuaded a relative of one of the men to paint another picture, which showed Ngaio's house in the background and a track leading up to it liberally sprinkled with red Craven A cigarette packets. According to one of the men involved:

> It was a bit of good-humoured tit for tat. Relief workers could not afford 'tailor-made' cigarettes, or even much tobacco. The picture was duly delivered and well received. Later, a carton of Craven A arrived at the quarry and was shared among the men—an appreciation from Ngaio Marsh.[25]

Ngaio's paintings were still largely concerned with the New Zealand landscape, even though the fiction she was writing at the same time was based in England. She retained her contact with the Group throughout the 1930s, and a photograph taken by Olivia Spencer-Bower in 1936 shows members preparing to hang one of the annual exhibitions. Ngaio is seated centrally, looking very *rive gauche* in a beret, tie and trousers.

By the middle of the 1930s Ngaio knew that although she would continue to paint and sketch for the rest of her life, she was never likely to achieve what she strove for as an artist. The success of her first novel proved that not only was this an expressive medium over which she did have control, but it was also a useful source of income. From *A Man Lay Dead*, published in 1934 by Geoffrey Bles, she earned an advance of £30 and 10 per cent royalties, which was about average for popular novels during that period. Bles published the first seven novels, but a substantial improvement in finances came with her move to William Collins in 1938. Ngaio felt guilty about leaving Geoffrey Bles, who had given her the encouragement she needed at the beginning of her career. But Edmund Cork felt that she would be better served by the larger firm, which was already successfully publishing and promoting his other Queen of Crime, Agatha Christie. Collins was able to offer an advance of £250 and royalties of 15 per cent for four detective novels. She remained with Collins for the rest of her publishing career and was also loyal to the American publisher, Little, Brown from 1940 onwards. From the start she was happy to leave the business side entirely in the hands of her agents, and accepted their efforts with humble gratitude. Ngaio always seemed pleased and surprised that anyone should want to publish her, and also made it clear that she considered haggling over terms an undignified activity. At the same time, she liked the things that money could buy, such as the new Chevrolet car she bought in 1938 after the move to Collins.

Work in the theatre was now being offered on a more regular and professional basis and added a modest amount to her income. New Zealand had a strong network of local repertory groups which maintained a yearly programme in local theatres and halls. Ngaio was often asked to be guest producer by these groups, and during the 1930s, when her father was still in good health, she gave her time freely. She was generally invited to produce 'one or two rather more venturesome pieces to appease the intelligentsia in their audiences and satisfy immortal longings in the odd administrative breast'. Attempts to persuade these companies to try a Shakespeare play met with solid refusal: no one wanted Shakespeare these days. But interest in drama was strengthened by the formation of the New Zealand branch of the British Drama League in 1932, which provided a focal point for small amateur companies to get together at festivals and competitions. Many of these drama groups came from isolated rural communities and involved churches and Women's Institutes, with a predominance of women. The opportunity to come together, however infrequently, to meet other people interested in theatre was of great value. Ngaio was asked to judge these festivals on a number of occasions, and a member of the Canterbury Repertory Society remembers that 'we were all very fond of Ngaio. She was unusually talented but she never talked down to anyone'. With her sense of humour and her understanding of the many problems involved in getting any show on the road, Ngaio was charitable in her judgements but always keen to raise standards and to fan any flames of real dramatic talent that she came across.

Bruce Mason the New Zealand dramatist and actor, who met Ngaio when she was judging a student drama competition, recalls her kindness and encouragement:

I first met Ngaio in Christchurch early in 1941, when I was a member of the Victoria College drama team, who visited Christchurch with a play called *The Intruder* by Maeterlinck. Our leading man was drunk, and finally could say nothing but the line, 'I do not know what ails me', which occurred twice in the text; he said it probably a dozen times before the play expired and the director, Pat Hildreth, had hysterics. Ngaio was adjudicating, and placed us third, of three. I shall never forget seeing her comfort Pat Hildreth, and can still hear her voice declaring, 'Your attitude is thoroughly professional, and that's what counts'.[26]

It was the same common-sense yet sympathetic view that made her march around with her friends to a London dressing room in the 1950s to comfort a young New Zealand actor after a dreadful performance, and to assure him that it would be better next time.

Ngaio's second novel, *Enter a Murderer* (1935), made convincing use of a great deal of her own theatre knowledge. Her third novel, *The Nursing Home Murder*, also published in 1935, again used recent experience to considerable effect. Ngaio had undergone an extensive gynaecological operation in 1934, attended by the noted surgeon Sir Hugh Acland and Dr Henry Jellett, a Dublin gynaecologist who had built up a considerable reputation in New Zealand and had been part of the social circle at Meadowbank ten years earlier. Ngaio had been on friendly terms with the Acland family for many years, having often stayed at Mount Peel, the family sheep station in the Southern Alps. Even so, Sir Hugh probably did not expect his patient to play practical jokes on him just after the operation—Ngaio smiled broadly from her pillows wearing a stubbly beard. She had smuggled some spirit gum and a false beard into hospital before the operation, and gave Sir Hugh a considerable shock. According to a close friend, he was still rather grumpy about the incident many years later, while being gently teased by Ngaio. Although she did not undergo a complete hysterectomy until much later, in 1974, this operation effectively destroyed any prospect of child-bearing.

With this fresh in her mind, she decided to base a novel on a murder in a hospital, and devoted her convalescence to writing it. Henry Jellett was the source of all the medical detail and together they constructed a highly paced novel. From this came a three-act stage play, *Exit Sir Derek*, which was produced by Canterbury College Drama Society in the Little Theatre of Canterbury University College in 1935. The last act included a simulated operation, and Dr Jellett made 'a startlingly realistic false abdomen with an incision and retractors to glut the horrified gaze of the circle'. Unfortunately the actor playing the patient was actually clamped by the nurse and lay in agony throughout the scene. The release of ether into the auditorium to add verisimilitude caused a member of the audience to faint and require real medical attention, and Dr Jellett was furious because a dropped rubber glove was picked up from the floor. But apart from these details, the play went very well and the decision not to try for further productions in England was unfortunate. *The Nursing Home Murder* continues to be one of Ngaio's most popular novels, and has outstripped all her other titles in sales. She also collaborated with Henry Jellett and other friends on a musical, *There She Goes*, for which she wrote several attractive songs including a wistful solo, 'Annie is Nobody's Darling', and a snappy duet called 'Red Pepper':

If you find your beau a mite too slow
Put some pep into your style.
If you part your lips and wag your hips then
He won't say wait a while.

Chorus:
Pep up! Just Pep up! Just Pep up all you've got!
With a Crawford smile and Mae West guile
And a style that's good and hot.
Then you pep up all you've got!

The score and the libretto have been preserved among the Marsh papers in the Alexander Turnbull Library, Wellington.

The next novel, *Death in Ecstasy*, followed in 1936, and although the author insists that all characters are fictitious, the plot has echoes of some actual events that took place in Christchurch. In the 1890s the 'Temple of Truth' was established in Latimer Square, Christchurch, and its Prophet of Righteousness turned out to have a fondness for wealthy but gullible widows. It was a relatively harmless confidence trick, but clearly became part of Christchurch mythology. In Ngaio's novel, which is set in London, the Church has a much more sinister role, involving a poisoned chalice and illegal drugs.

Much more innovative was her second theatre-based novel, *Vintage Murder*, which was published in 1937 before her next trip to England. Dedicated to Allan Wilkie and his wife, Frediswyde Hunter-Watts, this novel deals with a theatre company on tour in New Zealand and is based on the author's own experiences with the Allan Wilkie Company and the Rosemary Rees Comedy Company in the early 1920s. Even by the standards of a writer who was more than usually imaginative in the ways of death, the murder of theatrical manager Alfred Meyer is particularly grotesque. His head is crushed to pulp by a plummeting jeroboam of champagne which was designed to descend gently into a nest of fern and coloured lights on a table. This elaborate festivity was planned by the victim to celebrate his wife's birthday, and the table was set up on stage after the performance. The theatre detail is engrossing, but additional interest comes from the suggestion of the supernatural associated with the Maori tiki or greenstone fertility symbol that Alleyn gives to Carolyn Dacres as a birthday present. The Maori doctor, Te Pokiha, becomes an important witness, and after the case Alleyn goes to stay with him to learn more of Maori culture. The power of the New Zealand landscape also plays a part; Carolyn Dacres proves her innocence to Alleyn high up in the clear mountain air where 'it smells clean'. Essentially *Vintage Murder* holds to the classic formula of the enclosed world of a small group of people who know each other well, but unravelling the crime is enhanced by the use of unusual exterior detail. The novel proves that the crime formula hammered out in a host of English country villages can also work effectively in the unexpected venue of a small town in New Zealand.

Writing such a novel did, however, create problems for an author who deplored the New Zealand accent, was still uneasy about Maori characters, and who felt that even in 1930s New Zealand the urbane charm and upper-class accent of Roderick Alleyn would be as irresistible to everyone else as they were to her. Alleyn, at least, is portrayed as sensitive enough to feel ill at ease when he is drawn into the police investigation and suspects that Inspector Wade 'feels that I'm criticising him all the time. If I don't remember to be frightfully hearty and friendly he'll think I'm all English and superior . . . I would myself, I suppose, in his shoes'. The dialect baffles him but he tries not to reveal this (' "What, oh what," wondered Alleyn, "is the fine shade of meaning attached to this word 'crook'"?') Detective-Sergeant Packer develops an embarrassing case of hero worship which Ngaio should certainly have been advised to remove by her editors. The treatment of Dr Te Pokiha undoubtedly creates most unease in the contemporary reader, especially in the scene where he physically attacks the manager, George Mason, who has called him a liar. Alleyn's exclamation to himself, 'By jove . . . the odd twenty percent of pure savage', is barely recouped by his subsequent friendship with the doctor. *Vintage Murder* is undoubtedly intended to demonstrate sympathy for the predicament of the Maori people, trapped between two cultures, and Dr Te Pokiha's bitter remark has often been echoed in the fifty years since the book was published: 'We have become a side-show in the tourist bureau— our dances—our art—everything'. New Zealand writer Carole Acheson praised the novel in an article in the *American Journal of Popular Culture*:

> *Vintage Murder* is a far more ambitious novel than anything Marsh had attempted before, and clearly incorporates many of her responses as a returned expatriate, particularly her feeling for the land, sympathy for the Maoris and dislike of defensive and self-limiting colonial attitudes. The problem of combining a serious commentary on New Zealand with the stylised format of a detective story is overcome largely by changing the character of Alleyn, and making him the central consciousness of the novel . . . His personal desire to understand New Zealand and its people is given impetus by the murder investigation, and the usual tension between detective and suspects gains additional depth and interest by the conflict of three cultures. [27]

The snobbish attitudes that surface in *Vintage Murder* do not seriously detract from its effectiveness as a murder mystery, but there is a narrowness of vision in Marsh's view of New Zealand society that she never quite managed to shake off in the novels set in her native land.

By 1937 the need for travel was acute and Edmund Cork was encouraging her to become better known to English reviewers, many of whom thought she was either a man or a Maori. Five years had passed since her return to Christchurch and she was longing for new experiences and new acquaintances. This was more than just sentimental attachment to England; she wanted radical change and she described her feelings dramatically:

> The itch for travel is a chronic disease—incurable, insistent, some-times flaring up, sometimes more or less quiescent. It can't be explained. It can be appeased only by indulgence, or some such counter-irritant as hard work. The cure is, at best, temporary, the treatment curious. For a comfortable home, a rational existence, an ordered routine, and a chosen circle of friends; the patient must substitute a jolting train, a heaving ship, a muddled surge of complete strangers, and an incoherent mode of life. The peculiar hectic that rages in the travelbug's blood hankers after a set of conditions which, taken individually, are distasteful and exhaust-ing. Tormented, during treatment, by blistered heels, lost luggage and a perpetual search for somewhere to lay his head, why does this odd creature desire so ardently the renewal of all these un-comfortable conditions? Why, in retrospect, does he actually enjoy them?[28]

For her second trip to Europe Ngaio needed a new passport, and one was issued in December 1936. Her date of birth is given as 23 April 1899, her hair brown, her eyes blue, her height 5'10"; her occupation, novelist. Curiously, by the time her next passport was issued, in 1949, her eyes were hazel, her hair was grey and her height had decreased to 5' 9 3/4". Her occupation had also changed, quite correctly, to novelist and theatrical producer. But the date of birth in all her passports remained as 23 April 1899, a falsification she stoutly maintained all her life. Virtually all bibliographical refer-ences, including *Who's Who*, give this incorrect date of birth.

The reasons for this genteel deception are hard to establish. Many men and women are coy about age, but few actually go to the length of maintaining a fictional date on an official document such as a passport. A certificate of baptism with a blot over the year enabled her to maintain this vagueness; a tail of ink from the blot makes the final figure of the year look like a 9 instead of a 5. Quite probably Ngaio wanted to seem younger than she was at some time during the inter-war period, but even her closest friends were never taken into her confidence as to her reasons for this. Deducting four years from her age (and a quarter of an inch from her height!) may have been one of many role-playing exercises she engaged in as she developed her dual career as novelist and theatre producer, as well as her dual life in England and New Zealand.

The trip to Europe early in 1937 with her friend Betty Cotterill and Betty's friend Jean Webster was clearly going to provide more than enough raw material for a new series of books. They travelled around Europe in an old police car, and three months in Europe, visiting France, Germany, Italy, Austria and Luxemburg, cost them only £40 each. Ngaio gave a series of broadcasts about her travels when she returned to New Zealand, and again showed her gift as a travel writer in these pieces. One of her finest descriptions deals with their experiences in the small village of Beilstein in Germany where they had to stay for some time while Bet recovered from pleurisy. Ngaio watched the arrival of jack-booted officials, who nailed up a notice in the square demanding the ostracism of Jews in the village. The elderly Koppels, who kept a shop in the village, were afraid to go out during the day, and, unable to sleep one night, Ngaio was riveted by the sight of the 'large, hopeless face of Frau Koppel upturned to the night sky' at the door of their house. This incident, which also appears in her autobiography, is powerfully evoked, revealing a seriousness of vision that did not always emerge in her detective fiction. The three New Zealanders were advised by the hotel-keeper to leave Germany as soon as possible, and they were glad to take his advice.

Ngaio had completed her sixth novel, *Artists in Crime*, on board ship on the journey to Europe and it was published in 1938. It reveals more about the author than any other fiction she had so far written. In this novel Roderick Alleyn falls in love with a painter. Agatha Troy is already a well-known artist when Alleyn first encounters her on board a ship sailing across the Pacific from New Zealand. She is struggling with a quick oil sketch of the harbour at Suva, a sketch that her creator had already drawn in words from her own experience and later recorded in 'Portrait of Troy', the companion piece to 'Birth of a Sleuth':

On a voyage out to New Zealand from England we called at Suva. The day was overcast, still and sultry. The kind of day when sounds have an uncanny clarity, and colour an added sharpness and in-tensity. The wharf at Suva, as seen from the boat deck of the *Niagara* was remarkable in these respects: the acid green of a bale of bananas packed in their own leaves; the tall Fijian with a mop of hair dyed screaming magenta; this colour repeated in the sari of an Indian woman, the slap of bare feet on wet boards and the deep voices that sounded as if they were projected through pipes—all these elements made their impressions and I felt a great itch for a paint brush between my fingers.

The ship drew away, the wharf receded, and I was left with an unattempted, non-existent picture that is as vivid today as it was then. [29]

The description in *Artists in Crime* of the tall figure of Troy, with her short, dark hair, thin face and hands, 'absent-minded, shy and funny', seems very close to the Ngaio Marsh who absorbed that scene on the way back to New Zealand in 1932 and who had then been painting seriously for over ten years. Troy is first seen on the upper deck, wearing 'a pair of exceedingly grubby flannel trousers' with an unlit cigarette in her mouth. As she painted, 'her face was disfigured by a smudge of green paint and her short hair stood up in a worried shock, as though she had run her hands through it'. The painting of Suva harbour which Alleyn sees propped up in the lid of her paintbox is 'an almost painfully explicit statement of the feeling of that scene. It was painted very directly with crisp, nervous touches. The pattern of blue-pinks and sharp greens fell across it like the linked syllables of a perfect phrase. It was very simply done, but to Alleyn it was profoundly satisfying—an expression of an emotion, rather than a record of a visual impression'.

This is a revealing passage, not just because of the physical description of Troy, which so closely resembles her creator, but also because of the intensity of feeling that lay behind the painting. When Ngaio recognised that as a painter 'somehow I failed to get on terms with myself', it was an admission that her emotional responses could never find expression through her own technique, and indeed her ambitious but rather flat landscapes reveal none of the passionate love for the unspoilt New Zealand countryside that she expressed in words. The description of Troy's imagined painting links it to language, to 'the linked syllables of a perfect phrase', and there seems little doubt that by now Ngaio was finding words a much more malleable means of expression than paint.

Although Ngaio's agent Edmund Cork was slightly worried about Roderick Alleyn falling in love and eventually marrying, and contemporary reviewers wondered if he was going to become another Lord Peter Wimsey, Troy does not capitulate easily, and finds Alleyn's profession highly disagreeable. The fact that she is one of the suspects in the murder of her artist's model does not help the path of love to run smooth, and Alleyn conducts his investigation in a state of hypersensitive apology. He gets his murderer, but is resigned to continue waiting for the woman he really wants, Agatha Troy.

Death in a White Tie, published later in 1938, is an elegantly constructed mystery. The book is dedicated to Nelly Rhodes, ('to whom this book owes its existence'); details of the 'coming out' festivities and the London season were familiar to Ngaio through her friendship with this family. Nelly's daughter Maureen was presented in the 1937 season when Ngaio was back in Europe, and Ngaio herself was invited to a Royal Garden Party in June 1937, so this would have provided all the gossip and social chit-chat that makes the novel a fascinating snoop into the aristocratic world. A body found in the back of a taxi starts the unfolding of a complicated plot, at the end of which Troy finally accepts Alleyn's proposal of marriage. Ngaio has joked that this novel might be called 'the Siege of Troy' and indeed she is relentlessly, but tactfully pursued by the investigating officer. Alleyn is constantly aware of Troy's dislike of his profession, and he jokes wryly:

> If you painted a surrealist picture of me I would be made of Metropolitan Police notebooks, one eye would be set in a key-hole, my hands would be occupied with somebody else's private correspondence. The background would be a morgue and the whole pretty conceit wreathed with festoons of blue tape and hangman's rope.

Ngaio was once asked what she would do if Troy started to get in the way and needed to be disposed of. Without hesitation she replied, 'Why, murder her, of course, and have Alleyn investigate it'. But, she added reflectively, with just a tinge of regret, 'that could never happen in practice'. Fortunately the Alleyns' marriage remains another of Ngaio's idealised states; never a cross word is spoken and a perfect understanding is realised at all times. Troy remains an autobiographical element in Marsh's fiction: her physical appearance, her fondness for berets, cigarettes and curling up on the floor, her fear of physical intimacy and her uneasiness in social situations all reveal aspects of the author. Yet several of Marsh's fictional creations, including Roderick Alleyn, could be said to share characteristics of their creator, and it adds little to the novels to pursue such comparisons relentlessly.

Death in a White Tie was praised by the *Times Literary Supplement* as having 'a distinction that puts the author in the front rank of crime story writers'. Yet even in 1938 an element of snobbish prudery was being noted by the *Observer*, whose reviewer commented on 'a not very tolerant distaste for the broader aspects of writing and photography'. Was this New Zealander trying too hard to shake off her roots and adopt an aristocratic demeanour? Claire Tomalin identifies in Katherine Mansfield 'the mixture of adventurousness and anxiety she felt as a colonial coming to

One of Ngaio's sketches for Eileen Rhodes' children's novel 'Over the Edge of the Earth'.

England, and, not least, the curious attitude displayed by the English towards colonials'.[30] Undoubtedly Ngaio found herself in a doubly uneasy position; not only as a New Zealander but as someone from a very modest background being thrust into a social whirl of upper-class superiority.

Ngaio remained closely involved with the Rhodes family during 1937 and she spent a holiday with Nelly in Monte Carlo in October. She was also working with Nelly's eldest daughter, Eileen, illustrating a children's novel that Eileen had written called 'Over the Edge of the Earth'. The pen-and-ink sketches are exquisitely drawn, and reveal a bizarre visual sense. Unfortunately the book remains unpublished, probably because of the stark illustrative style and the strongly moral tone of the story.

Her extended stays with the Rhodes family in various country houses (as well as in a school that was taken over for the summer to accommodate this extensive family group, and which formed the background for *Final Curtain* several years later) gave Ngaio the material she needed for several novels. *Overture to Death* (1939) is set in the kind of idiosyncratic country village that she knew well. Character dominates the novel and although the murder is ingenious and rather gruesome, leaving poor Miss Campanula shot through the head with her blood spattered all over the village hall piano, the *New Statesman* reviewer accused the writer of treating crime fiction 'as a convenient vase to arrange her characters in'. Other reviewers admired her talent for developing character and were soon recommending that she forget detection and concentrate on straight fiction instead.

But the fund of plots for what she called 'tekkery' was still buoyant, and *Overture to Death* was quickly followed by *Death at the Bar* (1940) which derived from a tour of Devon and Cornwall in 1938 and an expert knowledge of darts acquired from her father. While he lived, the dartboard was a permanent feature of the dining-room in Valley Road and Ngaio used to join his friends in an occasional game.

Surfeit of Lampreys was published in the same year, revealing a sustained creative flow emerging from her experiences in England, just as she had predicted before she went. The murder of Lord Wutherwood still distresses some readers and indeed a meat skewer through the eye (even if it is a silver skewer of impeccable pedigree), is a queasy prospect. The impecunious Lampreys are lightly based on the Rhodes family, and the double flat described in the novel closely resembles their flat in Eaton Mansions off Sloane Square. Ngaio took expert advice from the surgeon Sir Hugh Acland about the mode of death, and he recommended that for almost instantaneous death, penetration of the skull through the eyeball was the most reliable method. Hence the ghastly sight which meets the young New Zealand visitor, Roberta Grey, as Lord Wutherwood breathes his last in the lift. Ngaio undoubtedly wrote some of her own life into this novel, and in view of her desire to appear younger than she was it is interesting to note that Roberta is presented as a contemporary of the Lamprey children rather than of their parents.

This novel again illustrates the ambivalence of Ngaio's cultural identity at this time. Roberta is initially overwhelmed by the sophistication and ease of the Lampreys' life in London, yet gradually realises that her own, 'colonial' virtues of common sense and energy are much more valuable in a crisis than any amount of elegant social chit-chat. 'You're a hopeless crew', says Roberta affectionately to her friend Henry, who agrees, 'We're museum pieces. Carryovers from another age . . . Our trouble is that we go on behaving in a grand leisured manner without the necessary backing. It's very dishonest of us, but we're conditioned to it'. Certainly Alleyn, whose judgement we are led to trust, finds much to admire in Roberta, and rather less in the self-indulgent Lampreys.

One more novel was to emerge from the experiences of 1937–38, the country house mystery, *Death and the Dancing Footman* (1942). This remains a favourite with Marsh's readers and it is indeed a shapely tale. American reviewers loved it: Will Cuppy in the *New York Herald Tribune* wrote, 'nobody in her racket begins to touch her for writing grace and few possess her skill at creating potential corpses and suspects, building a puzzle and other essentials of grand and lofty detection. There hasn't been anyone like her since the palmiest days of Dorothy L. Sayers'. Even the *Tatler* considered this novel 'on the plane of art'.

The 1937–38 visit gave Ngaio the opportunity to see more of her agent, Edmund Cork, and she developed great affection and respect for him. Edmund introduced her to other detective fiction writers and made her feel she had a place in the London literary world. Escorted by Edmund, she attended the installation of E. C. Bentley as President of the Detection Club in 1937, following the death of the first President, G. K. Chesterton, the previous year. With a mixture of hilarity and awe they watched the portentous ceremony, noting the symbolic weapons and the skull gleaming with a little red flashlight inside. Although everyone else was taking it very seriously, the visitors were definitely not sufficiently dignified:

> Mr. Bentley took the oath, John Rhode switched on the Skull, Freeman Wills Croft, who looked like a highly respected family solicitor, rather gingerly flourished the Sword, Anthony Gilbert displayed the Phial, and Miss Sayers, taking Edmund and me completely off our guard, loosed off her gun. The noise was deafening. I think I let out a yelp and I am sorry to record that dear Edmund, who has a loud laugh, laughed excessively.[31]

Ngaio was not made a member of the Detection Club at that time, as the rules required attendance at meetings, but she was invited to other events occasionally by Dorothy Sayers. She was finally admitted to membership in 1974, when unfortunately she was too ill to attend the function.

By April 1938, Ngaio was back in Christchurch, in a country where a new Labour Government elected in 1935 was striving to provide a welfare-based society that would never again permit the inequalities of wealth that had existed during the early part of the decade. A comprehensive social security system was introduced which would provide medical and dental care, substantial old age and sickness pensions, a 40-hour week and an extensive state-financed building programme. But consciousness of impending conflict in Europe was apparent, and the outbreak of war meant that the consolidation of this new welfare state would have to wait until the demands of another European conflict had been met.

The outbreak of the Second World War seemed to cause Ngaio's patriotism to flourish. She knew it might be many years before she could again visit England, but she longed to be there, sharing the experience of war. Ngaio wrote cheerfully to the Rhodes family, asking if Denys was now smelling of 'Brasso, sweat and prickly

Khaki', and pointing out that New Zealand, too, was suffering: 'All imports are forbidden except sausage skins and paper lace and a few oddments such as spare parts for sackbuts and a strictly limited number of sleigh-bells and, luckily for me, ink'. She often expressed her regret at not having been in England during the war, but whether reality would have accorded with her romanticised view of 'the gallant mother country' is debatable. When Billy Collins wrote to her in 1944 and mentioned the bombing of their offices in Pall Mall, Ngaio wrote back, 'Here in New Zealand we feel almost apologetic about our immunity from air raids. Your laconic sentence about your own offices in Pall Mall having gone is typical of so many English letters. One says helplessly that one is sorry and as usual regrets very sincerely that one has not been there during the last four cataclysmic years'.

Conscription was not introduced until after the fall of Dunkirk, but many New Zealanders had already volunteered for service and gone overseas at the end of 1939, including the celebrated Maori Battalion. A War Cabinet was established and New Zealand had a crucial role as supplier of food as well as soldiers to its beleaguered mother country. Nearly 140,000 people, 10 per cent of the entire population, served overseas, and there were more than 33,000 casualties. Only gradually, as the Japanese invasion forces spread down through South-East Asia, did New Zealanders begin to realise that their own nation could also be at risk. The fall of Singapore, the bombing of Darwin in Australia, and the presence of Japanese mini-submarines in Sydney Harbour made New Zealanders feel that they were coming close to the front line. For defence they had always depended on Britain, and Britain was now fighting for survival in Europe. Civil defence measures and rationing were introduced, and, as the wounded began to return, convalescent hospitals were established in many parts of the country. Ngaio became a Red Cross ambulance driver; looking thin and gawky in her shapeless uniform and brogues, she brought wounded soldiers from their ships to Burwood Hospital, inland. She was always ready to knock together entertainments for the services and, as might be expected, her patriotism emerged through her writing as well as through other, more direct contributions. These included a series of large murals of New Zealand scenery, which she presented to the hospital. They are now to be seen in the lounge of the Returned Servicemen's Club in Christchurch.

Local repertory societies were busy raising funds for the war effort, and Ngaio was engaged by several of them as a producer. Dunedin Rep asked her to produce *A Man's House* by John Drinkwater in September 1939, and the following August she worked with Ashburton Rep on Arnold Bennett's *The Last Hour*. She also directed Sutton Vane's *Outward Bound* for Canterbury University College, and Noel Coward's *Blithe Spirit* for Canterbury Rep. For several years Ngaio managed to involve her father in these productions, giving him small character parts to play: 'I used to walk round the set every night just before his entrance and there he would be, listening, with his ear at the door, for his cue. He would look at me and his eyes would snap and we would nod happily at each other and on he would go'.

During all this demanding theatrical work she was correcting the proofs of her latest batch of novels and preparing to undertake research for a new, non-fiction, commission.

The publishers William Collins were responsible for a substantial amount of non-fiction as well as fiction in the 1940s, and they showed considerable imagination in inviting Ngaio Marsh to contribute to a series of illustrated books for schools: 'The British Commonwealth in Pictures'. In collaboration with the historian R. M. Burdon, she produced a small volume on New Zealand, published in 1942. It contains twelve colour reproductions of landscape paintings by New Zealand painters, including two by Ngaio herself, one by her friend Olivia Spencer-Bower and one by her former teacher, Elizabeth Wallwork. There were also contemporary black-and-white photographs and several nineteenth-century engravings. Unfortunately the first group of pictures shipped to England for reproduction in the book was lost at sea. Another disappointment was that the rare colour film with which Ngaio had been supplied could not be processed in New Zealand, so only black-and-white photographs were used.

Intensely patriotic in tone, the 48-page book reveals Ngaio's deep love for her country and its people. She admits that 'New Zealand stands like a cranky little coda, at the bottom of the world', and that 'in some ways New Zealanders are still mid-Victorian Englishmen of good heart'. Just as in her fiction she liked to begin with characters, so she opens *New Zealand* with a description of a cross-section of the New Zealanders found at a country fair. She describes the run-holder (sheep farmer) and his family, leaning over the pens and inspecting the livestock; the hard-working cocky farmer (smallholder) with his children, having a day out; the auctioneer, the shepherds and the back-countrymen; the businessmen, newspapermen and strolling townspeople who have come to enjoy themselves at the fair. The book goes on to give a brief history of the two islands, and a description of the landscape. Surprisingly, in a short chapter on the Maori people, she compares them to the Celts, suggesting that 'in his passion for genealogy, his exquisite manners, his strong communal and tribal sense, his loyalty, his mysticism, his clannish feuds and his tribal gatherings, he is indeed closely akin to the Highlander, and in a certain cheerful inconsequence, to the Irishman'. While praising their culture, Ngaio recognises the problems of assimilating the Maori race into Western cultural patterns. She seems to see the merging of the two races as inevitable and desirable, an opinion which may have been acceptable in 1942 but which, nearly fifty years later, with the rise of Maori consciousness and a strengthening defence of their own unique culture, would find few supporters today.

The travel writer surfaces towards the end of the book, warning the visitor that the special joys of New Zealand may not always be obvious:

> The beaten track of tourists is not altogether the best track, and the unique landscapes of New Zealand lie a little way off it. Our thermal regions are probably less impressive than those of Yellowstone Park; our Alpine views lack the pretty floral foregrounds and charming chalets of the Austrian Tyrol and Switzerland. But Pohutokawa trees grow above bays of enchantment only in New Zealand, and nowhere else have I found any equivalent to the clear spaciousness of our mountain plateaux, or heard bird song as deep and moving as that of the New Zealand bush. This is a country so young that it impinges on the very ancient, and its clear and primordial landscape reaches back to emotions that have nothing to do with civilisation, but its spell—once felt—is not easily forgotten.[32]

Writing this modest, but sincere account of New Zealand and its people changed Ngaio's perception of her fictional base. She had travelled widely throughout the country while gathering material for her book, and probably knew it better now than she had ever done. The pressure of the Second World War led to a conscious recognition of her roots and she took the radical step of planning a novel with a distinctly New Zealand setting, involving a Maori village and a family who, although originally English, obviously intend to stay in their adopted country. For the first time her plot incorporates contemporary events.

The research for *Colour Scheme* took place at Rotorua and the surrounding districts, and Ngaio stayed with Marsh relatives who were then living in Hamilton, not far from the thermal area. Her cousin Stella Mannings, daughter of Ngaio's Aunt Amy, was married with three children: two boys and a girl. Stella's irrepressible younger son Roy (later nicknamed 'Bear') was then a grubby and energetic eight-year-old, and he was amazed by the tall and deep-voiced figure who came to visit. She made a salad with oranges in it ('Oranges? In salad?') and seemed to be the strangest person he had ever met. His older brother, John, was quiet, dreamy and played the piano. Usually shy, he clung to Ngaio's arm as they walked around the garden. The family connection offered by Stella and her children began to mean a great deal to this childless, middle-aged woman and her particular affinity with John was to shape both their lives profoundly in years to come. She wrote, in *Black Beech and Honeydew*, that she had sometimes thought of adopting a child. As the relationship with John deepened she began to look on him almost as a son, and on Stella almost as a sister. Ngaio's happiness with this new dimension to her life added energy to her fiction and certainly the use of the New Zealand landscape she loved had an invigorating effect on the next two novels.

Colour Scheme, published in 1943, is often regarded as her most interesting book and Ngaio considered it her best-written novel. Few crime novels can have such an unusual setting, or provide such a horrifying murder as death by boiling in a steaming mud pool. The novel adopts the familiar convention of a small group of people in an isolated locality, several of whom have good reasons for arranging the death of Maurice Questing. But what makes this country house party peculiar is that the characters are all staying in a ramshackle collection of wooden buildings beside an area of thermal gases and mud pools, in the North Island of New Zealand.

Instead of feudally regulated villagers and loyal servants in the background, there is a Maori village, self-contained and presided over by a former Member of Parliament, the distinguished Rua Te Kahu. Although elderly, he has 'an air of greatness':

> His head was magnificent, long and shapely. His nose was a formidable beak, his lips thin and uncompromising. His eyes still held their brilliance. He was a patrician, and looked down the long lines of his ancestry until they met in one of the canoes of the first Polynesian sea rovers.

An area of thermal activity is an alarming and unsettling sight for a stranger, with occasional bursts of steam shooting up from deep in the earth, mysterious, slow bubbling sounds heard down unexpected crevices and pumice rock that is too hot to walk on. Ngaio describes a region of solidified blue mud, sinter mounds, hot pools and geysers. The sulphurous smell was very strong'. There is also the great boiling mud pool, Taupo-tapu, 'dun-coloured and glistening, a working ulcer in the body of the earth. Great bubbles of mud formed themselves deliberately, swelled, and broke . . .' When Maurice Questing has disappeared and the thermal area is searched in the moonlight, it becomes even more mysterious and threatening, as wisps of steam float above the glistening, boiling mud, which never ceases in its slow, deliberate, bubbling sound.

In this novel, Alleyn appears incognito as a lumbago sufferer called Septimus Falls. He is already in New Zealand on security duties, and he arrives at Wai-Ata-Tapu in response to a letter about a suspected Fifth Columnist: two ships are torpedoed just offshore, and there is a strong suspicion that Japanese submarines have been given information from someone in the area. As well as finding the traitor, Alleyn also manages to discover who guided Questing along a doomed path through the mud pools to his death in Taupo-tapu. The fact that Questing was illicitly removing Maori antiquities from the restricted area of the Reserve, and had carried off a sacred object, Rewi's Axe, to sell at a profit, allows the narrative to link Maori legend to murder mystery. Legend recounts that the last person to see Rewi's Axe, a young Maori girl, lost her way at night and fell into Taupo-tapu. It is clear that to the Maori leader, Rua, Maurice Questing has received just punishment for his greed and insensitivity to Maori tradition. Alleyn, in summing up the case, gives serious consideration to what he calls 'the Maori element'. Throughout the novel the villagers are portrayed as dignified, welcoming and self-sufficient, although very poor. They respond to the uncomplicated kindness shown to them by the Claires, who run the hotel, and acquire a remote and powerful aura as their singing wafts across the thermal pools in the darkness. But they are not romanticised, and the problems of drink, petty crime and the abandonment of ancestral traditions are made plain.

Evidence that Ngaio had become fascinated by the Maoris she met while writing *Colour Scheme* is found in an unusual poem, never published, which she must have written about this time; it contains a reference to Mrs Te Papa, one of the characters in the novel. There are two drafts of the poem. The first one, crossed through, refers to 'I' throughout. The second version has transposed the experience to 'he', thus distancing the poem:

These then were the Maori people.
He was no further on than when he first began
Telling himself: it has to be me through them
Not them by way of us, which would be sheer
Impertinence. All right. He played it cool
And made himself endurable; himself endured
The smell, the lice, the creeping stale of beer
Scarcely distinguishable from the jakes.
All right.
He tagged along and no one seemed to mind.
You're good boy, eh? Boy, you got what it takes.
You couldn't say they made him look a fool.
They'd even given him a Maori name
Which seemed to be a compliment, a kind
Of bonus on a bogus brotherhood.
They laughed with him. Or at him? Well, they laughed.
By cripes he'd almost watched them fornicate.
You're in the mob. You're worth it. Boy, you're great.
Sometimes they'd tell him things that might be something.
He'd write them, folk-forlornly in his book.
They turned aside to snicker or to look
Sidelong. He picked there'd been some kind of sign.
He was no further on.

Mrs Te Papa, said to be ninety-nine,
Sat on the pumice shelf outside her shack.
Thinking herself alone she droned a threadbare song
Frail as a bone, a fossil leaf, a shell
of lost antiquity. He listened. It was gone.
He was no further on.[33]

CHAPTER 5

The Golden Age: 1943–47

In the South we suffer from the memory of a small but unmistakable Golden Age . . . the Golden Age in question was, needless to say, the Ngaio Marsh period in the Little Theatre at Canterbury University College, from about 1943 to 1948, and ending irrecoverably when the theatre was destroyed by fire in February 1953.[1]

The words are those of historian Professor John Pocock, who in 1957 engaged in a series of open letters with dramatist Bruce Mason on the state of New Zealand theatre. Published as *Theatre in Danger*, the pamphlet discusses the difficulties involved in establishing a national theatre, and the need for New Zealand writers to offer plays to New Zealand audiences on themes that help to explore their own national identity. Their debate arose from a cultural hunger created for many by their experience as students at Canterbury University, a hunger which spread out in a variety of directions and through a number of different talents. John Pocock recognised this:

Ngaio was indeed the sun in our firmament, but our activity was something much less heliocentric and more creative than a mere revolving round her. Some of us had ideas and developed lines of our own; there was a tradition to which we contributed; and I sometimes think we never learnt so much from Ngaio as when we disagreed with her—the highest compliment you can pay any teacher. It was the conjunction of a number of personalities, the others less mature and less creative but hardly less vigorous than hers, that made that theatre what it was.[2]

These remarks delineate a Golden Age in New Zealand drama.

91

Pocock is right to stress that valuable as Ngaio was as the stimulus at the centre, it was her willingness to take young people seriously, to foster new and untried talent and to value what the young had to offer, that was at the heart of her contribution to New Zealand culture. To produce Shakespeare triumphantly in the unsure world of 1943, while many of her young actors were waiting to be called to the Forces, and while she herself was still driving a Red Cross ambulance, was perhaps a subconscious celebration of the traditional values of English life that she had always cherished. And indeed the dramatic heritage of the Canterbury University College at Christchurch did seem to be seriously threatened at that time.

The Canterbury University College Drama Society had, in the 1930s, sustained a high level of dramatic production using staff and students, and under the strong influence of Professor (later Sir James) Shelley, some notable performances of Shakespeare were achieved. With Professor Shelley's guidance an assembly hall had been converted into the Little Theatre, later to be named the Shelley Theatre, with good lighting and even a cyclorama. This was to become a much loved venue for the student players of the later part of the decade. Unfortunately, with the departure of Professor Shelley to become head of New Zealand Broadcasting, the Drama Society fell into a very barren patch. The Little Theatre went dark, and although enthusiasts prevented the society completely falling apart and saved the famous cyclorama from destruction, the outlook at the end of 1941 was bleak.

Ngaio often told the story of the small group of students who climbed up the hill to 37 Valley Road on a hot day early in 1941, and asked her to produce *Outward Bound* for them. She agreed, and found she greatly enjoyed working with young people:

> Having no settled faults or mannerisms to correct, they started from zero and being extremely intelligent were soon passionately concerned with dramatic principles. Their gluttonous appetite for work and responsiveness under a hard drive were a constant amazement and their loyalty, once a relationship had been established, heartening above words. Their Little Theatre quivered with vitality.

Outward Bound, which was staged in July 1941, did not, in Ngaio's view, provide much of a challenge for these young actors, even though she had provided professional touches with music by Frederick Page, husband of her old friend the painter, Evelyn Polson, and a cast strengthened by her long-standing friend Dundas Walker, a seasoned actor who had worked with her before in amateur groups. Dundas also took a part in *Lonesome Life*, a one-act play by Harold Brighouse that Ngaio produced for Canterbury Repertory Society in September the following year. A nucleus of student actors began to form under her leadership during the next few years, and she also found time to direct Coward's *Blithe Spirit* for repertory societies in Christchurch and Wellington. Together with her war work and writing, these amateur productions meant that 1942 was a very busy year.

When the Drama Society asked Ngaio to work with them again in 1943, she agreed on condition that the play was *Hamlet*, in modern dress. They accepted her proposal, opening the door to something she had been longing to do for years— produce a Shakespeare play. The repertory companies had always been afraid of the Bard: 'He was, they all assured me, Box Office poison in massive doses'. But the Ngaio Marsh production of *Hamlet* quickly became a legend, and ran to packed houses in August 1943, with a revival in late November of the same year. How had someone who had never produced a Shakespeare play before, and had never worked with undergraduates, achieved such a high standard of performance?

Theatre is an ephemeral art, and it is impossible to capture and codify the particular combination of qualities that leads to an outstanding stage production. A study of Ngaio's rehearsal texts gives a great deal of information about her techniques, and also shows the enormous amount of work she devoted to each play before she even had the actors read through the first scene. Her small books on play production, *A Play Toward* (1946) and *Play Production* (1948), which were written during this 'Golden Age' of Christchurch theatre, show that she worked particularly hard on language, guiding the flow of words towards a series of climaxes and releases in order to grip the audience in the tension of the play. Acknowledging the influence of Stanislavsky, she stresses technique: 'the imaginative approach should not be a woolly impulsive affair depending on the mood of the moment. It should be forged clearly, step by step'.[3] She was well aware that unpredictability is

93

the hazard of the amateur actor, and recognised that 'the most difficult player is the one who, with a rich imagination and a strong but unstable emotional approach, is reluctant to learn technique. Such a player will be the slave of his own moods'. Perhaps thinking of the discipline required to write her own detective stories, she insists that 'acting is not a pumping up of emotion. It is a craft of which emotion is the raw material'. In *Colour Scheme*, one of the characters tries to explain the conduct of the famous Shakespearean actor Geoffrey Gaunt to an infatuated young woman, and says perceptively that 'the thing about actors, for instance, that makes them different from other people is that they are technicians of emotion'. This had to be impressed upon a group of enthusiastic amateurs, and the firm control established from the beginning was part of the training.

In *A Play Toward* the role of the producer is clearly laid out. Not until a vast amount of preparatory work has been done, often involving people on the production side, can the players be invited to attend: 'When the last page of your script is covered with notes and diagrams, your stage-manager has been given his scenic, property and light plots, and the play is orchestrated in your mind, you are ready for your players'. Her production scripts are impressive in their detail. Single pages of the text are pasted on the right-hand side of large, stiff-backed books; on the left are lively sketches illustrating the action of the scene. Stage business and actions are numbered and listed, and cues are given in colour. Ngaio often made cardboard models of the set to work out how to group the actors and how to handle rostra, which she frequently used. Black-and-white production photographs indicate how closely she managed to realise the imagined scene sketched beside the text.

As the rehearsals for *Hamlet* gathered momentum and the confidence of the student players grew, Ngaio found it easier to seek the help and expertise of other talented people then living in Christchurch. A number of *émigrés* from Austria and Germany had found their way to Christchurch in the 1930s, and many of them now gravitated to the hospitable world that Frederick and Evelyn Page created at their fine old house on the shores of Lyttelton Harbour at Governors Bay. In their garden congregated many poets, artists and composers, including the composer Douglas

Lilburn, who was then living and working in the city. He had been rejected for military service because of his weak eyesight. One of his best-known pieces, 'Landfall in Unknown Seas' (music to a poem by Allen Curnow), was given its first performance in the Great Hall of Canterbury University in September 1943 and during this period he began to work with the Drama Society. Ngaio had asked him to write incidental music for *Hamlet*, and he attended some of the rehearsals. His music, in Ngaio's view, made an immeasurable contribution: 'Douglas's sound was an organic part of the play and exquisitely adjusted to it. Without his music the productions would have been bereft indeed'.[4] Lilburn intuitively grasped what Ngaio was seeking in the music, and she responded warmly to his work: 'I remember my first delighted shock on hearing the magic he called up for the battlements at Elsinore: how the sound flowed into the play and was an articulated element of the dialogue'. A bonus was the presence of the celebrated international violinist Maurice Clare, who had recently formed the Wellington String Orchestra and was later to become Leader of the Boyd Neel Orchestra. Clare was interested in Lilburn's work, and went with him to some of the *Hamlet* rehearsals. He agreed to play the incidental music with some colleagues, and the score, for three violins and tubular bells, captured for the producer 'the very breath of the cold night air at Elsinore'. It was, she said, 'perfection'.

Another professional touch was added by the expertly produced programmes, printed by the Caxton Press in Christchurch. This small press, founded in the 1930s by the poet Denis Glover and his friends, played a seminal role in publishing contemporary writing in New Zealand. Ngaio maintained links with the Caxton Press for many years and the theatre programmes, usually designed by one of the students, are collectors' items. She always signed every first-night programme, a custom that endured until her last student productions.

Ngaio's production style may now appear over-dominant and re-strictive, but Keith Thomson, who was later to use many of her methods and techniques in his drama workshops with students in Australia and the United States, felt that her firm control and her total understanding of the particular interpretation towards which they were working were the only ways to build up the confidence of young actors who might never have read a line of verse drama before and didn't know stage left from stage right. Professor Thomson concedes that 'at the beginning you did exactly what she said, you were as putty. Later on it was possible to say I don't feel comfortable with this, and to try something different.'

Everyone involved in a Ngaio Marsh play quickly learned what professionalism in the theatre meant. She was fond of remarking that the difference between an amateur and a professional is that the amateur thinks it's fun. Her advice to the players is unambiguous:

> Actors will need—to be punctual
> to be provided with copies of the play, and
> in the case of the crowd, with
> accommodation for dialogue.
> It should be remembered—that one late arrival can mean loss of time for the directors, the actors, including the crowd, and the production as a whole.

Ngaio was confident in her company, and was particularly fond of the engineering students who were the stage crew. An actor in the company observed that 'for some reason—tradition perhaps—engineering students are a bolshie lot of brigands: but although erratic in their time-keeping and mildly sloshed from time to time, they never let her down and she knew they never would'. There was a lot of teasing and joking, and the cast placed small bets on how long the ash on her cigarettes would curl around before it fell off. Most of the students called her Miss Marsh, but as the relationship became closer, some began to call her Mum or Mumsie. Only the very elite corps ever called her Ngaio. All this gave her a warmth that had been lacking in her life for a long time. If Ngaio was good for the students, the process was not one-sided. Jack Henderson, who played Hamlet, thought that:

> Suddenly, quite unexpectedly, in middle age, in not particularly good health, she found herself being whirled about in a sort of student maelstrom. After the first terror had passed—on both sides—she found a kind of happiness which she had never experienced before.

Seated on the floor in the wings at each performance, mouthing the lines as they were spoken, Ngaio willed the actors to achieve a standard that they would never have believed possible. To Henderson her powerful presence was a mixed blessing:

> On the one hand, we had the reassurance of knowing that Mum/ Nanny/Godma was there, ready to render first aid if necessary including giving a prompt (the poor prompter never got a look in)—we were still only babies, remember, not yet weaned. On the other hand, a glimpse of an anxious face while tearing a passion to tatters was a shade off-putting. I quickly learned not to look at her at certain times.

The 1943 production of *Hamlet* gained much of its quality from this young actor. Jack Henderson was English but during the war he was sent to school at Christ's College in Christchurch, while his parents were in India. He first met Ngaio in 1941 during the school production of *Charley's Aunt*, when she came in to help with make-up. He remembers an extraordinary woman in the dressing-room: 'tall, thin, mannish in appearance, flat-chested, rather gawky (she did not move gracefully), dressed usually in beautifully cut slacks (less common then than now), large feet with shoes like canal boats, a deep voice—yet intensely feminine withal'. As a student at Canterbury University the following year he auditioned for *Hamlet*, and Ngaio responded to his 'edge, rancour, intelligence, a quivering sensitivity and a certain wry sweetness'. She trained him to control his delivery and 'to make his voice speak his thoughts'. In the final stages of rehearsal she brought him up to stay with her at the house so that she could give him additional coaching. Their friendship remained strong for several years, and although she was now forty-eight years old, and Henderson in his early twenties, they became very close. Henderson explained the relationship as a response to loneliness that they both, as only children, under- stood only too well. He felt that Ngaio was a substitute mother, an elder sister, a beloved aunt combined; she seemed to look on him as a substitute son or a younger brother, neither of which she actually had. The emotional bond was strong but Platonic; Ngaio was never demonstrative in her feelings. The attraction of men who were much younger than her was to be- come a familiar pattern in her life; they, in turn, were flattered by her attention. She had the ability to make all her friends, men or women, feel that they were the subject of her special regard. It is a rare attribute; an enhancement of the gift for friendship that few people have. Yet implicit in this outgoing warmth was a subtle rejection of shared intimacy. By making the other person the focus of her full attention, it was not necessary to return any confidences, and Ngaio continued to make herself emotionally unassailable. On one occasion when she reached out to comfort a weeping and desolate actor, he recoiled in surprise at this unexpected physical intimacy; it was a moment in life that he wishes could be re-run, in a different way.

The success of this first *Hamlet* proved to Ngaio that the talent existed in Christchurch to produce plays that she would not be ashamed of. She was now nearly fifty, and beginning to wonder whether life had anything new to offer. For her, the enthusiasm and support of her student players, together with the praise of many stern critics in Christchurch, gave her the confidence to keep going. She had faith in her student players to an extraordinary degree, and several years later, when Professor Keith Thomson wrote to her for advice in the choice of a play she replied that 'first, you should never underrate the potential of student players. After all, we managed a very successful Australian tour with two notoriously difficult plays, done by a student cast, and why shouldn't you triumph too?' A new generation of actors was to find Ngaio's methods too restrictive, and actor and director Mervyn Thompson wrote in 1980 with mixed feelings about her authoritarian regime. But in the Golden Age of the 1940s in Christchurch it was considered a privilege to be associated with the University Drama Society, and to be guided by someone who was willing to devote months to these productions. As early as 1943 Ngaio's status as a prime mover in the New Zealand theatre scene was recognised when she was involved in discussion about the establishment of a national touring company, and she met with other theatre people to try to launch the Group Theatre Project. The aim, to allow all New Zealanders to benefit from high-quality touring productions, was to remain a matter for lively debate and little action throughout the decade.

Crime fiction was now bringing in a satisfactory income, and Ngaio had been able to engage a housekeeper, Mrs Crawford ('Crawsie' was Ngaio's nickname for her) to help look after her father when she was away driving for the Red Cross or working on a play. Mrs Crawford was Irish, and her unusual turn of phrase amused Ngaio and her friends. Although she was an excellent cook, she dusted and washed so vigorously that ornaments flew and dishes cracked. 'Ah, the quality wasn't in it, Miss M'Dear', she would say to Ngaio as they surveyed the remnants of a china plate. 'But Crawsie dear, the quality *was* in it', Ngaio would patiently explain, and sadly gather up the pieces. A frequent casualty was an ornamental bowl surrounded by dancing cupids, and the heads of 'them cupids' often rolled and were stuck back on again. Mrs Crawford became devoted to Ngaio and with her husband as gardener they reliably maintained 37 Valley Road for many years, so that Ngaio could meet increasing public demands.

After *Hamlet*, Ngaio returned to her bread and butter, writing detective novels. *Died in the Wool* (1945) was completed between the last performance of *Hamlet* and the start of rehearsals for the next production, *Othello*, which was scheduled for the New Zealand winter of 1944. *Died in the Wool*, like the previous novel, *Colour Scheme*, is set in New Zealand, at an upland sheep station on the South Island. The problem of continuing to use Roderick Alleyn while Ngaio was more and more distanced from England was difficult, but the exigencies of war and a mysterious brief to check security in the Antipodes was a useful means of keeping Alleyn on hand during the war years. In *Died in the Wool* Alleyn is still stranded in New Zealand and estranged from Troy, and still hunting for German sympathisers. A humorous reference to Alleyn 'in a false beard, dodging round geysers', is a link back to the events of *Colour Scheme*.

The murder of MP Florence Rubrick, first knocked on the head and then suffocated in a wool bale, is one of Marsh's more gruesome killings, and the isolated setting adds a further touch of unreality to the crime. The novel sings with the mountain landscape that Ngaio loved to paint. On his way to Mount Moon station to investigate Flossie's murder, which had taken place fifteen months earlier, Alleyn drives up into the mountains and looks amazed over the vista before him:

> It was a great plateau, high itself, but ringed about with mountains that were crowned in perpetual snow. It was laced with rivers of snow water. Three lakes of a strange milky green lay across its

surface. It stretched bare and golden under a sky that was brilliant as a paladin's mantle. Upon the plateau and the foothills, up to the level of perpetual snow, grew giant tussocks, but there were no forests. Many miles apart, patches of pinus radiata or lombardy poplars could be seen and these marked the solitary homesteads of the sheep farmers. The air was clear beyond belief, unbreathed, one would have said, newly poured out from the blue chalice of the sky.

Ngaio had painted this scene several times, especially with the great mountain Aorangi, the 'Cloud Piercer', (Mount Cook), in the background. Looking out from his window that night, Alleyn witnesses 'the pageant of nightfall on the plateau. He saw the horn of the Cloud Piercer shine gold and crimson long after the hollows of the lesser Alps, as though a dark wine poured into them, had filled with shadow'.

Intriguing though the novel is, with its country house murder mystery again transplanted to an exotic setting, the interrogations necessarily take up a great deal of time, since Alleyn is building up a case from old evidence. The previous novel, Colour Scheme, did not suffer from this excess of interrogation and emerges as a much livelier piece of work. Alleyn tracks down the German sympathiser, who was also the murderer of Flossie Rubrick. When Alleyn writes to Troy of a landscape that sends shivers down the spinal column, Ngaio is leaving a door ajar for Troy to bring her painter's eye to the South Island, but it was not to be until 1980, in Photo-Finish, that Alleyn would share the spectacular sights of the Southern Alps with his wife.

The location of Died in the Wool is not specified and Ngaio must have built it up from a number of sheep stations in a district that she knew well. Certainly several of these outposts of the southern gentry, with their English trees and shrubs and their isolated and self-contained society, could have contributed to the fictional portrayal of Mount Moon, perched on its high, cold plateau, with 'the same men, the same routine, the same long evenings, the same smell of lavender and honeysuckle and oily wool'. The characterisation is interesting, not only in its retrospective view of the dominating, infuriating and highly astute Flossie Rubrick, but also in the presentation of young Clifford Johns, son of the station manager. Cliff is a sensitive child, who responds to music, books and pictures. Indifferent to arithmetic and games, he is hopelessly out of line with his schoolmates in the tiny local school he attends. The kind of kidnap that Flossie achieves, pulling him out of school and sending him to 'the nearest equivalent in the country to an English Public School' against the wishes of his father, a strong trade unionist, is not without a parallel in Ngaio's own life. In the novel Cliff accepts Flossie's patronage until the age of sixteen, playing on the Bechstein piano in her living-room during the vacations and making no objection to her plans to send him to the Royal College of Music in London for further study. But he suddenly rebels against the clear pattern laid down for him, so different from the world he knows on the high plains, where he feels he has a place of some kind. He pours out his resentment to Alleyn:

> When I tried to explain, she treated me like a silly kid. Then when I stuck to it, she accused me of ingratitude. . . . Nobody has the right to take a kid of ten and teach him to accept every-thing without knowing what it means, and then use that gener-osity as a weapon against him. . . . She'd got vested interests in me and she meant to use them.

At the age of sixteen, Cliff was beginning to understand what Flossie had done:

> I realised pretty thoroughly how hopelessly wrong it was for me to play at being a little gentleman at her expense. I realised that if I couldn't get as my right, equally with other chaps, the things she'd given me, then I shouldn't take them at all. I was admitting the right of one class to patronise another.

Fictional portrayals of children taken away from their families and educated for a particular purpose are not uncommon. Patrick White, in *The Vivisector* (1970), gives us such a child in Hurtle Duffleld, who grows up to be a famous painter. The resentment Cliff Johns feels is complicated by the disgust and pity that mingle on the last night he sees Flossie alive, and he 'wanted to get away clean'. Even Flossie's tears seem false. Yet when eventually Cliff is driven to regain her friendship and goes to the woolshed where she is practising one of her political speeches, she has already been murdered, and Cliff becomes a prime suspect in the intrigue that surrounds her death.

The three New Zealand-based novels of this period, *Vintage Murder, Colour Scheme*, and *Died in the Wool*, are remarkable for the amount of autobiographical material that they contain. While writing *Died in the Wool*, with its description of the transplanted Cliff, Ngaio was making plans that were remarkably similar. She had decided to give her cousin Stella's elder son, John Mannings, the best possible education in New Zealand, and arranged for him to leave home at the age of fourteen to become a boarder at Christ's College, the exclusive private boys' school in Christchurch. Effectively this removed him from his family and Ngaio started to groom him to be the kind of cultivated, polished Englishman that she had always admired. John was an introspective, impractical boy who was out of step in a school system that valued sporting prowess and masculine capability. Unsettled at school in Hamilton and at home with a father who did not understand him, John joined the wealthy sons of the New Zealand gentry in Christchurch. Ngaio did not realise that he was just as out of place at Christ's College as he was at home, and was surprised when he later confessed to being very unhappy during his years there. Intensely nervous, he stammered for many years before overcoming this problem. An accomplished role-player herself, she did not appreciate that, as a young adolescent, John did not have the same defensive techniques available. John remained at Christ's College as a boarder until 1950, when he began a course at Canterbury College but abandoned it to take up a commission in the Royal Artillery in England. Ngaio arranged an introduction to the Rhodes family so that John could follow a similar path to her own many years earlier. She remained a kind of motherly presence in his life, even when they were separated by long distances, buying him clothes in the London sales if she was there, and posting them to him with explicit instructions on how they should be worn. The strength of their mutual regard increased as Ngaio grew older, though John eventually moved to Australia to make his own life.

Adults often have clear and well-meant views about what is best for young people. John's father was anxious that he should have a better start in life than he had himself, and Stella knew that John's artistic side, particularly his love of music, would be nurtured by the excellent teachers at Christ's College. Ngaio was convinced that John would have a better future with an English-style upbringing: private school, British Army, financial career. And this is precisely what happened, although not quite as smoothly as she might have hoped. Friends who observed this developing relationship wondered if Ngaio was trying too hard to shape John's life into a mould that was cast in 1920s Britain rather than postwar New Zealand. Or was she, perhaps, awarding him a part in a stage play being directed by Ngaio Marsh, rather as she was later to do with a young actor, Jonathan Elsom, in 1960? The components of love are never easy to unravel, but the element of power is seldom missing.

If *Died in the Wool* appears to come dangerously close to her relationship with her cousins, the unfinished novel, *Money in the Morgue*, suggests another emotional crisis. There is no date on this handwritten draft, which extends to seventeen crown-sized pages and three chapters, but it is obviously from this period. A précis of the novel describes a Red Cross driver, Sarah Warme, who is attached to Mount Gold hospital, an isolated military hospital 20 miles from the nearest town. The wages clerk, Mr Glossop, is on his regular run to various hospitals in the area when his car breaks down after driving through a creek in flood. Obliged to stay overnight at the hospital, he places his moneybag containing £2,000 in the safe, but later he steals it. Unfortunately the matron sees him take the money, and he murders her. An ideal place for the moneybag fortuitously presents itself as a corpse is trundled past on a trolley, on its way to the morgue. Glossop assists the nurse with the trolley, and pushes the moneybag under the corpse. Meanwhile, various convalescent soldiers are lurking in the grounds, trying to get back into the wards after illicit expeditions beyond the confines of the hospital. Sarah, adjusting her cap in the driver's office, seems to be very interested in the resident doctor, Dr Luke, but the manuscript ends with Sarah's tantalising thoughts: 'We are too busy to fall in love . . . yet she waited for their interrupted, encounters with eagerness and a feeling of secret assurance'.[5]

This fragment is well structured and lively, with no apparent technical problems that might have prevented a satisfactory conclusion. But the draft is firmly crossed through on every page and no attempt seems to have been made to salvage any of the material and recycle it as a story or as part of another book. The future of Sarah, the Red Cross driver, must remain a secret for ever.

Ngaio had by now established a pattern that allowed her to write uninterruptedly in the evening and to cope with other work in the day. She sat in an armchair, not at a desk, and wrote on lined sheets of foolscap supported by a stiffly bound book. She often thriftily used up some of her father's old financial ledgers for drafts and notes. Early in her career she favoured an old fountain pen with green ink, 'a faithful old English fountain pen that cost a pound and has never been equalled by any streamlined gift number at eight times that price'. In later years she wrote with any implement that came to hand, and once complained to her friend and correspondent Lord Ballantrae that her wretched pen would only write when she sucked it. In her manuscripts the narrative flows smoothly down one side of the page and alterations and additions are noted on the preceding blank page. Corrections become more frequent as the pressure of the investigation increases. Anxious little sums punctuate the manuscript as it grows towards the required 70–80,000 words. Sometimes sketches on the blank pages reflect what is going on in the novel, but often there are affectionate drawings of her cats, who would have been keeping her company, or even curling up on piles of typed manuscript. Occasionally her mind wanders and there is a drawing of a stage set, or a few dinner-table plans offering various seating arrangements around her circular dining table. She worked best in the evening, when there were no disturbances, and, after breakfast in bed (she loved crisp bacon and fingers of toast), she would go over correspondence with a secretary and see the new pages, written in the small hours, being typed up. Even when she was in England, this writing pattern was followed.

Fiction now had to be laid aside as preparations got under way for the production of *Othello* scheduled for July 1944 in the Little Theatre, to be followed by a short run in Her Majesty's Theatre, Dunedin. Paul Molineaux, who had played Laertes in *Hamlet*, was Othello, and Jack Henderson took the role of Iago. Ngaio felt that for this production the actors were 'technically much better equipped' and she was satisfied to see that 'under intensive and strictly disciplined rehearsal the company began to take up an attitude nearer to that of the professional than the amateur theatre'. Poet Lauris Edmond, who had a small walk-on part in *Hamlet*, felt that the atmosphere was 'completely serious' and, having been turned down for the part of Emilia because of her New Zealand accent, she felt nervous at getting involved with 'those snobbish people in the Drama Club who speak with marbles in their mouths'. But Ngaio's charisma was unmistakable, and to Lauris she was 'one of the most vital people I've ever met—you feel as though she'd make an Egyptian mummy get up and act, she's so compelling. She talks about each character at times, but mostly she *does* bits, and at once you can see what is (or should be) going on in the character's mind'.[6]

Those disciplined rehearsals in the College buildings were not without incident, because in the lecture room beneath them a Senior Lecturer in Philosophy was labouring hard to impart difficult principles to his evening class. The noise of stage fights repeatedly brought him up the stairs in a high state of indignation. Ngaio always managed to calm him down, and the philosopher made a point of telling her after the performance that it had all been worth while. The long-suffering lecturer was the distinguished philosopher and social theorist Professor Sir Karl Popper, who considered Ngaio 'a marvellous producer of Shakespeare'. He gives her credit for transforming Paul Molineaux, one of his students, from a 'shy and clumsy youth' into an 'open and self-confident young man'.

Hard work by the actors, scrupulous preparation by the producer, and another inspired musical score from Douglas Lilburn created another success. This time the quality of the production was recognised by a professional manager, D. D. O'Connor, who was to bring out tours by the Old Vic Company and the Stratford-upon-Avon Players after the war. O'Connor offered to tour *Hamlet* and *Othello* during the long vacation, and in January 1945 the student players found appreciative audiences in Auckland and Wellington. On their return to Christchurch in February, both plays were successfully performed in the Radiant Hall before the beginning of term. This tour, with the sponsorship of D. D. O'Connor, established the Canterbury Student Players as a respected dramatic force in New Zealand. The support of a professional manager gave Ngaio confidence and prestige. Without his backing, the student players would have remained a cosy, domestic, amateur group, and the real successes of the 1940s would never have happened.

Ngaio was fortunate in having managed to persuade Douglas Lilburn to compose the music for these early productions. She often referred to the bitter-sweet quality of his setting for Desdemona's song before her death and how it never failed to move the audience. Paul Molineaux described it as 'a lament with its own stillness, full of potential disaster'. The relationship between Lilburn and Marsh was one of mutual respect, tempered with mutual caution. Ngaio knew that Lilburn was struggling to support himself as a composer, taking a few pupils and doing a little reviewing for local newspapers to provide a meagre income. In June 1945, when plans were well advanced for a production of *A Midsummer Night's Dream*, she wrote tentatively to ask if he would write music for the play. Ngaio suggested delicately, 'I myself have had a windfall lately and can think of nothing that would give me more pleasure than your music, if you would care to write it'. Her awkwardness in raising the question of a fee is finally overcome:

> I feel some hesitation and shyness in making my suggestion; which is foolish, for after all one would not be shy about asking a painter to make a picture, or a dramatist to write a play. May I then say quite bluntly that I realise the fee should be much larger than the sum the Drama Society is likely to have at its disposal, and that supposing you care to write the music, I should be very happy indeed to add 20 pounds to whatever fee is agreed between you.[7]

Lilburn undertook the commission, and in her formal tribute to him broadcast on New Zealand Radio in 1965 Ngaio affectionately describes him 'seated helpless at the piano with laughter misting up his spectacles' as the Rude Mechanicals danced to his music. She wrote a warm letter of thanks to him after the performance: 'It is difficult for me to say how completely your music realised for me, my feeling about the play. The first time we heard the preludes to the woodland scenes they anticipated so clearly the tempi of the verse to come that one experienced the strange and moving emotion that only arrives at such moments'. Typically for someone who relentlessly aspired to the highest of standards she went on to say that although the play went well and was financially very successful, she was conscious of flaws, and that 'if we could start working again it really would take enormous strides'. She remained

106

concerned about Lilburn's modest fee, and wanted the students to 'realise their indebtedness'. Although generous with her own time and money, she was also sensitive to the position of someone like Lilburn. In 1980, when Lilburn recorded the music for *Hamlet* and *Othello* as 'Canzonas I and II for String Orchestra', he sent Ngaio the record. On playing it she burst into tears, and wrote to him saying that she was glad she had been on her own when she received it, so many happy memories were released by his music.

The production of *A Midsummer Night's Dream* in late July 1945 was rehearsed in severe weather, with heavy snowfalls and extreme cold. Everyone involved was suffering from the chilly rehearsal rooms, although Ngaio wrote blithely that 'the fairies tripped winsomely in unheated premises'. The six-month gap between this production and the opening of Henry V for the students in association with Christ's College barely gave Ngaio a chance to embark on another novel. Instead, she worked on her booklet on production, *A Play Toward*, which Caxton Press published the following year. Essentially a practical handbook for actors and producers, the booklet struck the right note, with what the New Zealand *Listener* described as 'the taut assumption that we can in this country produce the best'. Jack Henderson, by this time established in theatre in Britain, wrote to say, 'I think it's bloody good', praise that she greatly valued—his letter was pasted into her clippings file.

During this creative and energetic period she also wrote a short story for the *Ellery Queen Mystery Magazine* in America. 'I Can Find My Way Out', published in August 1946, was the first of four to appear in *Ellery Queen*. Ngaio never found the short story form congenial, probably because her favoured method of starting a story meant beginning with a group of characters, and exploring how they interact. Such a technique requires time, and the short story needs a more direct approach. Several of her small output of stories were written during the 1940s, although publication dates are often later.

The Macbeth production in July 1946 saw Ngaio back in her favourite territory, Shakespearean tragedy. Norman Ettlinger played Macbeth and Keith Thomson played Banquo in a dark and stylised production which was galvanised by Douglas Lilburn's music for bagpipes—'he filled the theatre with witches'. Ngaio emphasised the powerful forces pent up within the play. The actors were startled at the intensity with which Ngaio acted out Lady Macbeth's passionate speech of temptation to her husband. This consciousness of evil emerged not only in the 1946 production but again when James Laurenson played the Thane in 1962, and finally in the violent imaginary production that is at the heart of her last novel, *Light Thickens*. Ngaio wrote about her experience of producing this play:

> As soon as rehearsals begin the actors find that they are dealing with contemporary affairs; that the savagery, the terrors and the beauties of the language, although they are set in a remote barbaric period, are expressions of the very elements that disturb the modern world. . . .
> The choice is the eternal choice between good and evil, the nightmare is the nightmare of power politics.

D. D. O'Connor also toured this production to Auckland and Wellington with considerable advance publicity. When the student players arrived in Auckland on 9 January 1947, they were greeted by the Mayor of the city at a civic reception and the tour ended in Wellington with a party hosted by Sir Patrick Duff, the British High Commissioner, Lady Duff, and the Prime Minister. The status of the Drama Society was high, and Miss Marsh and other members of the company were much in demand for interviews by press and radio. Ngaio did her best for publicity. When asked, 'What are your likes and dislikes, Miss Marsh?' she replied cavalierly that she liked fancy-dress parties, motoring, butterscotch, and brandy and ginger, and disliked formal parties, long meals and people with clammy hands. She knew that the press always preferred an image that was slightly larger than life.

Somehow during the past few busy months, Ngaio had organised the arrival of John Mannings as a boarder at Christ's College, fitting him out in uniform and equipping him with a bicycle. John was at Christ's for four years, and his younger brother Roy joined him in 1949. Ngaio obviously felt that their sister, Jean, should stay with her mother, an understandable view but one that caused Jean some feelings of disadvantage as she got older. For both boys the happiest day of the week was Sunday, when they would come up to 37 Valley Road for lunch, then play records on Ngaio's expensive gramophone and help to landscape the garden. By this time the house had been extended by a long, brightly windowed drawing-room which gave plenty of space for entertaining. Ngaio had mixed a brilliant delphinium-blue paint for the far wall, and a friend had painted a mural of *The Tempest* over the fireplace. Comfortably filled with chintz-covered armchairs, paintings and books, the room also had a warm floor, being one of the first houses in Christchurch to have underfloor heating. This was certainly one reason why Ngaio and her student guests liked to curl up on the floor when discussing a forthcoming production.

Stella Mannings, mother of John, Roy and Jean, drew much closer to Ngaio once John started school in Christchurch. She admired her famous cousin and appreciated the interest that Ngaio took in her sons. At the same time, her common sense did not allow her to accept all Ngaio's romanticised views of English society. Stella's childhood in England fascinated Ngaio, and she asked again and again to be told stories of Stella's early years as one of a large, and very formal, Edwardian family. Again, the lonely only child was trying to find a place in a large family, just as she had done with Nelly Rhodes and her children. Visiting John at school was not easy for Stella, as the trip from Hamilton meant a slow train journey and an overnight ferry. Once John left for school he was there until the end of term with only Ngaio nearby as proxy mother. Her experience of young boys was limited to her friendship with the Rhodes family twenty years earlier, but she was well able to act an appropriate part in a situation that required only intermittent involvement. She usually drove John back to school on Sunday night and stayed for evensong in the Chapel, to hear the music of the well-trained boys' choir. At this time her father was still alive but in failing health and given to fits of depression and irritation that John felt were often aimed at him. 'Popsy', as Ngaio called him during their final years together, made it clear to any young men around the house that their interest in Ngaio was unwelcome.

There had been no novel in 1946, and her agent was getting anxious. In between her other responsibilities, Ngaio managed to complete *Final Curtain*, which was published in 1947. In this novel she moved away from New Zealand and concentrated on Alleyn's wife Troy, whom he had left behind in England during the war. Troy, summoned to paint the portrait of a great Shakespearean actor to celebrate his seventy-fifth birthday, finds herself a guest in a very unusual household. Her canvas is set upon by a mischievous member of the extended Ancred family—an experience Ngaio herself used to endure when she stayed with the Rhodes family and returned to her manuscript to find that unsolicited extras had been added and improvements made. Troy is startled to find a pair of spectacles painted crudely on a haughty nose; then a green cow is added to the background, flying above the leonine head. Sir Henry Ancred is another of those larger-than-life Shakespearean actors who crop up in Marsh's novels, and are usually depicted rather dryly. In *Colour Scheme* Geoffrey Gaunt was dismissed as a technician of emotion, and in this novel Sir Henry is crisply disposed of as 'good in a magnificent Mrs Beeton sort of way. A recipe for everything and only the best ingredients used'.

Final Curtain contains a sensitively written chapter describing the reunion between Alleyn and Troy after an absence of three and a half years. They meet almost as strangers, and Alleyn has indeed wondered, on the long voyage back from New Zealand after the war, whether 'he and Troy might not find that the years had dropped between them a transparent barrier through which they would stare, without love, at each other'. He wonders if Troy is feeling the same mixture of anticipation and apprehension, but we already know that although engrossed in painting the portrait, Troy's anxiety is increasing: 'She remembered phrases spoken by other women . . . We were strangers again when we met . . . It wasn't the same . . . Would her reunion also be inarticulate?' After receiving news that Roderick is arriving in a few days she panics: 'I can't see his face . . . I can't remember his voice. I've forgotten my husband.' The quiet reconstruction of their marriage filters through the melodramatic relationships of the Ancred family, and the novel ends with Troy resting her arm on Alleyn's knees and concluding:

'Nothing is clear-cut . . . when it comes to one's views. Nothing.' He waited.
'But we're together,' she said, 'quite together now. Aren't we?'
'Quite together,' Alleyn said.

The experience of reunion after the long parting of war was one that many men and women shared, and Ngaio strengthens her characterisation of Alleyn by revealing his doubts and fears. He does not take Troy for granted, and he knows that his love for his wife will not spring to life again as easily as turning on a switch. Troy is always presented as distant and faun-like, re-treating into herself and her painting rather than revelling in society. Alleyn, although confident in his professional life, remains slightly unsure of his position in Troy's private world, and this self-doubt makes his character much more appealing.

Another unusual feature of *Final Curtain* is the use of poison by the murderer. Ngaio was adept at designing bloodthirsty ways of death, but she had hated and feared poison from early childhood. In her autobiography she writes of her terror of poison, which led her to tear up and burn in the garden bonfire a piece of sheet music whose last line was 'a cup of cold poison lay there by her side'. That song, one of her father's favourite parlour ballads, together with overheard rehearsals for the play *The Fool's Paradise*, about a woman who slowly poisons her husband, was enough to engender a lifelong phobia: 'to this day, on the rare occasions that I use poison in a detective story, I am visited by a ludicrous aftertaste of my childish horrors'.

Witty, humorous, with a mixture of country house murder, artistic insight and the romantic reunion of Alleyn and Troy, *Final Curtain* showed Ngaio in particularly good form. It reached a wide American public through pre-publication serialisation in the *Saturday Evening Post*, the popular weekly magazine. The *Saturday Review of Literature* remarked whimsically that it was 'purty ngai perfect', and although the Toronto *Globe and Mail* called it 'a better novel than a detective story', Julian Symons wrote that 'she uses the old formula brilliantly'. Ngaio's reputation in the United States was very high; in these years she was much preferred to Agatha Christie. Edmund Cork was advised by his American colleague Harold Ober that 'the Ngaio Marsh type of murder mystery is I think what editors are going to be looking for', and that Christie's character Hercule Poirot was beginning to detract from the reality of the stories. Cork had the difficult task of asking Agatha to remove Poirot from *Taken at the Flood*, which she did, only to find that the offer of publication had collapsed. Naturally Cork did not reveal Ober's confidential advice to either writer, but certainly the psychological exploration contained in the Marsh novels hit the right note for American readers at that time, even though in later years the absence of romance was to make her fiction less attractive to the magazines that still ran serials.

The remainder of 1947 was taken up with a production of *The Anatomist* by James Bridie for Canterbury Repertory Society in September, and with more thinking and writing about her chief concerns, Shakespeare and the stage. As her father's health declined she spent more time at home, but she used this opportunity to work on her booklet *Play Production*, which was published in 1948 with drawings by Sam Williams. It remains an eminently sensible introduction to the stage, and the experienced actor and director Elric Hooper feels that even now many actors and producers could find good advice there. Ngaio completely rewrote the pamphlet for its reissue in 1960.

The emphasis on clarity of diction and the player's duty to make himself heard is central to both *Play Production* and *A Play Toward*. Stress on voice work is essential, but Ngaio had a particular axe to grind in her concern for New Zealand speech. Pointing out that 'many New Zealand players do speak with half their voices and less than half their consonants' she required above all that every speech of every actor in her play should be heard by all members of the audience. But her diatribes against New Zealand speech in the pages of the New Zealand *Listener* in the 1970s indicate insensitivity to a change in attitudes that had escaped her understanding. In the 1940s Ngaio strove continuously to improve the quality of her actors' speech, and was recognised as achieving unusual clarity in her orchestrated approach to verse drama. The sound had to be right, but so also did the pace, and she often used the image of a rugby team passing the ball to encourage her untutored actors to develop pace and tension in the text. 'She had a horror of a scene dragging and insisted on speed in picking up a cue', according to Paul Molineaux, 'and it went a long way to establishing a credible interpretation of the text'. Audiences loved these lively and visually attractive productions; Shakespeare had proved to be good box office.

For those who came under the influence of Ngaio in Christchurch at this time, it was a very special moment in their lives. Paul Molineaux, later to become Director of the Security Intelligence Service of New Zealand, recalls the intensity and fire of his student years in Christchurch. Painter Douglas MacDiarmid, now resident in Paris, speaks of 'her powerful Shakespearean spell, exposure to which meant learning entire plays by heart, even at the lowest echelon to which my lack of acting prowess relegated me'. It was a visionary period, when Ngaio managed to foster the artistic development of many young people anxious to express themselves through writing, the theatre, painting and music. Infatuated with her as MacDiarmid was, he saw that 'she had the kind of forceful simplicity that could bring the goofiest undergraduate to his senses and the bigness of heart that every kind of student responded to'. The historian Professor John Pocock echoes this view:

> She was creative and charismatic, and each production was a discovery and an adventure; she was an inspiration to young people discovering the theatre, and immense loyalty and affection developed, which she didn't exploit. Because of this, she does have a special importance in the history of the arts in New Zealand, and in the lives of a whole succession of people, of whom I'm clearly one.

In the plays of Shakespeare Ngaio was to find a fulfillment that she had seldom encountered before. She threw into her productions all the emotional reserves that she normally kept safely locked away, finding in Shakespeare a legitimate outlet for passionate feelings. Here she could risk exposure in a way that she seldom allowed in her novels, always fearing a threat to her valued privacy.

The years ahead were amply to confirm her charismatic leadership and her outstanding abilities when working with students, but to reveal considerable weaknesses when she stepped outside this role into the harsher world of professional theatre.

CHAPTER 6

A World Opens Out: 1948–52

The end of the Second World War meant that travel restrictions were lifted and the artistic isolation of New Zealand and Australia came to an end. 'The cultural mood was optimistic and progressivist',[1] observes Professor Bill Oliver in the *Oxford History of New Zealand*. The year 1948 was to be eventful in many ways for Ngaio Marsh. The award of the OBE in June, for services in connection with literature and drama in New Zealand, and her appointment as Honorary Lecturer in Drama at Canterbury University College in December, were public honours that pleased her greatly. The visit of the Old Vic Company was personally stimulating and led to a new development in her theatrical career. But the death of her father in the same year, although not unexpected, was a loss she felt acutely.

Ngaio herself did not produce any plays during 1948, because of her father's uncertain health, but the year began with a burst of intense theatrical activity at the first residential Drama School to be held in New Zealand. This took the form of a summer school for actors and directors held at Wallis House in the Hutt Valley, outside Wellington, which was directed by Ngaio, assisted by Maria Dronke and Sam Williams. Those who attended were mainly young actors from the University of Canterbury and some from Wellington; hard work was expected of all participants.

Back in Christchurch she began another novel, *Swing, Brother, Swing*, and took an interest in a number of adventurous productions by the Drama Society. Pamela Mann, who had played Emilia in *Othello*, was then living with Ngaio and acting as secretary, as well as producing Congreve's *The Way of the World*. Restoration comedy was an unusual choice for the time but other students were also experimenting as producers. One of the most outstanding theatrical events of the decade was the first performance, on 24 April 1948, of the poet Allen Curnow's verse play *The Axe*, produced by John Pocock. Ngaio took a great interest in this play and Pocock cycled across Christchurch to discuss with her his plans for staging it, and to hear her suggestions on how best to approach the text. Several of the actors whom Ngaio had trained took part: Bernard Kearns, Michael Cotterill and Maryrose Miller. Pocock produced the play and took the part of the native leader Tereavai, defender of the old gods. In this fable of the island of Mangaia, in the Cook Islands, Curnow worked out a tale of conquest and savagery that he managed to relate not only to the bloody history of New Zealand in the nineteenth century, but also to the world war in which New Zealand had recently been involved. Curnow wanted 'to place New Zealand at the centre, the only possible place. Never mind the provincial cold-shudder at the thought that this is not the place at all, and never can be; that here is a centre of sorts, but not the centre, wherever that may be. The islander, even while he shudders, is feeling something at his own centre'.[2]

Curnow was one of the first New Zealand writers to strike out with an individual voice after the war, and *The Axe* reflected a sense of the reordering of traditional attitudes which was shared by the composer Douglas Lilburn and the poet Denis Glover, who were then still living in Christchurch. Professor Bill Oliver called *The Axe* 'a high point in New Zealand drama', and Ngaio thought it 'a most moving and beautiful production' and 'much the best play that has been written in New Zealand'. Curnow acknowledges Ngaio's support at this crucial time: '*The Axe* . . . owed a great deal to her encouragement and advice, at a stage when I was on the point of abandoning it'.

The award of the Order of the British Empire, on 10 June 1948, came at an important time for Ngaio personally and for the cultural development which seemed about to take place in postwar New Zealand. This recognition of Ngaio's work in the theatre and as a writer strengthened her public credibility. That the award was made before the death of her father was a source of personal contentment: he died in St George's Hospital, Christchurch, on 4 September at the age of eighty-five. She mourned his death deeply: 'to begin with, I was desolate'. But she recognised that 'he detested the disabilities of old age . . . I missed him dreadfully but I wouldn't have had him to go on any longer than he desired'. Now, the path was clear for her to seek some of the glamour of the woods beyond the garden wall, the vision she had depicted in her play 'Little Housebound' twenty-five years earlier. At the age of fifty-three, she was entirely independent for the first time, and opportunities were opening everywhere for literary and dramatic endeavours. The next three years were to change her from a small-town celebrity to an internationally known figure.

The emotional strain of her father's death, and the rigorous self-discipline she imposed on herself—she apologised to friends for weeping—coincided with the Old Vic tour at the end of 1948. It was one of the first companies to tour Australasia after the war ended and the actors, who included Laurence Olivier and Vivien Leigh, were welcomed with enthusiasm. Ngaio was impressed by the high standard of their performances in Christchurch, and in an article, 'Shakespeare in New Zealand', she wrote:

> The visit of the Old Vic Theatre Company has changed the dramatic face of New Zealand in a few weeks. Before these players came we had no standard in theatre work. Now, we have the highest. Before the Old Vic came, New Zealanders under the age of thirty who had never left this country had no conception or experience of first-rate acting. Now, they have known it and to its scrupulous touchstone they will do well to subject not only their own future work on the amateur stage but that of any visiting companies and, above all, that of their National Theatre when it is brought to birth.[3]

For the first time she publicly committed herself to the idea of a national theatre, and the debate was to continue for two decades.

The elation of seeing Laurence Olivier as Richard III on stage in Christchurch was matched only by the ferment into which Ngaio and her student actors were thrown by the unexpected invitation to entertain the Old Vic Company in their Little Theatre, and to perform something for them.

Ngaio had been running a series of acting and production workshops at Canterbury College during 1947 and 1948, using Pirandello's *Six Characters in Search of an Author* as an exercise. The talented actress Brigid Lenihan had emerged from these classes, and

Ngaio decided to use Brigid, Bernard Kearns and other actors from the class to perform not Shakespeare but Pirandello for the Old Vic Company. To some extent this was a gamble, as she was much more experienced in dealing with Shakespearean texts. Yet she herself had felt a deep response to this play and her actors were brought to share in it, especially Brigid, whose performance as the stepdaughter was considered outstanding.

Laurence Olivier and Vivien Leigh were also entertained at 37 Valley Road (collected by John Mannings and driven up at great speed in Ngaio's car) and this was the occasion when Vivien tried on Edmund Kean's coat, which had come to Ngaio from her grandfather, the theatre-loving Edward Seager:

> It was made of tawny-coloured plush-velvet and lined with brown silk that had worn to threadpaper and torn away from its handsewn stitching. Pieces of tarnished gold braid dangled from the collar and cuffs. It was tiny.[4]

The coated fitted Vivien Leigh perfectly; but if it really was Kean's coat, he must have been very small indeed. Ngaio once brought it out for Jack Henderson to try, but he could not get it on without damaging it. Ngaio valued the Oliviers' visit and the inspiration the Old Vic Company brought to her actors so much that she gave Olivier the coat as a present: 'Gramps was a good judge of acting: he would certainly have approved'.

As a further tribute, she wrote the script for a farewell to the company which was broadcast on New Zealand Radio. Olivier and Leigh read extracts from some of their most famous roles on stage and in film, and the script ended on a stirring nationalistic note, stressing the value of cultural links within the Commonwealth.

Ngaio's fifteenth novel *Swing, Brother, Swing*, which appeared in 1949 and was published as *A Wreath for Rivera* in the US in the same year, had been slowly reaching completion during 1948 and was eventually sent off to Edmund Cork. It is dedicated to her friend Betty Cotterill, with whom she visited Europe in 1937, and is set in London just after the end of the Second World War. Ngaio may have been too preoccupied with her father's declining health to carry out her normally meticulous research for this book. Although she attempts to give the novel a contemporary feel, with references to food rationing, six-year-old dresses and the 'exhausted aftermath' of the war, it is clearly based on her pre-war memories of London, where she danced at jazz clubs like the 'Metronome' with the Rhodes. Ngaio had not visited England for eleven years, and this is quite apparent from her approach. The plot is weak and trivial, the setting inappropriate, and in comparison to the originality of her New Zealand-based novels, *Swing, Brother, Swing* appears a retrograde step. Admittedly there does seem to be a slight change in attitude from her earlier 'high-society' novels, *Death in a White Tie* and *Surfeit of Lampreys*, with the aristocratic characters now being much more harshly treated. Alleyn has little patience with the drum-playing Lord Pastern, telling him that he is 'probably the most quarrelsome man in England', and that his 'notorious eccentricities' and 'loudly publicised domestic rows' had made him contemptible. In fact, all the characters seem extraordinarily out of touch with the real world. As a fairly lightweight society crime story set in the 1930s it would have been acceptable, but set in the grey and dreary London of the years following the human and physical destruction of the Second World War, the plot seems ridiculous and the atmosphere of privilege and snobbery insensitive. A trip to England was clearly long overdue if she was to continue to set plots there with any kind of conviction. And, fiction apart, she was in need of that surge of energy and freedom she always felt when the Inter-Island ferry cast off its moorings from Lyttelton Harbour, on the first stage of a journey to Europe.

But first, an unexpected theatrical opportunity presented itself. D. D. O'Connor, the producer who had supported the Canterbury Student Players on their first tour of New Zealand in 1945, had heard about their impromptu performance before Laurence Olivier and the Old Vic Company. Generously he suggested that the students should tour Australia with *Othello* and *Six Characters in Search of an Author* in January and February 1949, under his management. Several venues were proposed, but eventually the tour was restricted to Sydney, Canberra and Melbourne. The tour caught the imagination of the press on both sides of the Tasman Sea, and Ngaio described the company on the *MV Wanganella* as they rehearsed on the boat deck: 'much excited, greatly possessed of that sense of partnership inseparable from all well-augured enterprise in the theatre . . . we tingle with anticipation but maintain a cool and hardy demeanour'.

On arrival in Sydney harbour in the early hours of 10 January 1949, the company were fêted as celebrities. It was pouring with rain, but the Sydney *Bulletin* reported the event in swashbuckling style:

> The New Zealand Canterbury Players practically swam ashore on the first lap of their pilgrimage to Australia. They arrived on probably the wettest day in human knowledge. They are led by Ngaio Marsh, who is, by now, hot on the trail of a new murder mystery, who killed the sun? . . . Ngaio is tall, lean and tweedy. Her skin, eyes and profile can support a beret with distinction. Her deep contralto voice is kept on an even keel. At the Lord Mayor and Lady Mayoress's welcome she was 'shot' so often by the camera and newsreel boys she must have begun to feel like the victim in her own tragedies.

The first day in Sydney was a social whirl, starting at 10 a.m. with a party given by Sydney University Dramatic Society: then there was the mayoral reception at 3 p.m., a reception given by the Italian Opera Company at 4.30 and a press conference for Ngaio at 5 p.m. Invitations to parties, barbecues, picnics and other social events flooded in. At a party given by the wife of the Vice-Chancellor of Sydney University, Ngaio was referred to as 'the lioness of the evening', who 'purred amiably'. This was the season for the 'New Look' in clothes, with long, full skirts and picture hats. Press photos show the New Zealand actresses very much following the fashion. Ngaio dressed superbly, in smart dresses, huge hats and kid gloves.

As usual, there were practical problems in setting up productions in strange theatres. An unforeseen disaster was the theft of some of the *Othello* costumes before the opening night, together with the stage manager's new dinner jacket and a wallet. Fortunately borrowed costumes were obtained in time for the opening night, but Ngaio was annoyed by suggestions in the local newspapers that this had been deliberately engineered as a publicity stunt.

Although none of the actors who made up the Canterbury Student Players were professionals, they were nevertheless a group of forty very experienced Shakespearean actors. They had benefited from playing in a number of Ngaio's productions and from the

119

regular workshops she had run during the previous years. Paul Molineaux, Bernard Kearns, Pamela Mann, William Scannell and Brigid Lenihan were all well seasoned in major roles and Bob Stead was a reliable and capable manager. Dundas Walker, the old friend of her parents, by now a very elderly statesman indeed, accompanied the students to help with make-up and to act as a beneficent father figure to calm first-night nerves.

Even given the fact that Australia had not received any serious companies from outside for many years, the press reviews of both plays were ecstatic. The Pirandello play was reaching a completely fresh audience, just as Ngaio had first seen it in London in 1930. The Sydney *Sun* was full of praise:

> Acting of the type for which the theatre really exists was seen in Sydney last night . . . Here was the fresh wind of inspiration and dramatic intensity, producing exhilaration and excitement—a rare phenomenon in our local theatre. Here is theatre in the van, as these revolutionary dramatic spirits of all times have tried to make it.

The Sydney *Herald* praised the company's 'consistent vitality', their 'order and strength' and the 'speed and flashes of bravura'.

A warm welcome, packed houses and an enthusiastic press greeted the company when they stepped off the train in Canberra on 31 January. They opened with *Othello* but again it was *Six Characters* that seemed to impress the audience most. The Canberra *Times* reported that 'nothing like *Six Characters in Search of an Author* by Luigi Pirandello has been seen before in Canberra . . . the production reached a standard rarely seen'. The High Commissioner for New Zealand and his wife entertained the actors, but Canberra was a hot and arid construction site in 1949, and the company were glad to move on to Melbourne, with its gracious old nineteenth-century houses and strong theatrical tradition. Coincidentally the Stratford-upon-Avon Players, forerunners of the Royal Shakespeare Company were also playing *Othello* in Melbourne at the Princess Theatre, but according to the reviewer for the Australian *Listener*, 'as a production of Shakespeare, it has almost everything to learn from Miss Marsh's work for the New Zealand student players at Melbourne University'.

Apart from another round of parties and receptions an unexpected invitation came from the Kozminsky Gallery to ask Ngaio to open an exhibition of paintings by a young artist recently arrived from Bombay, Allen David. In her short address she promoted the idea of increased international links. She stressed that because of their geographic distance from the world's cultural centres, it was up to Australians and New Zealanders to establish and strengthen lines of communication in the arts. For Ngaio and many of her generation in New Zealand, the standard had always been Europe, and she was never to alter this view. Her interest in making it easier for artists to travel to and from Europe and within the Commonwealth was always aimed at achieving the standards of 'home'. She never seemed to realise that the postwar generation of Australians and New Zealanders did not wish to imitate, but to initiate. In Australia the 'cultural cringe' of the 1950s was finally dispatched by a powerful artistic surge of writers, painters and performers during the 1960s. Contemporary writers such as David Malouf, Thomas Keneally and Judith Wright were writing from an imaginative response to their own landscapes, not in imitation of European models.

The successful tour by the Canterbury Student Players brought them prestige in New Zealand because of their recognition overseas. The fact that they had been favourably compared to the Stratford-upon-Avon Players and the recent Old Vic tour was enormously encouraging. Their reception in Australia established the Student Players as a force that could return to New Zealand convinced of their worth, and confident that a New Zealand theatre could develop from such modest beginnings.

The company returned to Christchurch on 10 March 1949 after three months on the road, having given 140 performances to audiences totalling 25,000 people. Ngaio was quoted as saying that the tour had been 'an unqualified success' and she hoped that similar Australian companies would soon be visiting New Zealand. Theatre in Australia was to need several more years before it reached the high standard of the Canterbury Players. One of the most influential forces in developing it was Keith Thomson, who was instrumental in founding the university theatre in Adelaide, energetically developing their society, and encouraging the Adelaide Theatre Festival.

Among the letters waiting for a reply when Ngaio returned to

37 Valley Road was an invitation from Canterbury University College to become an Honorary Lecturer in Drama. This public recognition of her valuable work with young people and of the high standard of her productions was important to Ngaio, who always felt rather in awe of university people, while not realising that they were also in awe of her.

Ngaio's confidence was built up still further by the acceptance of four of her student actors to engage in theatre work in Britain. Her star, Brigid Lenihan, was already working in British rep, having followed Laurence Olivier's advice to Ngaio: 'Don't let her go to drama school; she's got all that, she has star quality. Let her sweat it out in Rep'. Pamela Mann and Bob Stead were among a small number of students selected from around the world to study production at the Old Vic Theatre School, now opening for the first time since it was bombed in the war. Bob's wife Mizzy accompanied him, as did technical designer John Knight, who was later to marry Brigid. Jack Henderson had already returned to England, followed soon after by D. D. O'Connor's first wife, whom he subsequently married. It was a small scandal, which startled Ngaio and was the kind of behaviour that upset her deeply. Ngaio had loved Jack in a complicated way that was less than romance but more than a professional relationship, and she hated to see him behave in what she considered to be a dishonourable way. She certainly felt that her much-valued association with O'Connor as manager was being put in jeopardy. For all her ability to chart the most complex emotional dilemmas in her novels, she repeatedly proved unable to recognise them when they actually confronted her. A mixture of naivety and a desire to think the best of everyone made her surprisingly vulnerable when faced with extremes of passion and misery in real life. No matter how convincing her woman of the world act, Ngaio still seemed to want to cast a warm, fantasy glow over people she liked. The situation was eventually resolved when Dan O'Connor married again. He continued to give Ngaio financial backing, and Jack was restored to his place among Ngaio's group of friends.

It was time to be back in England; time to leave the cosiness of Christchurch for the bracing anonymity of the metropolis. There was a great deal of theatre to catch up on, and her new book, *Swing, Brother, Swing*, was coming out in April. The Canterbury Players gave her a special farewell performance in the Little Theatre on 30 May called 'Bottom's Dream: A Bytte in One Act'. This useful spoof, adapted from the Bard by Bob Gormack, managed commodiously to incorporate characters from several plays well known to the cast, including Macbeth and his Lady, Othello and Desdemona, and, of course, Bottom.

Two days later, having left her house in the care of her cousin Stella and her husband, Ngaio set off for England. She was accompanied by Pamela Mann, who had been her secretary for some time and was now bound for the Production Course at the Old Vic. The intention was for her to continue as secretary during the voyage, to help Ngaio make progress on her next novel, *Opening Night*. Again, Dan O'Connor generously helped with expenses, and was making preliminary moves to initiate his ambitious undertaking, a Commonwealth drama company, a scheme in which Ngaio was to play a leading role.

The voyage began as usual with the cumbersome route of overnight ferry to Wellington, overnight train to Auckland, and the ferry to Sydney, where they joined the *Orion* for the voyage to England. Winter was upon them in the south, and press photographs taken in Sydney show Ngaio wearing the sumptuous sealskin coat that had so impressed her young admirers in Christchurch: 'the most glamorous coat I ever saw', said Keith Thomson. When she went to buy it she brought Pamela with her, and bought her a fashionable imitation ocelot coat. This was to sustain Pamela through many cold English winters, and wrapped up in it, she queued all night on the pavement outside the Old Vic for tickets when the theatre reopened on 14 November 1950. Meanwhile, wearing their marvellous coats and wide-brimmed hats, they looked like international film stars on the streets of Sydney. In the two days they spent there, they managed to see *Annie Get Your Gun*, an English vaudeville show, and two films, as well as dining splendidly at 'Le Coq d'Or'. After a brief call in Melbourne, they were soon steaming across the Indian Ocean and had settled down to the pleasant routine of shipboard life. Pamela recorded in the journal she kept of the voyage that 'Ngaio and I work in the morning. Kind people come up and discuss the weather then say they'll "led us ged on with it". In the afternoon we are hearty. Wish we could stop rolling'.

123

Opening Night is another theatre mystery, and it evolves very naturally from the author's recent experience with actors on tour. Her talented protégé Brigid Lenihan, who had already arrived in London, was much in her thoughts. The heroine of the novel, a penniless actress just arrived in London from New Zealand, seems an amalgam of Brigid and Ngaio, but in the view of Pamela Mann 'the girl's diffidence and scruples are far more typical of Ngaio herself'. Although the novel was started on the *Orion*, it clearly has a tang of postwar London that the previous novel lacked. The character of Martyn Tarne is so convincingly developed that the murder appears an irritating intrusion rather than the climax of the plot. *Opening Night* was strong enough to stand without the investigative crime framework and the characterisation, with the tensions between the actors firmly drawn, is ripe for further development. Julian Symons is correct when, in *Bloody Murder*, he praises the first half of this novel for its 'brilliant picture of the intrigues taking place before the opening of a new play', and regrets the loss of mood after the official investigation starts.

Sexual crimes had not entered her novels up to now, but the marital rape suggested here is disturbing and was certainly still considered fairly problematic in 1962 when a BBC memo about a possible radio dramatisation records that the novel 'has possible drawbacks for a Saturday night audience . . . it has wife-rape as a central incident; but such stories as the *Forsyte Saga* have probably made this acceptable'. The BBC reader, Arthur Russell, 'thought that for a detection series the non-appearance of Roderick Alleyn until page 147, well over halfway through, would be a weakness, but acknowledged that to cut the exciting backstage story . . . would do violence to a good novel'.[5] Russell's impression is that Alleyn was reluctant to join a cast list where he really had no part to play. Fortunately *Woman's Journal* proved to be made of sterner stuff than 'Auntie BBC' in coping with marital rape, and serialised the novel between March and May 1951.

But in July 1949 the novel was still developing well on the top deck of the *Orion*, while in the afternoons Ngaio played deck games and joined in the entertainments with Pamela. She compared a successful charade evening on 10 July, awarding the prize to Father Walsh, who had played Queen Victoria; Pamela's charade of Moses in the bulrushes came second. The ship called at Colombo, giving them a chance to order silk dresses at Ramsamy's in the morning and collect them before they re-embarked in the evening. The last week on board was a festive round of cocktail parties and private dinners: 'no breaking in for austerity England' noted Pamela in her journal. Ngaio's dinner party in the restaurant was a great success.

The ship docked at Southampton at 5 a.m. on 16 July 1949, and waiting for them on the quay were Denys and Terence ('Teddy') Rhodes and Bob Stead. Swept off to Mount Offham, the country house in Kent where the Rhodes family were then living, Ngaio and Pamela arrived at 'a scene of incredible confusion. The annual village fête was in progress in the garden, the band was making an unbelievable noise, children were running around in fancy dress and the lawn seemed to seethe with people. The Rhodes family was assembled en masse to greet Ngaio . . .' As the visitors emerged, somewhat startled, from the car, Eileen said casually, 'We've invited a few people to meet you—hope you don't mind'. It was the kind of offhand greeting that Ngaio must have half expected, and she was immediately drawn once again into the quirky, humorous world of the Rhodes family.

For Pamela, arriving in England for the first time, the country-side, the house and the people were like a dream. She was experiencing the same amazed sense of being in a moving picture that Ngaio had felt when she first arrived twenty years before. After dinner on their first night there was something completely new to gaze at—a television set. Neither had seen one before.

Three days later they were in London, renewing contact with D. D. O'Connor and the Steads. Ngaio needed a flat, and was fortunate enough to find one at 56 Beauchamp Place, in Knightsbridge, very near the premises rented by 'Touch and Go' twenty years before. As well as bringing back memories, the flat also had that suggestion of fantasy necessary for Ngaio's contentment:

The flat was over an enchanting clock shop. During the night I could hear minuscule chimes, single tinkling bells, a gong, musical-box confections and the punctual wheelhorse observations of a dependable grandfather. There was even a French clock that tootled a little silver trumpet. . . . It was like the setting for a Victorian fairy tale. . . . [6]

The flat was to be shared with Bob and Mizzy Stead, and the project in hand was to advance Dan O'Connor's scheme to form a British Commonwealth Theatre Company, with Ngaio as director and Bob as business manager.

Although she flung herself immediately into the theatre world, with late suppers at the Café Royal and a trace of the old gaiety, the changed face of bombed and battered London affected Ngaio deeply. The BBC lost no time in contacting her, and in September she broadcast a talk, 'London Revisited', which records her responses to the 'kind of inertia', the 'air of fatigue that seems to lie over most things'. She found the change in people more noticeable than the change in the appearance of a city she had loved. The talk ends:

> What can a New Zealander have the cheek to say about the waste-lands behind St Paul's? Only that one turns away from them with a kind of astonishment that a people who suffered this nightmare outrage should be as they are, in good heart after all. What an impertinence to say that one finds them 'a little tired'.[7]

Life soon established itself at a brisk pace for Ngaio, as writer, broadcaster and theatre producer. She felt obliged to give her full support to her publisher's celebration of the 'Marsh Millions' at the end of July. Ten of her novels were published simultaneously by Penguin, in conjunction with Collins, with 100,000 copies of each, making a million Marsh copies. Sales received a tremendous boost from the attendant publicity. Ngaio was photographed with the Chairman, Billy Collins, at a cocktail party given for the launch, looking sophisticated and at ease, although she admits that 'it was astonishing, this time in England, to find myself broadcasting and being televised and interviewed and it was pleasant to find detective fiction being discussed as a tolerable form of reading by people whose opinion one valued'. She must have been particularly delighted with the comment of an anonymous *Times Literary Supplement* reviewer: 'there is no doubt that Miss Ngaio Marsh is among the most brilliant of those authors who are transforming the detective story from a mere puzzle into a novel with many other qualities besides the challenge to our wits'.

Although those who met Ngaio at these formal events remember her as dazzling, expensively dressed, with dashing hats and accessories, those who knew her best understood what an effort such public appearances required. At a reception arranged in her honour in London, Edmund Cork, concerned at her late arrival and knowing how punctual she usually was, went to the restaurant door to look outside. There was Ngaio, impeccably dressed, walking up and down the pavement, unable to bring herself to enter. Had she been an actress, one could have said that she felt under-rehearsed for her part and was reluctant to take the stage. In Christchurch the presence of her young acolytes gave her confidence and a clearly defined role as teacher and guide. In London, while she enjoyed meeting distinguished members of the literary and theatre world, she was less sure of herself. But she knew the part to play, and she played it well, conscious that her publishers expected a certain public performance from time to time. The style and polish of literary parties in elegant venues was always a stimulating change, and once she had made the effort to attend she usually enjoyed herself.

The summer of 1949 continued to find Ngaio immensely busy. She decided to help the British export drive by ordering a new Jaguar car to use while she was in England, and to follow her out to New Zealand when she departed. This was a cream-coloured Mark V convertible, so highly powered that Ngaio and Bob Stead thought about entering it for the Monte Carlo Rally, then still considered to be 'a gentleman's hobby'. This idea did not come to fruition but the car duly arrived in Christchurch with its GB plates still in place, and immediately became the most desirable vehicle in the South Island. Even so, Ngaio thought nothing of allowing Stella's son, young Bear Mannings, who was then only eighteen, to borrow the car to take his girlfriends to dances, and occasionally she received worried phone calls from astonished bystanders who had just seen the car flash past in a cloud of dust with a cheerful young man at the wheel.

In England, Ngaio drove the car down to Mount Offham for weekends with the Rhodes family. In London, work on the novel continued late at night, often after visits to the theatre, when the streets were quiet and social life was over. *Opening Night* was making spirited attempts to escape from the detective fiction strait-jacket and launch itself into the uncertain currents of the serious novel, and Ngaio had to act with particular firmness to bring it, regrettably, into line. Pamela brought the first draft up to

Edmund Cork in early August, and to celebrate its completion they indulged in an excess of theatre-going.

Both Pamela and Ngaio kept a record of the plays they saw during 1949–50, and Ngaio's scrapbook consists of the theatre programme pasted on the right-hand page of a large book, with her comments and sketches of design details recorded on the left. The theatre journal gives up in September 1950, but records that in the fourteen-month period from July 1949 to September 1950, Ngaio saw sixty-two productions, sometimes two a day. Her commentaries are often pungent, as in her verdict on the open-air production of *The Tempest* in Regent's Park: 'pedestrian production with little movement and artsie-craftsie floozies as dancing chorus'. She quite enjoyed *Black Chiffon* with Flora Robson at the Westminster Theatre—'suspense held overlong without relief—fair production'—and found Goetz's *The Heiress* at the Theatre Royal with Peggy Ashcroft and Ralph Richardson 'excellent . . . with two star players a possibility for us'. But she hated Miller's *Death of a Salesman*: 'I disliked it intensely and thought it phoney but it's drawing the crowds'. After charitably dismissing *The Young and Fair* at St Martin's—'doesn't altogether escape a Girl's Own Paper flavour'—the London theatre scene was fairly well exhausted, so she moved on to Stratford, where Anthony Quayle was directing a season. This was much more challenging, and she enjoyed the whole atmosphere of Stratford, with walks along the Avon and trips into the surrounding countryside. Her favourite production was *Much Ado About Nothing* with Quayle as Benedick and Diana Wynyard as Beatrice: 'on the whole—delightful'. She was fascinated by the set and by the decor: 'magnificent production and decor and lovely clothes. Ingenious set opening and closing like book wings with portable units and platforms'.

Briefly back in London for a few days in late August, Ngaio joined Dan O'Connor for a visit to the Edinburgh Festival. There she saw Tyrone Guthrie's famous production of Sir David Lindsay's sixteenth-century morality play, *The Three Estates*, which had a profound effect on her theatrical style for years to come. Ngaio found it 'the best show I've seen', and was fascinated by the three-sided thrust stage, and the actors coming and going through the audience 'with immense gusto'. On her return to London she mopped up *The Beaux Stratagem* at the Lyric, *Fading Mansion* at the

Duchess ('interesting and at times very impressive'), *The Third Visitor* at the Duke of York's ('frightful thriller'), *The Sleeping Beauty* at the New Lindsey Theatre Club ('poorish and amateurish'), followed by another draught of the heady brew on offer at Stratford. Michael Benthall's *A Midsummer Night's Dream* was 'an exciting show . . . but overloaded with extraneous props'. *Othello* was disposed of in one dread word, 'dull'. *Cymbeline* was better received: 'exciting production with notable use of colour and set pieces', but the highlight of the visit was clearly Tyrone Guthrie's production of *Henry VIII*, with Anthony Quayle as the King. What fascinated Ngaio particularly was Guthrie's brilliant use of crowds, with fluid movements and 'bit-parts dickied up to great effect'. Much that she learned from Guthrie's productions was put into practice in her large-scale Shakespearean productions in Christchurch throughout the 1950s and 1960s.

It was hardly surprising that while she was revelling in practically every available theatrical production, an invitation from the presitigious BBC Director Val Gielgud to write a play for a new autumn series should go without response. His elegantly framed invitation asking for 'an originally written play of the type which I believe you would supply à merveille' went on to declare 'a longstanding admiration for your work, a mutual publisher and my professional background which incites me to make a suggestion which I hope may not be altogether disagreeable to you'. Despite this flattering overture, Ngaio was unable or disinclined to write a play for October transmission, but she did start to broadcast regularly and to take part in a variety of radio programmes such as *Woman's Hour, Talk Yourself Out of This* and *London West Central*. Her pleasant, deep voice, sense of humour and lively conversation made her ideal radio material, and during the whole of her twenty-month stay in London she broadcast regularly on the Home Service, the Light Programme, the World Service, and occasionally on BBC Television.

The press had started reporting on the British Commonwealth Theatre project, and in a lengthy interview in *The Evening News* on 25 July 1949, Ngaio described their plans to form a non-profit-making company which would give young British actors a chance of going overseas to play alongside Commonwealth players, 'weaving a strong drama thread between Great Britain and the

Dominions'. Ngaio talked about a touring company of actors drawn from all over the Commonwealth, which would visit Australia and New Zealand first, then Canada and South Africa. It was a huge undertaking and only someone of Ngaio's phenomenal energy and charisma could have taken the project as far as she did.

Meanwhile Ngaio's Beauchamp Place flat was becoming a focal point for New Zealanders in London. The dramatist Bruce Mason and his wife Diana came to stay; Biddy Lenihan, John Knight and John Pocock came to dinner. Allen Curnow strolled across from Bayswater to discuss the possibility of having his verse drama, *The Axe*, staged in London. Soon afterwards Fred and Eve Page, accompanied by Sylvia Fox, arrived and took a flat in Notting Hill Gate. Pamela Mann was enchanted with the easy-going lifestyle of Chelsea at that time. She walked along Chelsea Embankment one hot Sunday morning with the Steads, the Masons, and Ngaio to a riverside pub where everyone was drinking out of doors. It was, says Pamela, 'so completely unlike a New Zealand Sunday morning'.

Ngaio, who always loved cats, had acquired a Siamese kitten called Ptolemy. She used to exercise him on a blue jewelled lead, striding through Knightsbridge, tall, elegant, and beautifully dressed. The sight so amazed Bruce Mason that he commented on it in letters twenty years later. It must have seemed a long way from her lifestyle during much of the 1930s and 1940s in Christchurch, where the highlight of the week was often Sunday supper followed by a game of Lexicon with her father and the two elderly Walker brothers. And unlike her earlier prolonged stay with the Rhodes family she was now entirely independent. She spent memorable weekends at Mount Offham, such as the visit in September when she attended a hop-pickers' campfire and concert party organised by Teddy Rhodes, but also made new friendships in quite different spheres.

This dramatic change in lifestyle, and even in her appearance, was to become part of Ngaio's regular visits to England. More than an expatriate, she cultivated a dual identity, signing hotel registers in New Zealand with a flourish as 'Ngaio Marsh, London', and in England, as 'Ngaio Marsh, New Zealand'. To those who knew her only in Christchurch, curled up on the floor of her house wearing comfortable trousers, chain-smoking companionably with her students, or pottering around the garden in old shoes, the glamorous studio photographs taken in England seemed to be of a different person. Ngaio always took care to dress carefully for the parts she was to play, wearing well-cut tweeds for weekends in Kent and sophisticated dresses for theatre life in London. Unlike many tall women, she was not afraid of high heels when dressing for an occasion, or of showing her excellent legs to advantage in coloured or lacy stockings. She liked hats and wore them with an air, her well-defined features and tall figure ensuring that heads turned whenever she entered a room. Yet, back in Christchurch, she seldom wore fashionable clothes except for a special event such as a first night of one of her plays, and even then she was more likely to be dressed for work backstage.

Along with all the other new possibilities that were opening out that year came an unexpected approach from Owen Howell, a solicitor nearing retirement who had prepared a stage play based on *Surfeit of Lampreys*. Since the 1935 staging of *Exit Sir Derek* in Christchurch, the play based on her novel *The Nursing Home Murder*, no attempts had been made to dramatise any of Ngaio's novels. Ngaio and Pamela went for lunch to Howell's converted mill outside London, where they also met his two children, Peter and Gillian, both of whom were actors. Ngaio was in favour of the project, and although she had nothing to do with the production, followed with interest the progress of the play after its acceptance by Molly May at the Embassy Theatre, Hampstead, for performance in the autumn of 1950. She also began to take an interest in the career of Peter Howell, who at that time was playing Hamlet in a production for the West of England Theatre Company. Ngaio was already beginning to look around for likely young actors to form the basis for the Commonwealth Theatre Company, and she decided to see more of Peter's work. Invited to the Beauchamp Place flat to work on Hamlet with Ngaio, Peter found it 'the most amazing experience . . . it was a kind of therapy for both of us . . . she used to say it kept her hand in. I certainly loved it'. In grooming Peter Howell to play Hamlet Ngaio may have been trying to find a replacement for Jack Henderson in her affections; certainly the role of mentor to sensitive and talented young men was one that she adopted with particular acuity.

At the end of September she was to see one of her great stage heroes acting and directing in London, when Donald Wolfit opened his Shakespeare Season at the King's Theatre. Ngaio was critical of what she saw: 'frightful scenery and costumes . . . dire supporting company'. Wolfit's *King Lear* was 'uneven but magnificent', and Pamela Mann, who accompanied Ngaio, found it hard to understand how such power could be conveyed while cardboard boulders wobbled as he leaned on them. But the flamboyance of Ben Jonson's Volpone must have suited Wolfit's style perfectly, and both Ngaio and Pamela thought it 'exciting, vigorous, and authentic in spite of characteristic gross faults in staging. Wolfit gives a great—repeat great—performance here'. Ngaio no longer responded to Sir Donald's bravura approach to Shakespeare and she was acutely aware of the lack of discipline in his performances. It must have been a ready topic of conversation when her old friend the actor-manager Allan Wilkie visited her for lunch on 30 September. Wilkie was writing his autobiography, and Ngaio agreed to provide the Preface. This is among her papers, with its vivid description of 'a bullet head, a large frame, a drooping cigarette and a voice of particular resonance, reduced at moments of disaster to a terrifying hiss, letting forth streams of particularly inventive blasphemy'. It speaks of the memoirs as a unique record, as indeed they were, and concludes:

> Many a more solemn and pretentious book tells us far less about the living theatre than this. It will be read with pleasure by anyone who has the smell of greasepaint in his system or gets a jolt under his diaphragm when the curtain rises on a play.

Unfortunately Wilkie never saw his book in print, and although the editor at Faber and Faber, T. S. Eliot, found it 'a nice book' (his rejection note was left in the manuscript by mistake and found by Ngaio), he did not recommend publication. Despite efforts by Ngaio and her friends the autobiography was never published, and now seems to have disappeared. As an account of a barnstorming actor-manager, setting off with his wife and company to perform in unpromising venues from the Far East to Canada, from America to New Zealand, it would have made an important contribution to theatre history. Even Ngaio, generally so reluctant to criticise anything to do with the world of publishing, commented on the short-sighted policy of those who were not prepared to take a risk with an unusual author.

Pamela Mann had started her course at the Old Vic in October but still came to Beauchamp Place to help Ngaio with her typing and correspondence. Weekends with the Rhodes at Mount Offham became less frequent as engagements in London increased, particularly broadcasting. But Nelly Rhodes and various members of the family occasionally came up to London to see Ngaio, and on 9 October there was a lively group of 'Lampreys' in the studio audience at the BBC to support their friend in *Talk Yourself Out of This*. Conversation at dinner in La Speranza afterwards mainly concerned a proposed trip to Monte Carlo at the end of October. The Plunket family had rented a converted Saracen fortress at Eze above Monte Carlo for two weeks, and had invited Ngaio to join them.

This fortress was obviously the inspiration for *Spinsters in Jeopardy* (1954): 'a vast house that seemed to grow out of the cliff . . . moonlight and shadows, black as ink, were thrown across its recessed face'. Nelly and Ngaio disliked the position of the fortress and came down to the old hotel where they had stayed before. This was their third holiday in Monte Carlo together, and, strolling along the promenade, there was some sadness while they thought of the people who were not there: Tahu Rhodes had died in 1947 and Toppy Blundell Hawkes, her friend from Meadowbank days who had also been her escort in 1920s London had died of septicaemia as a young man in 1935. As Ngaio regretfully noted in her autobiography, by 1949 'our quartette had become a pair'.

Ngaio had to be back in London for a *Woman's Hour* interview at the beginning of November, and for another radio assignment: to provide the commentary for the opening of an exhibition by New Zealand painters, sculptors and potters at New Zealand House. She prepared her script with care, setting the scene on a misty evening on the Strand to convey the feel of London to her overseas listeners. She took the opportunity not only to praise the work of these young artists who had come to England to develop their talent on the strength of bursaries from the New Zealand government, but also to stress how important it was for them to return to New Zealand. The exhibition was opened by well—known New Zealander, the political cartoonist Sir David Low, who stated unequivocally that 'no country can build up a culture if all its best talent always leaves it'. But Ngaio made the point that the opportunities had to exist if young people were to return, saying to her listeners, 'once again, it's over to you, if you want to have them back'. The choice was to affect her personally when in 1951 she turned her back on the possibility of a successful career in British theatre, and brought her British Commonwealth Theatre Company to an Australian and New Zealand public that did not always seem to value the offering.

Further broadcasting followed on a regular basis, including a *Books to Read* programme on 28 December. The producer, Mary Treadgold, sent Ngaio 'a catholic selection of books, as befits an immediately post-Christmas broadcast'. In case her reviewer should think five books rather a lot to cope with over the holiday, she briskly encouraged her 'to discover your own method of achieving this', and then slipped in a sixth book for good measure. Although this programme paid the relatively high fee of 15 guineas, it demanded a written script in advance and a read-through on 21 December before the broadcast a week later.

By this time Pamela Mann was too much involved with her production course at the Old Vic to continue acting as secretary, and the post was handed on to another of the Canterbury Student Players, Rosemary Clark-Hall. She was training as a figure-skater in London, and came to Ngaio in the afternoons. They were to work together intermittently for the next few years, and when Rosemary returned to Christchurch as Rosemary ('Roses') Greene, wife of Michael Greene, she became secretary and friend for the remainder of Ngaio's life.

For most of 1950 Ngaio and Bob Stead worked hard at assembling the company they needed for the proposed Commonwealth Tour, now scheduled for Festival of Britain Year, 1951. There was still a huge amount of organisation to do, and the difficulties of assembling an international cast were far greater than she anticipated. Peter Howell realised that the whole project was almost impossible:

> Ngaio, wonderful as she was, maybe wasn't as brilliant because she hadn't got experience of knowing exactly the way the London theatre worked. And how the hell do you find people who are

prepared to go away for a year, and how do you find the right plays?

But in the spring of 1950 none of these problems seemed insoluble, and during the day Ngaio and Bob worked hard together to establish the company. During the evenings, long into the small hours, she wrote *Spinsters in Jeopardy*.

Eventually a cast list representing Britain and five Commonwealth countries was assembled: Australia, Canada, South Africa, New Zealand and India. Notable names included actor Basil Henson, who became a member of the National Theatre, London, and John Schlesinger, now better known as a film director but then recognised as a fine actor who liked to show his amateur films to other members of the company. Jon Bannenberg, who acted and stage-managed, became a ship designer. Some were tempted, but in the end it was for many people, 'too far, for too long'.

Although Ngaio had not accepted Val Gielgud's invitation to write a radio play the previous year, she was interested in a proposal from D. G. Bridson, then Assistant Head of Features at the BBC, to write a half-hour feature to celebrate the centenary of the founding of Christchurch on 16 December 1850. She accepted the commission.

Given Ngaio's own family history, it is not surprising that she proposed to tell the story of a typical nineteenth-century immigrant family seeing the advertisements in England for the Canterbury Association, enduring the long voyage out, facing the immense vista as they climbed the hills above Lyttelton Harbour, and finally managing to establish themselves in a new life in New Zealand, 12,000 miles from home. Professional to her fingertips, she started work immediately, and on 15 August Rosemary Greene wrote to the BBC that Ngaio was already well advanced on the first draft. On 23 August she sent a rough script, and dispatched the final script on 14 September. R. D. Smith, who was handling the project while Bridson was on holiday, wrote immediately to Ngaio saying that 'Overseas Directors like this very much and so do I'. He requested a few minor script changes, which she made the same day, and returned it with a modest note saying, 'I'm so glad you think it's all right'. The programme received the attention of the best producers and performers available to the BBC, and had a musical score composed and conducted by Antony Hopkins.

Recordings were still made on cumbersome discs, and elaborate plans were necessary to ensure simultaneous worldwide broadcasts. The programme, 'The New Canterbury Pilgrim', sounds over-formal and stately now, but was entirely suitable for its rather nationalistic purpose at that time. Not only was Ngaio thinking of her ancestors, Edward Seager and Esther Coster, who were among the earliest pioneers, but also of her own response to that arrival at Lyttelton Harbour: 'when one comes up over those hills, and looks down on the Canterbury Plains, it is one of the most remarkable entries into a country that you could possibly have. It's quite extraordinarily beautiful'.

Ngaio regarded the first night of *Surfeit of Lampreys* on 21 November at the Embassy Theatre, Hampstead, with mixed feelings. She had approved Owen Howell's adaptation, but knew that a delicate touch from the cast was essential. Pamela Mann, who had finished her course at the Old Vic and was working at the Embassy Theatre as secretary to the manager, Molly May, did not feel confident about the way the production was shaping up. She recorded in her journal: 'First night of Ngaio's *Surfeit of Lampreys* at the Embassy. Don't think it is going to be very successful'. *The Times* reviewer was not enthusiastic, finding that 'the play is one more instance of a novel transferred to the stage as though the business involved no sort of theatrical problem'. The novelist herself was disappointed: 'much too heavy-going . . . the set was extremely lugubrious'. Owen Howell had caught some of the flavour of the Lamprey dialogue, but according to his son Peter, the play was extremely difficult to cast: 'The Lampreys are indeed wonderfully fey, mad and funny, but they're not easy to get right—even a much better director might have found it difficult'.

But a useful contact had been made at the Embassy, and the failure of *Surfeit of Lampreys* was followed by an interesting proposal from Molly May that Ngaio should produce *Six Characters in Search of an Author*, a play that always inspired her. Brigid Lenihan was still in London and naturally Ngaio wanted her to play the part of the stepdaughter that she had performed so powerfully in Australia and New Zealand, but the management insisted on an English star. The part went to Yvonne Mitchell, to the producer's great disappointment. Peter Howell played the Producer, and Bruce Mason had a small part as the piano-player.

He remembers his performance as 'a repertoire that must have been the weirdest ever: the Romanian Dances of Bela Bartok, and the Tritch-Tratch Polka of Johann Strauss'. His memories of the rehearsals shed considerable light on the difficulties Ngaio had to face in coming to work as an outsider, in the professional London theatre:

> I, as a member of the cast, was completely aware of the patronising attitude of the English cast to what Charles Lloyd Pack (playing the Stage Manager) witheringly described in the play as a 'bloody amateur'. This was how the cast viewed Ngaio at the first rehearsal, though not at any later one. There was a deathly silence at the first rehearsal when Ngaio explained to the British contingent that 'in New Zealand we have six weeks to prepare a play.' No one looked at anything but their own noses. She soon put them right, and made it perfectly clear that first, she knew her job, and second, would stand no indiscipline.[8]

Apart from a rambling and unrelated piece in *The Times*, which reads as though the reviewer had not actually attended, virtually all the newspaper reviews were favourable. To the *Evening Star*, 'the production by Ngaio Marsh provides the best version of the play that London has seen', and Maurice Wiltshire in the *Daily Mail* praised it as 'an extremely difficult and fascinating entertainment'. *The Herald* saw the play as 'movingly developed' and the *Graphic* looked to the future, claiming that 'if Miss Ngaio Marsh continues to devote as much attention to producing as she has devoted to writing, she will soon be as well known on London stages as she is on the bookstalls'.

With this encouragement, Ngaio must have thought very seriously about Molly May's offer to direct a season of English Comedy at the Embassy in the summer of 1951, Festival of Britain year. But the departure date for the British Commonwealth tour was now fixed at 15 February 1951, and in declining the Embassy Theatre's offer, Ngaio effectively realigned her loyalties to the Antipodes and to the furtherance of New Zealand theatre.

Time was now beginning to press alarmingly, and Ngaio started to refuse invitations to broadcast on the BBC. One invitation she did not decline, however, was to lecture at the Royal Society of Arts on 12 December 1950. Her topic was 'The Development of the Arts in New Zealand', and she was awarded the Society's silver medal for her paper. In April 1952 she was made a Fellow of the Royal Society of Arts, a prestigious and much-valued appointment.

Christmas 1950 flashed by and the treasured invitation to spend the holiday with the Rhodes family in Kent had to be refused. She said goodbye to the family during a hasty weekend visit in early February, and after a farewell party for the company at Dan O'Connor's flat, they were off.

Tensions between members of the company were kept at bay during the voyage but surfaced with a vengeance when they reached Australia. On board ship, Ngaio distributed copies of her latest novel, *Opening Night*, and settled down to daily rehearsals, work on *Spinsters in Jeopardy*, and observation of the behaviour of a group of actors on board a ship. Notes and sketches indicate that she must have been turning over possibilities involving a theatre company on board ship that suddenly required the services of Roderick Alleyn to solve a murder. Antagonisms within the group were probably close to this by the time the tour was over.

The season in Sydney was a heart-breaking contrast to the successful tour Ngaio had led there two years before. Shaw's popular play *The Devil's Disciple* was poorly cast and had bad reviews. Peter Howell remembers 'bitter, miserable actors' and Ngaio admitted that the play 'grew colder and colder in my hands the more I tried to blow some warmth into it. Dissonances of all sorts broke out in the company, the houses faded, gnawing anxiety and depressions settled among us'. The *Sydney Morning Herald* thought the cast like puppets, and blamed the director: 'Her powerful personality dominates practically every single conception and robs the whole effect of spontaneity'. Ironically, Ngaio had written in her theatre journal when she saw the play on BBC television in July 1949:'Play obviously a winner any-where'. Not only was she wrong about the play; she was unable to handle professionally trained actors with the same confidence that made her such a success with amateurs. Criticism of the director mounted and her lack of expertise in financial management surprised and alarmed Dan O'Connor, who was backing the tour. Ngaio's old friends among the company gathered round her pro-tectively and this made matters rather worse. *Twelfth Night* went down better in Sydney, but Ngaio had decided to move swiftly on to New Zealand, and to add *Six Characters* to the repertoire. In an interview broadcast on Radio New Zealand in early August she was still full of idealism, still hoping that her nucleus of actors would help to inspire local talent and fire the amateur societies. Even then she was looking forward to the establishment of a national theatre, and to the building of new civic theatres throughout New Zealand.

After a positive opening in Auckland the company went on tour, encountering a mixture of fortunes that even Ngaio's optimism, now gravely shaken, could not overcome. In Christchurch, where there should have been strong support, houses were mediocre and tickets were given away free to charities. But they were booked for a six-month season and they played it out, coping with neglected, dirty theatres, half-empty houses and primitive technical equipment. Ngaio's description of the last performance of the tour, in Blenheim in the north-east of the South Island, is full of heartache. The confident, energetic leader of the past two years was defeated by a hopeful dream that turned into a disaster. It was hardly surprising that nearly two years were to pass before Ngaio produced another major play.

In 1988 Peter Howell accounted for this as 'a direct result of biting off more than she could chew; eventually out of her idealism and ambition came an almost impossible task. Whereas an acid, tougher person, with more experience of the London scene and how to pick people might have made it work'. By the end of the tour Ngaio was weary and disillusioned. On a radio interview in February 1952 she spoke sadly about the uncomfortable, out-of-date theatres with their inadequate facilities that had finally defeated her idealistic plan to bring high-quality live theatre to all parts of New Zealand. Ronald Walker, writing in the journal *World Theatre* at that time, recognised the British Commonwealth Theatre Company tour as 'a significant event', but reported sadly that 'after a good start this company ran into many of the obstacles that beset those not intimately connected with the interests that own the few available theatres, and it failed to become the permanent institution that we hoped'.[9]

The years between 1948 and 1952 had marked much happiness and achievement for Ngaio Marsh, but this section of her life, which started so confidently with her student players touring Australia, ended in painful failure. It was to be her Canterbury University students who would restore her faith in herself as a producer, at a time when her special talents were badly needed.

CHAPTER 7

Phoenix from the Ashes: 1953–59

The aftermath of the British Commonwealth Players' tour left Ngaio physically and mentally exhausted. A further blow grieved her deeply: an unexpected fire destroyed her beloved Little Theatre in Christchurch on 13 February 1953. All the costumes, records, scenery and equipment that had been painstakingly gathered together over a decade were lost, and the interior completely burnt out. For Ngaio it was not just a practical disaster; the Little Theatre represented more than four walls and a cramped stage. Here she had struggled with her early productions, and here she had seen her actors grow and mature under her guidance. The Little Theatre held memories that were infinitely precious, and she wrote movingly about the loss:

> If it were true, as some people hold, that sound does not alto-
> gether die but leaves an echo of itself on walls and in the fabric
> of such places as our Little Theatre, what phrases, what jetting
> sounds went roaring up that night: Othello's opulent agony, the
> ghost's booming expostulations, wings in the rooky wood,
> Clytemnestra's death cries, Puck's laughter, the symmetrical
> bleating of Lady Wishfort and Faustus' cry of 'See, see where
> Christ's blood streams in the firmament.'What a bonfire![1]

If ever the University Drama Society had needed someone of Ngaio's vision and influence it was now. She hoped this unfortun-ate event might lead to the building of a new theatre at the university, which was then still located in the centre of Christ-church. A small but flexible, well-equipped and comfortable theatre, seating about 400 was the ideal venue that she had been recommending for several years. But the University of Canterbury

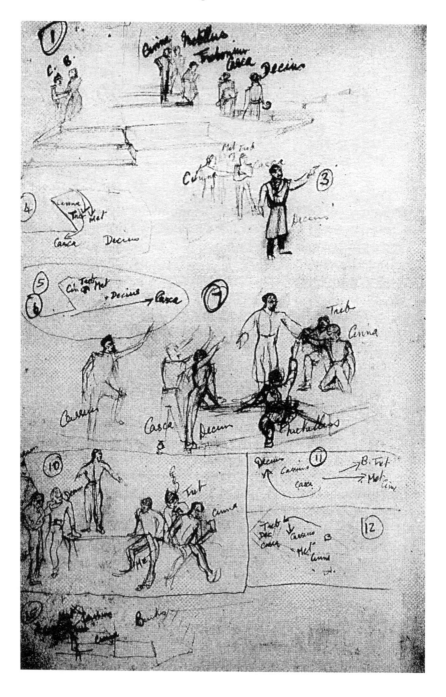

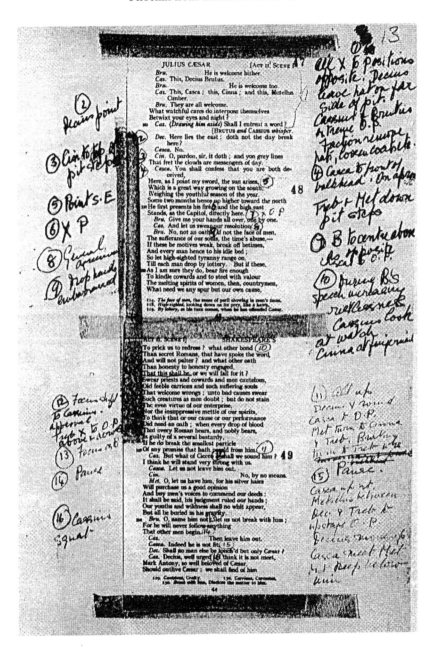

The director's production script for Julius Caesar. *Text (right) corresponds to a sketch on the blank page (left).*

was not then prepared to move in this direction, and Ngaio realised that 'if there had been the smallest possibility of rebuilding, the interim could have been straddled fairly easily but it soon emerged that there would be no replacement. We were in the wilderness and likely to remain there'. Not until the opening of the Ngaio Marsh Theatre at the new university campus on the outskirts of the city in 1967 were the student players to have their own home once more.

A production of Julius Caesar had been planned for July 1953, and by special permission of the University ('a compassionate if short-lived gubernatorial impulse') plans were made to create a theatre in the round in the sombre Victorian Gothic Great Hall, normally used only for formal occasions such as degree days and examinations. The recent memory of Tyrone Guthrie's productions in Edinburgh and Stratford gave Ngaio the confidence to ask the army to construct a three-sided block of steeply raked seats. There was no fixed stage, but rostra, with a revolving central section operated by hidden stage-hands, allowed great flexibility, including a spectacular fall by Caesar from the top of the structure. The layout facilitated the flow of street scenes and battles through the audience, an unexpected theatrical technique that Ngaio introduced to the Christchurch audience.

In many ways, the enforced change in acting style brought a welcome challenge to the producer and her actors. The cramped stage of the Little Theatre had fostered a cosy intimacy between actor and audience, but the large cast that was needed to fill the Great Hall, with an audience of nearly 1,000, made everyone rethink their methods. A Radio New Zealand interview of 13 July 1953, recorded during the clash of short swords at a final rehearsal, found Ngaio in confident mood, enjoying the great dramatic sweeps of colour that the new venue allowed. The role played by the crowd fascinated her, and she wrote dialogue specially for them. She also divided the crowd into different blocks of colour according to the colour of their cloaks. Swirling around the rostra, this Roman citizenry produced an impressive kaleidoscope of sound and colour, and the audiences loved it. Not only was the production a huge artistic success, showing the Christchurch audience for the first time how Shakespeare could be released from the restrictions of the proscenium arch: Julius Caesar was also profitable at the box office. The proceeds enabled the student players to find their feet and start replacing materials they had lost in the Little Theatre fire. Ngaio had worked furiously to make this production a success, but characteristically she praised her young actors:

> Homeless, without records, scenery, wardrobe, properties or any focal point, it might well have disintegrated . . . it was now that student resilience asserted itself. Instead of retiring upon desultory play-readings in some dejected classroom, the Drama Society, cocking a snook at calamity, rose from its ashes.

Such phoenix-like resurgence does not happen without dynamic leadership, and after the disappointments of the Commonwealth Players this call upon her production skills and artistic inspiration restored Ngaio's belief in herself and increased rather than drained her energies.

About this time an important new friendship came into her life, bringing qualities that she badly needed and helping to dispel a sense of isolation and depression after the Commonwealth Players tour. She was also missing the zest and variety of her life in London, and the introduction to two expatriate Russians, Vladimir (Val) Muling and his wife Anita, led to an exceptionally close bond for many years. Cultivated manners and the suggestion of aristocratic connections in the old world never failed to impress Ngaio and, just as her own personality struck the Christchurch students as the height of sophistication, so the Mulings affected her.

In fleeing Estonia during the Russian Revolution, Vladimir Muling had moved East and had worked as a customs official for the British government in China for many years. Here he met and married Anita, another expatriate, and they moved to New Zealand after the Second World War. In Christchurch, Muling worked as a clerk for a local heavy machinery company but longed to establish a specialist bookshop. Ngaio encouraged him in this ambition, but it was never to be achieved.

Val became a close confidant and although Ngaio did not usually discuss her writing with anyone, she began to talk to Val about work in progress. Soon, on his regular Saturday visits, he was reading and discussing the novels as they developed. It was a meeting of minds such as Ngaio had never enjoyed before, and it became obvious to friends close to her that, at the age of fifty-eight, she had fallen deeply in love. They worried about her vulnerability but Ngaio's training in reticence must have made the situation bearable. Her friendship with Val was not affected by a court case from which Muling was acquitted; if he did have homosexual leanings (he was accused of soliciting in a local park), he was very much the kind of man to whom Ngaio was drawn. Many of her young actors were homosexual, and she obviously felt very much at ease in their company. For a basically insecure woman like Ngaio, creating and recreating herself for every situation, a homosexual friend offered excellent companionship but no threat to her precarious emotional balance. Val Muling was also married, which made him doubly secure. Val managed to overcome the subtle mental barriers erected by Ngaio to defend herself against intimacy; her flattering interest in other people generally enabled her to remain in control of the situation. His friendship gave her both liberation and stimulus: he and Anita opened up to her the world of Oriental art and Russian church music and they shared Ngaio's cultural interests with intense energy. She knew Val Muling for barely ten years but his photograph travelled everywhere with her, and after his death Anita remained a close friend.

The Mulings brought a kind of glamour to what had settled into a fairly routine life for Ngaio in Christchurch. They were genuine exiles and to some extent Ngaio understood their displacement, feeling, as she often did, strong emotional ties to people and places on the other side of the world. In exchange for stories of life in Russia during the time of the Czar, she introduced the Mulings to a genuine New Zealand sheep station, Mount Peel. The huge empty spaces of the high plateaux reminded the Mulings of Russia and the visit took on a symbolic quality for them. Ngaio had packed a picnic so as not to impose on the Aclands but after they had wandered about the estate for a while Lady Acland invited them into the house, where a fire was blazing in the dining-room. She was anxious to be hospitable, but rationing was still in force and alcohol was in limited supply. Then she remembered a bottle of vodka left over from a birthday party and went to fetch it from her son's bedroom. There was much fuss as brown bread from the picnic was laid out to accompany the vodka, and then Anita Muling asked Lady Acland if she had an unwanted goblet. The atmosphere became electric as, with her back to the fireplace, she clenched the glass between her teeth and, in one dramatic movement, downed the neat spirit, snapped the stem off the glass and threw it into the fire. 'That is how we drink vodka in Russia', she announced to the astonished company. Little wonder that Ngaio was so fascinated by them both.

Ngaio had been continuing with her latest novel during the New Zealand summer, and despite all the claims on her time since the theatre fire, she had managed to complete it before the final rehearsals began after Easter. *Spinsters in Jeopardy* was published in the United States at the end of 1953, and in London the following year. Inspired by the Saracen fortress where 'The Lampreys' had holidayed in 1949, *Spinsters in Jeopardy* involves a new character, the Alleyns' son, Ricky. Although he is not mentioned in the previous novel, *Opening Night*, Ricky appears as if by magic as a small boy of about five years old. His vocabulary is remarkably well developed for his age, and the precociousness of a comment like, 'we are lavishly wide awake in the very early morning in a train. Aren't we, Daddy?' strains the reader's credulity. Yet his panic in the train when left on his own in the compartment for a few moments is entirely convincing, and some of Ngaio's own childhood fears seem to be remembered here. Ricky becomes useful to the plot, since his ill-advised kidnap leads Alleyn to the headquarters of an illegal drug factory in the Alpes Maritimes. The novel is more of a thriller than a detective yarn; elaborate black magic rituals take place in the fortress, with robed figures and drug-induced orgies. Troy's place in the novel is as a mother, not a portrait painter, and her character and emotions are explored more fully than is normally the case in Alleyn's straightforward detective investigations.

Meanwhile, public debate continued in New Zealand about the desirability of a National Theatre and a National Orchestra. The Labour Prime Minister Peter Fraser had made an encouraging commitment to a National Theatre in the late 1940s, in the period of new thinking just after the Second World War, but his government was defeated and subsequent administrations did not share his views on the importance of government support for the arts. The Community Arts Service Theatre, sponsored by the University of Auckland, toured valiantly in the North Island from 1947 to its demise in 1962, adopting the barnstorming approach and performing in any venue available, from tents to school classrooms. The considerable effort involved in taking live theatre to small, isolated communities was appreciated by local people but no government subsidies were available to make the actor's lot easier.

Then, in 1953, with the recent failure of the British Commonwealth Players as a warning, Richard and Edith Campion returned home to New Zealand after training at the Old Vic Theatre School, and bravely established a new professional touring company, the New Zealand Players. Based in Wellington, the New Zealand Players gave their first performance in the Opera House, but they never found a permanent venue. The high costs of touring eventually defeated them, and the company disbanded in 1960. The Campions had insisted on the highest standards for their productions, and costumes and sets were lavish. Life on the road was always filled with problems, and one of the Christchurch student actors, Michael Cotterill, who joined the company after leaving Canterbury University, remembers an exhilarating mixture of weary days driving the lorry, followed immediately by quick rehearsals and performances.

Ngaio Marsh had held high hopes of the Campions' venture, and she supported it warmly in a lecture given in 1955: 'Its approach is modern, vigorous and inspired by certain vitality and freshness of attack—a kind of youthfulness that is the most precious raw material in the theatre'.

During the early 1950s Ngaio took an active part in the call for government subsidy for the arts, but she remained worried about the monolithic structure that might emerge from the founding of a National Theatre. She feared government interference and voiced her suspicions in public:

> If the State is content to appoint a director, supply the money and then retire, and if the director is a man in a thousand, a man like that great Irishman of the theatre, Tyrone Guthrie, of the highest ability and integrity, who refuses to lower his flag an inch, however fierce the wind of criticism may blow, why then you may get a good National Theatre.[2]

And she was concerned that a National Theatre in New Zealand could lead to a smug, inward-looking approach to the arts, which

TOP LEFT *Rose Marsh with her daughter Ngaio.*

TOP RIGHT *Ngaio with Tip, the spaniel. She is wearing the uniform of her first school.*

RIGHT *Ngaio as a prefect at St. Margaret's College, Christchurch, New Zealand.*

Early amateur dramatics in Christchurch with parents and friends. Ngaio and her mother are on the right, and Harry Marsh is fourth from the left.

A Life Class at the School of Art, Christchurch, attended by Ngaio Marsh.

Painting holiday on the West Coast with the artists Richard and Elizabeth Wallwork. Ngaio is in the centre with her painting box; Richard is holding his oil-painting of Ngaio sitting on a rock.

The stalkers' camp in the Upper Rakaia in 1927 which provided the basis for the short story 'Morepork' fifty years later. Ngaio is at the front. Tahu Rhodes is on the right.

RIGHT *The joint proprietor of 'Touch and Go' in Beauchamp Place, London, in 1930.*

BELOW *With the Rhodes and Plunket families at a seaside holiday in Kent. Nelly Rhodes is in the centre, with Toppy Blundell Hawkes, Ngaio and Tahu on the right. The five Rhodes children are also in the photograph.*

LEFT *French chic—the suit that Ngaio bought from her winnings in Monte Carlo. The winning ticket is shown below.*

BELOW *The 1936 Group Exhibition in Christchurch, Ngaio in the centre, wearing a beret. Left to right: Rata Lovell-Smith, Phyllis Bethune, Mr. Bethune, Dr. Lester, Billy Baverstock, Margaret Anderson (holding 'Figures from Life' by Tosswill Woollaston), Mr. Henderson, Rosa Sawtell, Louise Henderson. Missing is Olivia Spencer-Bower who took the photograph.*

TOP *'Midsummer Muster, Mount Gold.'*

BOTTOM *'Springtime in Canterbury.' These large murals were painted in the early 1940s by Ngaio Marsh and were presented to Burwood Hospital.*

Ngaio Marsh in 1943, aged 48.

ABOVE *By the end of the 1940s, Ngaio's house in Christchurch had been extended and the garden well-established. This was her life-long home.*

ANTONY
&
CLEOPATRA

WILLIAM SHAKESPEARE

University of Canterbury

DRAMA SOCIETY

CIVIC THEATRE

July 1959

Playbill for July 1959 production of 'Antony & Cleopatra' by the University of Canterbury Drama Society, produced by Ngaio Marsh. The inside of the playbill (below) is autographed by the producer.

DOMITIUS ENOBARBUS		David Hindin
EROS		Ian Kirk
SCARUS	Friends to Antony	James Laurenson
PHILO		Murray Alford
MECAENAS		Huntly Eliott
AGRIPPA		Gerald Lascelles
DOLABELLA	Friends to Caesar	Paul Baudinet
PROCULEIUS		Mervyn Thompson
THYREUS		Stephen Erber
MENAS, a pirate and friend to Pompey		Barrie Atkinson
TAURUS, lieutenant-general to Caesar		Ross Pye
ALEXAS		Ian Kirk
SELEUCUS	Attendants on Cleopatra	Alistair Clark
DIOMEDES		Robert Ludbrook
MARDIAN, a eunuch		William Carter
SOOTHSAYER		Paul Goddard
CLOWN		Paul Goddard
CLEOPATRA, Queen of Egypt		Annette Facer
OCTAVIA, sister of Caesar		Wyn Jones
CHARMIAN	Attendants on Cleopatra	Jill Callister
IRAS		Jeanette McClurg
MESSENGER		Peter Berry
BOY		Richard Porter
CAPTAIN		Max Hickey
SOLDIERS		Gary Blake

Peter Nicholls, Ken Davy, John Langden, Paul Spong

LADIES IN WAITING   Dian Morse,
Nicola Le Cren, Barbara Jones

EGYPTIAN GIRLS   Marianne Dalhoff,
Margaret Tyndall, Diana Thorpe

> The music accompanying the play was specially written for the production by the Musical Director, Frederick Port. This is the society's third major production for which he has composed, synchronised, conducted and recorded the musical score. The Society greatly appreciate Mr Port's share in the success of the production.

Titlepiece designed and executed by Stephen Erber

STAGE DIRECTION	Michael Sheppard, Bruce Dormer
MUSICAL DIRECTOR	Frederick Port
	assisted in recording by David Hindin
STAGE CREW	
	Will Keily, Grant McAlpine, Trevor Clark, Hugh Boyd
PROPERTIES	Michael Edsall
	assisted by Colin Zeff, Douglas Bennie
PROMPT	Margaret Swarbrick
CALL-BOYS	Betty Cotterill, Barrie Gimson
MAKE-UP	Jean McGregor, Jean Muirhead, assisted by Grant Wright, Andrew Sharp, Margaret Rollerson, Elizabeth Roberts, Hilary Briggs, Elizabeth Eames, Vivien Hart, Elizabeth Bondy, Penny Oliff, Angela Goulter, Ann Mayer, Elizabeth Hamann, Rosemary Mathias, Jon Elsom
WARDROBE	Margaret Cameron, assisted by Irene Adcock, Mary Buller, Pamela Firth, Dermot Holland, Judy Mandon, Barbara Nicholls, Robyn Royds, Ruth Rundle, Ann Ballin
PRODUCER'S SECRETARY	Margaret Swarbrick
BUSINESS MANAGER	James Facer
FRONT OF HOUSE	John Gimson
PUBLICITY	Barrie Atkinson, assisted by Annette Facer, Steven Furlonger, Keverne Trevelyan
GALA PERFORMANCE	Robert Scott
REHEARSALS MANAGER	Ian Kirk
TREASURER	Mervyn Glue
SECRETARY	David Hindin
CHAIRMAN OF DRAMA SOCIETY	William Carter
PRESIDENT OF DRAMA SOCIETY	Professor J. C. Garrett

THE PLAY PRODUCED BY

Two of her first productions with the Canterbury Student Players. Jack Henderson played Hamlet (left, seated beside Ngaio) and Iago (below, far right). Paul Molineaux played Othello (below centre beside Ngaio).

TOP LEFT *The successful Australian tour of 1949. Dan O'Connor (centre) promoted the tour. Ngaio is on his left, Pamela Mann on his right.*

TOP RIGHT *Brigid Lenihan, 'our bright star' on the Australian tour.*

RIGHT *Ngaio in tweeds in England, 1950s.*

ABOVE *Portrait of a director: rehearsing Hamlet (1958) with Jennifer Barrer and Mervyn Glue.*

BELOW *Student players on tour. Pamela Mann is left of Ngaio in this photo.*

Sketch in manuscript: grooming a horse. (Mugar Memorial Library, Boston University.)

A sketch of Roderick Alleyn by Ngaio Marsh, on the pages of her hand-written draft of Death at the Dolphin; *it shows Alleyn interviewing the mysterious Mr. Conducis.*

letters.) Then, if the key word were "night" (the number of the combination)

```
A  B  C  D  E  F  G  H  I  J
1  2  3  4  5  6  7  8  9  0
K  L  M  N  O  P  Q  R  S  T
1  2  3  4  5  6  7  8  9  0
U  V  W  X  Y  Z
1  2  3  4  5  6
```

DOLPHIN   THEATRE
4 5 2 6 8 9 4   0 8 5 1 0 8 5

NIGHT   GLOVE
4 9 7 8 0   7 2 5 2 5

who a book hinged unit covered with black.

A page from Ngaio Marsh's handwritten manuscript of Death at the Dolphin, *working out the safe combination.*

TOP *A prize-winners party at the Savoy for the Collins 'Detective Dons' competition, 1962.*

BELOW *Ngaio loved fast cars. She imported this black Jaguar XK150 into New Zealand and drove it with panache until she was in her 80s.*

Ngaio Marsh with Frank Sargeson in the Katherine Mansfield Memorial Garden in Wellington after she had presented him with the Katherine Mansfield Memorial Award for 1965.

RIGHT *Ngaio on her travels.*

In 1977 the Mystery Writers of America named Ngaio Marsh as Grandmaster. She is seen here with the 'Edgar' award (a small china bust of Edgar Allan Poe) sent to her after the awards ceremony in Los Angeles in 1978.

The writer at work in her armchair at home.

would work against the interplay of artists between Europe and the Antipodes that she had always sought to encourage: 'It is necessary for our young actors, writers and painters and musicians to get themselves out into the mainstream of western culture and make what they can of it'.

The debate spilled out into the literary magazine *Landfall*, the New Zealand *Listener* and New Zealand radio. *Landfall* had become an influential voice in cultural affairs since its founding in 1947 by the poet Charles Brasch, and in its pages many arguments were put about the national role of the performing arts. Professor John Pocock discussed the relationship between firmly established and highly regarded local amateur groups, such as the Canterbury College Drama Society, and a proposed National Theatre. Would such a company absorb too much energy from the scattered urban centres of two sparsely populated islands? Would professionals regard themselves as superior, and share with British actors a 'patronising contempt for the amateur'? Could a structure be devised which would allow rather for a devolution of expertise, so that a central theatre would advise and support amateur groups throughout the country rather than drive them out of business?

Ngaio continued to emphasise the need for adequate buildings. While recognising that it was 'just possible for a group of integrity, whether government sponsored or under its own steam, making endless compromises in staging and mounting, to play in our present ill-equipped smaller halls', she wanted to see civic authorities building small, well-designed theatres that would be a pleasure for the audience and professionally rewarding for the actor. She went on to say publicly:

> I know that to put the playhouse before the players is to put the cart before the horse. But in New Zealand we have the players. We have numbers of talented young men and women who would make the stage their job if they could. The team of horses is here but without adequate theatres there is no cart to which they can be harnessed.[3]

Those decaying theatres, described by Ngaio in 'A Note on the Status Quo' in 1947, with their rotting backdrops, silted-up sinks, floors littered with rat droppings; these theatres which had defeated the British Commonwealth Players in 1951, haunted her still.

The debate continued, and nothing happened to improve the situation for the Canterbury College Dramatic Society in 1953. But the success of *Julius Caesar* had left the student players in Christchurch with sufficient funds to look to the future with confidence, and they started to search for a venue for their next productions.

Ngaio retreated to begin work on her next novel, *Scales of Justice*, which has an ingenious plot hinging on the esoteric fact that no two trout have identical scales, a piece of knowledge passed on to the author by a member of the Royal Society. Crime writers love to use unusual information of this kind, and Ngaio had thriftily stored it away for future use. The writing of *Scales of Justice* was to engross Ngaio through late 1953 and 1954. The novel contains a particularly brutal murder, where Colonel Carterette is struck on the temple with a golf club as the murderer floats down the river in a punt, idly swishing at the daisies; the *coup de grâce* is then delivered with the point of a shooting stick—'deliberately pushed home and sat on'. One of Ngaio's relatives remembers coming across the author out on her terrace with a shooting stick impaling a selection of melons, trying to establish, with the help of a retired police officer, how the murder could actually have been carried out. She was always meticulous in her researches.

On the surface, *Scales of Justice* may exhibit the familiar delight of the classical detective story writer in small English villages with their rigidly stratified society, but a careful reading reveals that the perfect picture-book village of Swevenings is, in fact, bursting with snobbery, suspicion, adultery and secrets, to say nothing of that dreadful crime, catricide. (Commander Syce accidentally dispatches one of his neighbour's cats while practising archery in his garden.) Although Alleyn is called in to the case by the aristocratic Lady Lacklander, the person who snobbishly says, 'It is a help, Mr Alleyn being a gent', is in fact the social-climbing murderer. And the ancient scion of the village, Sir George Lacklander, not only passed secrets to the German government while a member of the Foreign Service in the 1930s, but drove a young man to suicide as a cover for his guilt. When Lady Lacklander says dismissively about Kitty Carterette, 'You never know . . . with that sort of people what they may do', Alleyn smartly replies, 'Nor with other sorts either, it seems'. Marsh's romantic view of the feudal English village was at last beginning to crack, and the only person to emerge honourably from the mesh of hatred and deception is Nurse Kettle, the district nurse who is outwardly tolerated but secretly despised by the superior set. Her gentle infatuation with Commander Syce and his bashful fondness for her suggest that the ridiculous class-consciousness of the village of Swevenings might have one or two chinks in its defences. The BBC read this novel in July 1955 with a view to a dramatised version on radio, and a filed memorandum reads: 'We should have to eliminate the appalling snobbishness'. A truer reading of the novel would be that the appalling snobbishness is accurately depicted and firmly ridiculed by the author.

The writing of *Scales of Justice* had to be laid aside for the celebration of Christmas. For Ngaio Christmas had a special significance, and in *Black Beech and Honeydew* she describes the various little rituals that were part of her childhood celebrations. Christmas in the Southern Hemisphere is difficult for the European to imagine. The English cultural heritage that was carried out to New Zealand insisted on snow, holly and blazing fires, in a reality of drought, heat and blazing skies. For those who wanted to feel that England was 'home', and this still included many New Zealanders, old-fashioned traditions had to be maintained, even to the roast turkey and Christmas pudding. For the Marsh family, those traditions were sacrosanct. When Ngaio encountered a real English Christmas for the first time in 1928 she was enchanted, and the memories of English country house Christmases with the Rhodes family were to remain with her always.

'The Christmas Tree' began in the 1950s as an informal party for her Christchurch friends and their children. These were mainly theatre people, but other friends were also invited. Anna Page, daughter of Evelyn Page, the painter, still vividly remembers the first Christmas Tree that she went to as a very small girl. The spruce tree was extravagantly covered with decorations at a time when, she recalled, most people were making do with little twists of paper from cigarette packets. Ngaio started to buy toys and other presents on her overseas travels, and her friend Sylvia Fox remembers one voyage when a wicker property hamper bursting with dolls and toys accompanied them across the Pacific. As the years went by, Ngaio established her own traditions. The children were served a proper meal in the dining-room by her housekeeper and extra servants brought in for the occasion. The best china and glass was used for this meal, which took place while the adults were having drinks in the drawing-room. Then a record played church bells and carols to summon the children to the tree and, with the curtains drawn to block out the dazzling sunshine outside, Ngaio lit the candles and distributed the presents.

And what presents they were. Each child received a huge cardboard box decorated by Ngaio containing lots of different items. She would ask parents for a list of suggestions earlier in the year, and more often than not, all the items would be included. Sometimes a little ceremony would be involved; one person given a full-sized cricket bat (quite a prize at the age of ten) was sent on a treasure hunt to find the ball. While the children played with their new toys, the adults were summoned to dine.

As the years went by other customs grew up, and one that particularly delighted her was the play the children performed for her. Sometimes there would be a children's story such as Oscar Wilde's 'The Little Prince', or a comic spoof of a well-known play. Ngaio's secretary, Rosemary Greene, and the parents worked hard on these offerings; Michael Greene proved invaluable, with his gift for excruciating puns and Shakespearean masterpieces such as 'Macbath' and 'Cleopatter, or Corn in Egypt'. The Christmas Trees continued for more than a generation, and Anna Page brought her own daughter, Charlotte, to one of the last gatherings. The Rhodes connection was not forgotten. Teddy Tahu Rhodes, grandson of Nelly and Tahu, attended while he was a pupil at Christ's College in the late 1970s, renewing the association between Ngaio and the Rhodes family that had lasted for over seventy years.

Happy though she was in her role as producer of Christmas magic, Ngaio must often have thought hard about those families which disappeared down her steep garden path, leaving her alone, waving, at the top. It was the same solitary figure that Elric Hooper remembered occasionally standing to one side and watching at cast parties after productions, an essentially lonely woman who seldom revealed to other people the extent of her own emotional needs. She usually spent Christmas Day alone, reluctant to intrude on friends.

The imagery of Christmas continued to be important even though Ngaio had ceased to be a believer many years before. Her nativity play for children, *The Christmas Tree*, was written in the early 1950s for Nelly Rhodes and was first produced by Ngaio with

Sunday School children in Addington Church in Kent. It was produced a few years later in Christchurch by Pamela Mann. The play, not surprisingly, relates firmly to an English Christmas: 'all over England, in big houses and little houses, in churches and shops and pubs there are trees like ours'. What gives the play an original twist is the comparison of the 'child-Christ's birthday tree' to the Cross:

SECOND VOICE: If you took away the shining ornaments and candles and stripped away the green and all the branches except two, high up, one on each side, the tree would still be there.
THIRD VOICE: But it would be a different one to look at.
FIRST VOICE: It would be the tree of Christ the Man.
SECOND VOICE: It would still be shining.
THIRD VOICE: You can see it now, shining on the Altar.
FIRST VOICE: It would be a cross.
[*Organ plays one verse of' 'There is a green hill far away'.*]
THIRD VOICE: At the heart of every Christmas tree all over the world tonight, there is the other Tree, the Cross of Christ the Man, God's Tree.
SECOND VOICE: It's green at Christmas and bare on Good Friday, but it's still the same tree.

The play continues fairly conventionally, with children dressed as angels lighting candles on the tree, the telling of the story of the coming of the shepherds and the Wise Men, and the final use of the tree as a symbol of birth, death and renewal. *The Christmas Tree* was published by SPCK in 1962.

Ngaio admitted that she had written the play as though it were a fairy tale, and found it hard to explain to people that she had no religious convictions. When she attended Christmas Midnight Mass at Birling Church during her next trip to England she found it full of young people, and was led to feel 'rather out of date with my Georgian doubts'. The struggle with religion was very real to her and emerges in letters to people with whom she was particularly close. During the war, writing to Denys Rhodes, she was clearly still strongly influenced by her father's 'truculent rationalism' but longing for more than this, and for confirmation that human beings are justified in seeking some kind of spiritual goal. In writing to him about 'the terribly muddling business of Christianity' she revealed that:

> I, myself, your senior by twenty years, have been dumbly plodding along this thorny track for some time and have come to no conclusion for myself. I can only produce more platitudes. It seems to me that the materialistic attitude (maintained stockily by Popsy) breaks down before the impulse that has been evident in human beings throughout their history, to refuse to accept it lock, stock and barrel. You may call this impulse merely an instinctive desire to ward off death but I do not see it as that. Surely an entirely materialistic being could have no such impulse.

Ngaio seemed happy to accept the Christian Church as part of the fabric of a society she supported, yet all her life she wrestled with the conflict between emotional response, which for her was usually connected to sacred music, and rational rejection of dogmatised spirituality. The easy path of Church of England doctrine that was open to her was not meaningful after she had outgrown her ardent schoolgirl beliefs. Yet she lacked the confidence to cut a swathe through the forest and create a new path. The idea of a traditional village church was attractive; what troubled her was her own place in the congregation. On her last visit to Birling Church after her serious operation for cancer in 1974 her friends felt that she was on the point of going to the communion table. She was unable to bring herself to do so, even after being so afraid of death only a few months before. Her scrupulous honesty made it impossible to use religion as a crutch and she never altered from this position. But turning Christmas into theatre, with the Christmas Tree parties for her friends and their children, was aesthetically pleasing as well as personally significant, and these celebrations were maintained until just before she died.

Apart from her Christmas parties for children, Ngaio also had a high reputation for her cocktail parties. In 1950s New Zealand, cocktail parties in private houses were considered to be rather smart affairs, and an invitation to 37 Valley Road carried considerable social cachet. As her cousin Stella and her family were staying with her, Ngaio decided to do some entertaining. The Christchurch gentry were invited, along with all her friends. Bear Mannings was then waiting to be called up for the New Zealand Air Force, and John was destined for officer training in England after spending a short time at Canterbury University College. They were asked to help serve the drinks.

With his Air Force friend 'Snowy', Bear circulated enthusiastic-ally, serving from an elegant claret jug full of a fragrant, neat cocktail. He maintains to this day that no one told him that the mixture had to be diluted. In a short time half the company were wildly drunk. The other half, who had been served from jugs containing only the mixer, looked on in amazement as wives slid gently to the floor and husbands grew noisy and aggressive. One woman collapsed under a hedge in the garden and her outraged husband strode past without offering a hand to help. The voices of the Dean and the Bishop could be heard fading away into the shrubbery, as each earnestly tried to persuade the other to take the Communion Service the following morning. Several hours later an elderly neighbour was discovered lying under the piano, found by her dog who had come over to investigate her absence. A guest who had managed to struggle home passed out while ringing to say thanks for a wonderful party, and found herself sprawled at her desk twelve hours later. The select dinner party to follow was enlivened by Bear and Snowy chasing baked potatoes around the floor with forks, at which point they were finally banished. Ngaio was convinced that Bear had deliberately doctored the drinks as a practical joke, and she was furious. On this occasion her sense of humour left her completely, and the subject was not discussed for several years. She did take her position in Christchurch society seriously, and although she liked her parties to go with a swing, this one would be remembered for all the wrong reasons.

Early in 1954 Ngaio packed up her drafts of *Scales of Justice* and embarked once more for England. The house was left in the care of Helen and Lyall Holmes and their young family, who were waiting for their new house to be built. They inherited the resident custodian, Tom Twitchit, a large tortoiseshell cat, and one of a long line of much-loved felines. Ngaio missed her cats when she was away, and often found that without really trying she assumed tem-porary responsibility for other cats when she was in London.

This voyage to Europe was one of her most satisfying experiences at sea. She was travelling aboard the Norwegian freighter *Temeraire*

Ngaio Marsh

which she joined in Adelaide, Australia, along with ten other passengers and a friend, Essie Molonie, who was willing to act as secretary for the voyage. Discerning travellers often chose the leisurely pace of cargo boats at that time, finding the few rooms available for passengers and the absence of enforced social life more to their taste than the opulence of a commercial liner. For a writer working on a book it was ideal, and Ngaio was delighted with the *Temeraire*: 'she was old-fashioned, odd and good'. After an extended voyage through the Suez Canal and the Dardanelles the ship anchored at Odessa to discharge its cargo of wool, and then sailed on through the Mediterranean to Spain, finally depositing Ngaio and her secretary rather unexpectedly at a small port in Wales. Bob Stead, who had returned to England after managing the British Commonwealth Players tour, drove from London to collect them. The *Temeraire* not only provided the opportunity to complete and polish *Scales of Justice*, but also supplied much of the inspiration for *Singing in the Shrouds*, a shipboard mystery which Ngaio was to write two years later.

During Ngaio's third extended stay in London, she leased houses in Hans Road, near Harrods, and in Clivedon Place, off Sloane Square. Her school friend Sylvia Fox, who was also in England at that time, joined her for company and to help run the house. It was a quiet and relaxing period, with long days spent writing or reading, and frequent evenings at the theatre or trips to Stratford, which Ngaio described as 'to me, the loveliest road in England'. Shortly after her arrival Ngaio addressed an International Conference on Historical Research in the Theatre, and visited the Bristol Old Vic as part of the event, but for much of the time she worked hard at her writing and was difficult to entice out of the house, even to exhibitions like the Cecil Beaton photographs at the Victoria and Albert Museum. Sylvia and Ngaio did manage a holiday in the West Country, staying with Denys Rhodes and his wife Margaret in Devon and then driving across Dartmoor and into Cornwall. The social side extended to drinks with Princess Margaret while staying with the Rhodes family in Kent. Professionally, she was recognised by the Crime Writers' Association, which presented her with a 'Red Herring Award' for *Scales of Justice* (1955) at their annual dinner in May 1955—it was runner-up to Winston Graham's *The Little Walls* which won the main prize.

By now detective fiction had given Ngaio considerable financial security, although she never felt that she could afford to stop writing. In 1955 her advisers established Ngaio Marsh Ltd as an independent company. Sales of paperbacks, hardbacks, radio serials and dramatisations amounted to a substantial income: she could order her clothes from the famous designer Hardy Amies, her groceries from Harrods, and support herself very comfortably through her writing. Yet she saw income only in terms of what it could buy: 'I shall never learn to look upon money in any other terms than those of its purchasing potential'. And she never intended to rest on her laurels. In the revised edition of *Black Beech and Honeydew* she refers to the advice of Ulysses in Shakespeare's Troilus and Cressida, who warns that time is passing and it is not fruitful to 'seek remuneration for the thing it was'. In other words, keep working.

In 1955 she began a novel that involved a great deal of the atmosphere of the part of Kent where her friends the Rhodes now lived. The village portrayed in *Off with His Head* is remarkably like Birling, which Ngaio knew well. The village smithy still stands below the church, and within its quaint exterior there is a working forge where modern equipment coexists with the ancient tools described in the novel. There is indeed a group of standing stones near Birling, but it nestles in a quiet hollow beneath the great chalk escarpment that lies north of the village, and not in the grounds of Mardian Castle. The fictional village of Mardian is associated with ancient mysteries that centre on the traditional dances of the Mardian Morris Men. Performed on the winter solstice, the secrets of the morris dance are jealously guarded by the Andersen family, who particularly resent the curiosity of the pushy German folklore scholar, Mrs Anna Bunz.

Ngaio researched the background very thoroughly for this book and her library in Christchurch contains several reference books on folk dance and ancient customs. It was a very cold winter in 1954–55, and Ngaio was snowed in while staying with her friends at Birling Place. Intense cold permeates the book; bonfires blaze in the snow, and in the smithy 'gusts of hot iron and seared horn and the sweetish reek of horse-sweat drifted out to mingle with the tang of frost'. At Mardian Castle it is colder inside than out, and the midwinter sun is 'faint as an invalid' or 'like a live coal in the western sky'. Snow squeaks underfoot as unknown footsteps are heard at night beyond frosted window-panes. The village of Mardian is said to be the coldest place in England, which corresponds to her own experience. The penetrating cold, the heavy, lowering skies full of snow and the early fall of darkness bring an almost primeval sense of nature's menace and the need to combat the power of winter with dance and blood sacrifice. It is as though the winter cold was driving mid-twentieth-century man to clash swords and strike the ground in order to defeat the deadly, vice-like frost. The transition from a decapitated rabbit to a headless old man seems entirely appropriate to the bizarre scene in the courtyard of Mardian Castle, with its ancient dolmen silhouette against the dark sky and flames dancing on the snow. That the violent murder should have resulted from a mundane clash of interests relating to a proposed new road through the village and whether or not the forge should become a petrol station provides an irony matched only by the vicar nervously condoning the Morris Men's pagan revelries because a collection is taken for the belfry roof.

Off with His Head is an unusual novel and deserves better than categorisation as simply another piece of formula fiction. Roderick Alleyn and Fox unravel the mystery in the end, but the enduring nature of the ancient village and its pagan rites is ultimately more memorable than the routine task of identifying a murderer. The detailed nature of criminal investigation seems almost incidental to a fascinating plot. The manuscript was delivered to Edmund Cork at the end of her stay, with all the usual doubts and misgivings: 'I'm in such a stew over it, not knowing if it's deadly dull or passable'. She had followed Edmund's advice about more action and violence in her novels, although Val Muling used to encourage her to develop character more fully.

Although not normally given to conspicuous displays of wealth, Ngaio's modest affluence allowed her to be generous to her friends and relatives. John Mannings (now using the surname Dacres-Mannings) was by this time a young officer in the Royal Artillery, and she occasionally sent him telegrams to entice him away from barracks for a treat. The arrival of a telegram, it appeared, was the only way to get released from parade. John had some leave to take, and Ngaio proposed either a week's moderately expensive stay in France or a few days of intense luxury. They opted for luxury, and the theatrical director side of Ngaio came to the forefront. She brought John and her secretary to Paris, where they stayed at the Georges V. It was first class all the way, including a car and driver at their disposal for the whole stay. There were visits to Versailles, Fontainebleau and the *Folies Bergère*. Only once did Ngaio's 'woman of the world' performance crack, when she mistakenly swept her party into a high-class brothel for dinner. As the meal went on, waitresses appeared in progressively more scanty and diaphanous apparel. Ngaio maintained her sang-froid until one of the ladies invited John to remove her bra as she served dessert; the dinner came to a brisk conclusion. It was, John remembers, an excellent meal . . .

Back in England, there was a final burst of Shakespeare at Stratford. Ngaio saw four plays, the highlight being Laurence Olivier's performance as Macbeth. There were after-show dinners with the Oliviers and the Quayles; a feast of good company and good productions to remember on the long trip back to New Zealand, which was already booked.

Drama in New Zealand was not entirely forgotten. During 1955 Ngaio was approached by the New Zealand Players in Wellington who wanted to give a Christmas season of *The Wyvern and the Unicorn*, a play for children that she had written the previous year. Sadly this season was cut short by an outbreak of polio in New Zealand, but the play was well received, and five years later it was remembered when the search was on for a Christmas Opera to be commissioned for the New Zealand Opera Company.

The last few months of this long stay in England involved some light-hearted broadcasting on a number of BBC panel games, and an edition of *Frankly Speaking* with fellow guests John Betjeman, Maurice Richardson and J. B. Boothroyd. By February 1956 Ngaio and Sylvia Fox were on the high seas, and to Sylvia's amazement the sedentary writer was suddenly transformed into an active participant in deck games and other entertainments. As a well-known figure, she was generally given the social accolade of dining at the Captain's table with other guests of note. She took a wardrobe of dinner dresses and enjoyed the social mix of a liner. Sylvia loathed it all and hid away with a book whenever possible.

On board ship, Ngaio immediately began work on the next novel. This was to be *Singing in the Shrouds*, a book that had taken shape on the *Temeraire* and had been at the back of her mind for over a year.

The innocent decks of the *Port Wellington* were used to plan out the intricate moves of this far from straightforward mystery, where Alleyn is defeated by an alcoholic and obstructive captain. 'I set up the scaffolding for my next book during the voyage', she told a reporter, on arrival in Melbourne. 'It is to have a ship-board setting, so I spent most of my-time finding out how this vessel ticks. I didn't tell everyone what I was doing, but I think they suspected. They kept saying: "don't put me in it."' This was the voyage when an elderly lady gently approached Ngaio as she sat, notebook in hand, on the upper deck and asked her in perfect seriousness if she always knew who the murderer was. This enquiry amused the author greatly and she tactfully explained that detective fiction writers generally worked all this out before they began. Unruly though Ngaio's stable of characters may have been at times, and anxious to take on a life of their own, she always knew what their designated fate was to be.

The *Port Wellington* docked in Melbourne in March 1956, and by the end of the month the indefatigable Miss Marsh was deeply involved in preparations for *King Lear*. This performance, which took place in August, was the first of a number of productions given in the Civic Theatre, Christchurch, an uncongenial venue which Ngaio described as 'a theatrical joke in bad taste'. The only way to reach out to a distant audience of 1,100 people was to use the aprons designed to take massed choirs and orchestras, and on these thrust stages Ngaio wove the patterns that were the foundation of her orchestrated action. The rehearsals took place in unheated boat sheds near the River Avon, where gusts of icy wind and an earth floor made it all too easy to imagine Lear's sufferings on the 'blasted heath'. For Ngaio, who felt the cold and was prone to bronchitis, these rehearsals were a struggle.

King Lear had been the producer's introduction to Shakespeare many years ago. Her governess Miss Ffitch had given it to her to read; no *Midsummer Night's Dream* fairies were to enchant this little girl, but the startling impression of a world of cruelty and madness, inexplicably expressed in poetry of great beauty. It is often said that the only truly satisfying production of this great play is the one that exists in one's own imagination, and Ngaio may well have thought this as she struggled to achieve tragic grandeur beneath the nymphs and shepherds decorating the lofty walls of the Civic Theatre.

Mervyn Glue was King Lear, and many of Ngaio's experienced actors came to help. Gerald Lascelles, Bill Scannell and Annette Facer played France, Edgar and Cordelia, respectively, and two talented newcomers worked with Ngaio for the first time, Elric Hooper as the Fool, and Jonathan Elsom as Oswald. These young men were to become some of Ngaio's closest friends, and their careers were inextricably part of her own life from then on. Although the Civic Theatre may have made an intimate acting style difficult, Ngaio's stage effects were powerful; so powerful that one night during the blinding of Gloucester, when a bloody, gelatinous lump was flung to the floor, a member of the audience collapsed and had to be carried out.

During the next three years Ngaio settled down to an agreeable routine in Christchurch. An annual production of Shakespeare with the student players took up three or four months of the year, and the rest of her time was devoted to her writing, her house and her garden. In 1957 she produced *Henry V*, which she had first staged in 1945, and just managed to complete *Singing in the Shrouds* (1959) before the play began. In *Hamlet*, the following year, Elric Hooper and Jonathan Elsom were groomed for greater things, taking the roles of the Prince and Laertes. Jonathan, a fine arts student at that time, was flattered by the attention Ngaio gave to his costume designs for this group of productions. She always took seriously the contributions of her students, in whatever form. The world of theatre stayed with her for her next novel, *False Scent* (1960), which was being completed as rehearsals went ahead for *Antony and Cleopatra* in 1959. A smaller but rewarding task was the rewriting of *Play Production* for a new issue as a 36-page pamphlet for schools, to be published the following year. Full of good practice and sensible, realistic goals, *Play Production* is a minor classic of its kind.

Although many years had passed since Ngaio had considered herself a painter, she was called on from time to time to open exhibitions and comment on contemporary art. Douglas MacDiarmid had an exhibition at the André Brooke Gallery in Christchurch in 1959, which Ngaio opened for him with great aplomb. She took a lot of trouble for events such as this, dressing up for the occasion and adding a personal note to her speeches. Later that year she was invited to give the second Annual Art Lecture sponsored by the Auckland Gallery Associates. In a lecture which raises a number of interesting questions, she discusses attitudes towards the visual arts in New Zealand and calls for better understanding of works of art:

> If we are to keep our sculptors and painters in New Zealand we must be prepared to think as intelligently as we can about what they are up to. Our interest must be lively enough to explore and adjust and become better informed. We must discard from strength and not from prejudice. As far as the layman is concerned, taste, after all, is the final arbitrament. It is upon the level of taste in any society that the progress of the visual arts depends. The better informed the taste, the greater the integrity of the work that informs it. It is upon this delicate and inevitable ambivalence that the future of aesthetics in New Zealand depends.[4]

There was also good advice to writers in a New Zealand Radio talk, *My Poor Boy*, which was subsequently printed in the *Listener*. Warm, humorous and sympathetic, she addresses a letter to an imaginary young person who has asked her how to become a writer. She warns that writing is hard work, often drudgery, and that 'one generally finds in the long run that one's best work is the stuff that has been ground out between the upper and nether millstones of self-criticism and hard-labour'. She gives the classic advice to the aspiring wordsmith: get busy and do it:

> If you wait for fair weather, inspiration and no external interference, you will never begin it. You may be able to write a novel, you may not. You will never know until you have worked very hard indeed and written at least some part of it. You will never really know until you have written the whole of it and submitted it for publication.[5]

In 1958, Elric Hooper left Christchurch and went to London to train at the London Academy of Music and Dramatic Art (LAMDA), financed by a bursary obtained on Ngaio's recommendation. Jonathan Elsom followed him a year later. She missed them both and looked forward to their letters, but other youngsters were coming on, including a history student from the North Island who elected to study at Canterbury University because of Ngaio Marsh and her work in student theatre. Having got to Christchurch, he was too shy to audition during his first year, but finally climbed on to his bicycle and rode up to Valley Road to audition for *Antony and*

Cleopatra in his second year. He lost his way, arrived late and flustered, and was thoroughly daunted by this august figure in her elegant drawing-room. His name was James Laurenson and when he got the small part of Scarus-Decitus he was 'over the moon'. He would probably have been surprised to know that meanwhile Ngaio was writing to Jonathan in London about 'agonisingly difficult auditions for *Antony and Cleopatra*', but noted that 'a newcomer, Jim Laurenson is very promising indeed as Scarus-Decitus'. She made Jonathan still feel part of it all, by adding, 'I wish I could discuss the décor and the dressing with you'. For Laurenson, the experience altered his life; he decided from then on that his future was going to be the theatre.

Family affairs also concerned her at this time. John Dacres-Mannings was staying with her for an extended period having been taken seriously ill while serving with the army in Germany. His brother, Bear, accompanied him on the ship back to New Zealand and after a brief visit to his parents, who were then living in Tauranga on the North Island, John came to stay with Ngaio, where he found the English atmosphere of Christchurch much more congenial. Ngaio was concerned to get him started again in a new career, and although worried about his health and his future prospects, she was happy to have him near her, even for a few months. Bear returned to his career as a pilot with the New Zealand Air Force, and was destined to spend some time in Africa training pilots for the emergent nations of the 1960s.

Life was falling into a convenient pattern; there was even time to design her own Christmas cards and have them printed by the Caxton Press. Surely it was time to disrupt all this, and take in a heady draught of Ngaio's special elixir, travel.

CHAPTER 8

The Public Figure: 1960–65

The year 1960 at last proved to Ngaio that her achievements as a writer were internationally recognised. *False Scent* had been published in New York on 16 December 1959, just in time for Christmas, and immediately became a modest success, selling 12,000 copies by the end of June 1960, in company with such bestsellers as *Exodus* by Leon Uris, *Hawaii* by James Michener, and *The Devil's Advocate* by Morris West. Her forthcoming trip to Europe was being extended by invitations to Japan and America in order to visit publishers and readers. Only in New Zealand, it appeared, was her fiction regarded as negligible.

Ngaio said goodbye to Christchurch with feelings that were more complex than usual. During the past few years she had at last become settled in a strong network of supportive and congenial friends and her work in theatre in Christchurch was bringing her much personal fulfilment. To say goodbye to this, as well as to her house and to the students of whom she was so fond was, she felt, 'one of those moments of truth one hears so much about'. Sylvia Fox, Betty Cotterill and the Mulings saw her off at the railway station in Christchurch and she needed the short train ride to Lyttelton Harbour to prepare a public face for the parting from her student actors, who were waiting to give her a boisterous fare- well. Most painful of all must have been the parting from Val Muling, whom she was destined never to see again. The desire to escape to fresh fields was tempered this time by an acceptance of her place as a New Zealander and a recognition that her own country had much of value: 'as one grows older, one likes the illusion, at any rate, of tranquillity. It is a pleasant country to come home to'.

The journey to Europe was a marathon: she departed from New

Zealand on 27 February 1960 and arrived in Southampton on 8 June. From Sydney she sailed to Indonesia and Singapore, where she stayed for a few nights at the famous Raffles Hotel, met friends of the Mulings and briefly met the Wolfits. The next ports of call were Hong Kong, Yokohama and Tokyo. While she was in Tokyo the New Zealand ambassador, Mr J. S. Reid, entertained her at a formal dinner in the Embassy, where she was introduced to prominent people from the world of books and international affairs. With her guide and translator Shinko, Ngaio was given an extensive sightseeing tour, including a visit to Hiroshima.

Japan was overwhelming—the shrines, the gardens, the mist-wreathed hills, and the sense of tradition appealed strongly to her, although she disliked the profound American influence. She watched a group of village actors on an improvised stage celebrating a Spring Festival, and accompanied her guide to a dancing lesson. The following unpublished description of this experience was probably intended to be read as a travel article:

JUDO AND THE DANCE

It must be true that the games people play are a kind of reflection of their personalities. Look at these two boys. Their delicate fingers flicker and jab at each other with excruciating accuracy. They probe and twitch. Every now and then they are galvanised into spasmodic action and their audience of thousands shouts with metallic abruptness. They are beautiful in their white coats and scarlet and black sashes. They bow to each other with punctilious venom and when the bout is finished are gay and genial. It's only when we are threading our way out of this vast arena that I notice there are no other Western faces in the auditorium.

Outside the rain drives down like a slantwise bamboo thicket. 'There are no taxis. Better for us the electric,' Shinko says and we barge our way through the turnstiles and strap-hang past half a dozen stations. A woman with a baby on her back is fast asleep, smiling vaguely. At the station there is a taxi. It dives into a maze of dripping back streets. Shinko and the taxi driver chatter like castanets. Like all taxi drivers, he is friendly and interested and keeps turning his head at terrifying moments to smile and nod at me. The traffic is abominable. Now we are in a lane so narrow that there is scarcely room for us.

'Hi-hi', Shinko says, and we stop. She gives him an infinitesimal tip as he stands bareheaded and bowing in the rain.

There is the usual hazard of keeping Japanese slippers on Western feet with undivided stockings. The stairs are very steep. When we get to the top Shinko whispers something almost unintelligible which turns out to be to the effect that I am not expected to imitate her. She then falls to the floor like a leaf and kow-tows. She rises and I follow her into the tiny studio where she kow-tows again. A gramophone is playing traditional music. A very old woman sits by a charcoal brazier, smoking. She and I bow to each other. The teacher comes forward and two middle-aged ladies. More bows. Shinko explains (I recognise the familiar sounds, smiles and gestures) that I find no difficulty in sitting on the floor. A mat is laid down and I am given tea. The lesson proceeds. One of the middle-aged ladies dances 'Moon Viewing'. The teacher seems to give her hell and stops her repeatedly, illustrating the hand and head movements. The recorded voice and instruments skip from note to unanticipated note but for me at least it is beginning to make sense and the dance is exquisite. The dancer stops and kow-tows, apologising for her mistakes. The second lady does a dance about animals and is also given hell. Then Shinko dances. At first it is about a landscape. Trees, a stream, mountains and clouds are delicately acknowledged. Then she, too, dances 'Moon Viewing'. How elusively and yet how precisely she sees the moon. She is corrected, much more gently, and dances again. A man comes in, bows, and sits by the brazier. He is the teacher's husband. He and the old lady, who is a celebrated dancer, chatter with great animation while Shinko dances again. Then it is over. I get up, a female Gulliver among these lovely Lilliputians. I thank them. Shinko murmurs a translation and with many formalities we take our leave.

Outside it is still raining.

On the way back, Shinko says, 'Ma-am. Please tell me. What did you think of my dance?'

How difficult it is to tell her.

Letters back to friends in Christchurch are full of detailed descriptions, often illustrated with pen or pencil sketches, of buildings, gardens and people. Her interest in Oriental art, which had been fostered by the Mulings, encouraged her to purchase a large painted screen which was shipped back to Christchurch for her. The Mulings were asked to unpack it on arrival to ensure that it had travelled without damage from Japan. They were mystified to see that the beautiful, hand-painted panels chosen by Ngaio elegantly depicted the services offered by geisha girls and their appreciative patrons. Ngaio, responding only to colour and design, had not been overly concerned with the subject matter, and the deferential art dealer did not explain the scenes. But everyone agreed on the beauty of the paintings, and the screen was handsomely displayed in Ngaio's long drawing-room along with porcelain ornaments and some rugs that she also bought in the Far East.

The long, slow trip across the Pacific on board the *Chusan* was broken only by a brief call at Honolulu, and the peaceful time on board ship allowed Ngaio to make good progress on her next novel, *Hand in Glove*. She was also finishing off a lucrative article on New Zealand for the glossy American magazine *Holiday*. On this trip she was propositioned by a ship's officer, who invited her to his cabin on the pretext of a cocktail party. Fortunately, remarked Ngaio with satisfaction, he was a small man, and she put him in his place with her dignity only slightly ruffled.

Ngaio disembarked in San Francisco on 15 May and after staying for a few days at the Fairmont Hotel and addressing various groups of admirers, joined the 'shabby comfortable train' that was to take her across America to New York. This venerable train was very much to her taste, 'like an old grande dame sweeping across the USA to Chicago and New York'. She arrived in New York on 19 May and was treated like a celebrity from the outset. *False Scent* was still selling well, and throughout the week she spent in New York there was a constant round of interviews by newspapers, magazines and radio. Her suite at the St Regis Hotel was filled with flowers and Ngaio was made to feel like a star.

Her friendship with her American agent Dorothy Olding at the Harold Ober Agency was now renewed. They had first met in London in 1954 and Dorothy was to become one of Ngaio's most valued friends even though, as with many of her personal associations, meetings were punctuated by long absences. Dorothy's dry humour was exactly on Ngaio's wavelength and they enjoyed each other's company. Even at the height of her public success Ngaio had to make a conscious effort to cope with publicity and curious interviewers, and she valued Dorothy's support and guidance. A highly respected doyenne of the New York literary scene, Dorothy appreciated Ngaio as a writer and as a person. Dorothy escorted her through the many social events arranged in her honour. One duty Dorothy did not expect was to be asked to take her to Greenwich Village, then a very fashionable centre for the young and off-beat. With the typical uptown New Yorker's view that anything below Penn Station was off the end of the earth, Dorothy had never been to Greenwich Village. But Ngaio was determined to go, despite a holiday weekend, pouring rain and an absence of cabs. With great reluctance Dorothy led the way to the subway. Drunks lurked in shadowy corners and sinister groups caused her to walk swiftly, but Ngaio was greatly entertained. At the sight of someone urinating in a murky underpass she announced with satisfaction, 'Now I've really seen the seamy side'. It was all a good preparation for the performance of *The Threepenny Opera* that they were going to see. Her next suggestion, a walk through Central Park on the way home, was firmly resisted: Dorothy had experienced quite enough local colour for one night. But the crime writer was still eager for atmosphere and before she left New York she spent the evening in a police patrol car in Harlem, finishing up at a precinct in the Bronx at 1 a.m.

For Ngaio, suffering from the snobbish 'high culture' attitudes of the New Zealand literati to her fiction, recognition as a writer by the *New York Times*, the *New York Herald Tribune* and *Newsweek* surprised and pleased her. The guest list for the luncheon party given by her American publishers, Little, Brown on 23 May represented an influential cross-section of a dynamic and powerful publishing world. *Newsweek* was slightly awed by her 'queen-motherly kind of charm', but was in no doubt that 'what her royal patent derives from is 21 of the best whodunits ever written', and the *New York Times* simply called her 'New Zealand's best-known literary figure'.

Given this admiration for her work, it is all the more surprising that many New Zealanders continue to see her contribution to culture only in her theatre work, and reject the novels as being outside the literary flowering of the postwar years. The attitude towards the detective novels as perhaps slightly disreputable seems completely at odds with the opinion of her American public and the international world of detective fiction lovers. Yet one can understand the position of writers and critics in a young country such as New Zealand, trying hard to be taken seriously on an international basis, and finding that by far their best-known contemporary author is renowned for her detective fiction, most of which is set in England.

Ngaio's visit to her American editor, Ned Bradford at Little, Brown in Boston, completed her brief American tour, and on 1 June she embarked on the *Bremen* for Southampton. She finally arrived in England on 8 June, having left New Zealand more than three months before. The Atlantic run had not been enjoyable; the company was uncongenial and she was exhausted after all the activity in the United States. But arrival in London never disappointed; she once remarked that 'to come back to London for anyone who knows and loves it, is like getting a dose of some powerful heart-stimulant'. This was just as well, because British interviewers were as anxious to meet her as the Americans, and there were several long interviews on BBC radio and television, including one on *Woman's Hour*, as guest of the week.

By July she was resident in a rented house in Montpelier Walk, in Knightsbridge, her favourite part of London, and destined to be the future setting for the wanderings of Lucy Lockit, a real cat who was the model for the crime-solving cat in *Black as He's Painted* (1974). Old friends were soon calling round. Elric Hooper and Jonathan Elsom were both still at LAMDA and she was anxious to know how they were getting on. Jonathan was then in lodgings in Earls Court and Ngaio may have felt that he still needed space to find himself before being thrown into the tough world of professional theatre. By offering him a room at the top of her house for £5 a week she provided both a home for Jonathan and company for herself. In a slightly bashful attempt to fend off gossip, she called him her godson and he called her Godma. It could be said that Ngaio directed Jonathan to be her escort as she had directed him in her productions. She coached him to get rid of the last vestiges of his New Zealand accent and polished up his etiquette for encounters with the aristocracy. However, for Jonathan, it was a magical time. He considered himself Ngaio's 'squire', driving her around London and escorting her to the theatre. He dined with her at night and kept her supplied with theatrical gossip, occasionally bringing home his fellow students to meet her.

While in London Ngaio always liked people to stay with her and invited her cousin Stella to join her. Stella arrived that summer for a six-month stay, and Ngaio enjoyed showing her the sights and

taking her to the theatre. Ngaio had just taken delivery of her distinctive black Jaguar XK150 sports car, a famous marque and very
highly powered. She had always loved fast cars and this one was
eventually shipped back to New Zealand where she drove it with
great panache until cataracts eventually made her admit that it was
unsafe for her to drive. Edmund Cork, Ngaio's agent, opposed the
purchase, fearing that she would see herself off in an enthusiastic burst of speed. Certainly the car took some getting used to;
Stella remembers one of its earliest outings to the Portobello
Road and a dented mudguard as the new owner tried to park.
Within the city Ngaio liked Jonathan to drive her and he would
potter over to Harrods to get the lamb chops or even drive it to
LAMDA occasionally. Only after several months did Ngaio realise
that the car was not insured for him, probably because he was
under twenty-five, and she took her place at the wheel again. It is
a measure of Ngaio's financial priorities that the purchase of the
Jaguar gave her no qualms whatsoever (she had bought it under a
special export scheme to minimise tax), but buying an art-nouveau
necklace of gilt and semi-precious stones that she had seen in a
local jeweller's caused considerable anxiety. Eventually, after
much indecision, she bought it, and wore it often on formal
occasions. Ngaio had very little jewellery but she did have some
favourite pieces, such as her double row of pearls, her cameo
brooch and the wishbone ring that Allan Wilkie had given her.
These can be seen in nearly all her photographs.

During the second part of 1960 Ngaio worked hard on a number of projects. She was now well into *Hand in Glove*, which was
becoming a kind of comedy of manners with very little crime,
she was drafting the first version of *Black Beech and Honeydew*, her
autobiography, and the success of *False Scent* on both sides of the
Atlantic had led to interest in a version for the stage. Ngaio started
work on this with Nelly Rhodes' eldest daughter, Eileen Mackay.
They interrupted their work to travel together to the Passion Plays
at Oberammergau in August, accompanied by Jonathan Elsom and
Eileen's daughter, Kate. Ngaio insisted on travelling in old-fashioned
style on the Blue Train for part of the journey. She valued the
experience of seeing the plays but although many people
around her were in tears by the time of the Crucifixion, she was un-
moved by the performance. Teutonic thoroughness did not awaken a

response in her; her religious doubts remained unassailed. Memories of Christmas Communion celebrated in the bush to the sound of tuis and bell birds were more significant to her own spiritual needs. She was rather more moved by finding that some of the actors in the play really were wood-carvers and craftsmen in the town, and made several purchases at their workshops.

On her return to London she found that her diary was full for the rest of the year. There were engagements to speak at literary luncheons and to attend formal functions arranged by the New Zealand government. She particularly enjoyed being present at the opening of an exhibition of paintings by her former student actor, Douglas MacDiarmid, during Commonwealth Week in November 1960. The idea of the Commonwealth still meant a great deal to her and she liked to help celebrate the achievements of artists from overseas.

Theatre contacts now extended to an ambitious group of young actors calling themselves 'the group of three: theatre of today'. Charles Vance (best known for his productions of Agatha Christie plays), Vance's wife, Imogen Moynihan, and Raymond Hawthorne (now an important figure in New Zealand theatre), having amazed rural Norfolk with a summer tour of modern plays, had decided to form a small company to tour in Hawthorne's native New Zealand. Not only would they tour; they would also offer structured training for young actors and provide professional openings for people wanting to go back to New Zealand after training overseas. All these aims were bound to appeal to Ngaio and she welcomed their approach with an enthusiasm that astonished them. Charles Vance, who first saw her in Christchurch in 1948 when he was a humble prop-carrier on the Olivier tour, was still slightly starstruck when he went to see her in 1960: 'Ngaio was a big lady. She had a huge heart and cared more about theatre, performance and making things happen than almost anyone I have ever met. She was an incredible inspiration and wouldn't let you give up on anything. She cherished youth and valued young people'. Unfortunately 'the group of three: theatre of to-day', despite its patron, did not manage to get to New Zealand. But Ngaio continued to give generously of time and money to anyone who approached her with worthwhile projects, and although she never forgot the bitter experience of the British Commonwealth

Players' tour, she still longed to see professional theatre established in New Zealand.

Christmas 1960 was spent with the Rhodes family in Kent. Shortly after Ngaio returned to London a letter arrived from Anita Muling in Christchurch telling her that Val had suffered a severe stroke. Fortunately Stella had not yet returned to New Zealand; with her intuitive understanding and love for her cousin, Stella was able to offer Ngaio help and encouragement. Val did not survive the stroke and died shortly afterwards. In March Ngaio wrote to John Dacres-Mannings, who was then living in Sydney: 'As you divined, his death has been a most grievous blow and it's hard indeed to believe that my argumentative, brilliant and affectionate little friend will never come shouting up the hill again on Saturday afternoons'. The Acland family, remembering how the Mulings had been affected by the countryside around Mount Peel, generously offered a place for Val in the graveyard of the family chapel on the estate. On her return to Christchurch Ngaio went with Anita to plant roses on Val's grave at Mount Peel: it was a moving experience for them both. Their friendship remained strong for the next twenty years.

Stella left for New Zealand early in 1961 and Ngaio absorbed herself in work. A true professional, she was skilled at directing herself in a public role that kept her inner feelings for Val Muling safely locked away. Jonathan was busy at LAMDA but usually tried to be back for the evening meal, which was prepared by a cook who came in every day for the purpose. At weekends Ngaio often went to Kent to see the Rhodes, and Jonathan visited his own relatives in the country. When in London, they went to exhibitions together, strolled around the city, went to the theatre or the cinema, and watched television. On Saturday afternoons Ngaio enjoyed nothing better than settling down to watch the wrestling, and with plates of fruit cake, cheese and strong cups of tea, she and Jonathan would stretch out on the two settees in the sitting-room ready to provide grunts and groans for the performers.

A trip to Stratford was always a treat, and on 22 April Ngaio and Jonathan represented New Zealand at a civic reception held to celebrate the Bard's 397th birthday. They took part in a pa-rade through the town and drank convivial toasts at a luncheon representing a wide range of civic dignatories and theatre people.

Then Jonathan was packing his bags to begin his career as a professional actor, spending the summer in rep in Suffolk before moving on to Dundee Rep, which was then being managed by Jack Henderson, Ngaio's first Hamlet. Knowing that actors in rep were expected to provide their own suits, she bought Jonathan a tailored suit that saw him through many productions.

Time was beginning to run out and the passage home had to be booked. She managed to find time for a short Aegean cruise in October 1961, accompanied by the secretary who was working for her in England, Joan Pullen. This was a great success; she wrote to Jonathan that she was 'in a state of unexampled bliss'. Never having been to Greece before, Ngaio for the first time saw classical art and architecture outside the pages of books and museum cases. Less satisfactory was the long-awaited performance of *False Scent* at the Connaught Theatre, Worthing, on 23 October 1961, performed by the local repertory company. No matter how hard Ngaio and Eileen had worked on the dramatisation of this novel there still seemed to be flaws, and Ngaio was filled with more than her usual misgivings. Arthur Barrett played Roderick Alleyn in a production directed by Guy Vaesen. Although the play was reasonably successful, it had one serious drawback: the death of the heroine at an early stage of the action. Naturally most leading ladies found this unappealing. Ngaio and Eileeen were dissatisfied with the version put on in Worthing but Ngaio had no time to do further work on it. Copious notes from Eileen and others who had seen the play were sent to Ngaio when she was back in Christchurch and they indicate a general awareness that there was something fundamentally wrong:

> The temptation to imagine that the blame for any unsatisfactoriness at Worthing lay with the Alleyn or the Florrie or the production is a dangerous temptation. Of course a more thoughtful production than is possible in one week will help and of course more accurate casting will help. But not enough.

Hopes of a London production remained high throughout 1962, but the right combination of circumstances never seemed to occur, and *False Scent* was never staged in the West End. Tempting though it was to postpone her departure in hopes of a firm arrangement with a London management, letters from Wellington were urging her back to begin a phase of work which would establish her as a public figure known throughout New Zealand.

Saying goodbye to the little house in Montpelier Walk was painful, breaking again the close ties that she had made in England. She sent a poignant last-minute note to Jonathan, telling him that all the luggage had gone off, 'and as I look out on the lights over the little pub and hear people going past, I think of the last 18 months which have been so happy here, and particularly of you, my dearest adopted godson, who contributed so much to that happiness'. Lucy Lockit, the cat, had been found a good home, but not before she surprised Ngaio by bringing into the house a little wooden fish which she played with on the carpet. Like so many of the small details woven into *Black as He's Painted*, it was taken from Ngaio's closely observed world.

Letters she had received from New Zealand composer David Farquhar in the past few months ushered in an exciting new project for her, and *False Scent* faded into the background. The proposal was to turn Ngaio's children's play, *The Wyvern and the Unicorn* into a Christmas Opera, with music composed by David Farquhar, from Wellington. The Arts Advisory Council of New Zealand, which was to fund the commission, together with the New Zealand Opera Society, agreed to contribute towards production costs. The whole enterprise was a major investment in New Zealand talent that was to cause both delight and antagonism locally before the culmination of the endeavour in a performance before Her Majesty the Queen on 7 February 1963 in Auckland. Ngaio was enthusiastic from the start, and wrote to David Farquhar in September 1961 that she was 'very pleased indeed' for him to go ahead along the lines he had already outlined to her, and that she 'would like to have a shot'[1] at writing words for the songs in Acts II and III.

Ngaio left for New Zealand on 30 November 1961 as planned, aboard the *Ceramic*, and docked in Wellington on New Year's Day 1962. This year brought theatrical success with an acclaimed production of *Macbeth* and also with the opera *A Unicorn for Christmas*, first performed in December. Furthermore, academic approbation was offered at last when the University of Canterbury invited her to deliver the Macmillan Brown lectures in April. This prestigious lecture series had been founded to commemorate the distinguished New Zealand scholar Professor John Macmillan Brown (1846–1935).

The three lectures, entitled 'The Three Cornered World: Shakespeare in the Theatre', deserve better treatment than they have received. After being broadcast by Radio New Zealand in May, these lectures seem to have been completely forgotten. Yet they sparkle with insight, humour and a genuine understanding of Shakespeare and his interpreters through the centuries. The lectures deal in turn with the producer, the actor and the audience. Ngaio describes the producer's role as that of a lens, collecting all the aspects of the play and projecting them through the actors to the audience. She quotes from *Julius Caesar* to describe the life of a producer as 'a phantasma or a hideous dream', and goes on to explain this deeply felt experience:

> I may be straining at a comparison but I must say that this speech does express with horrid accuracy, the terrors of Shakespearean rehearsals. For the producer, there will occur only too often, baleful nights and days when the play seems to come apart and fall to pieces. However careful his preparation, however great his own devotion and that of his company, he will, at one stage or another be visited by this nightmarish experience. [2]

And she humorously goes on to describe her imagined view of the beleaguered Shakespeare at rehearsals, clutching his script, at the mercy of producer and actors: 'Look Will, what the hell am I meant to make of this one?. . . I mean to say, old boy, what does it *mean?*'

Her erudition is lightly worn, and is combined with understanding of the actor on the stage. She discusses voice, movement and the actor's role as though she were the conductor of an orchestra, always stressing the rhythm, the climaxes and the flow of Shakespeare's dramatic poetry. By insisting on the training needed to master the voice, with a two-octave range, breathing control, colour and tone, she is very much in line with contemporary Royal Shakespeare Company practice, which places great stress on voice work with a team of specialist coaches.

In the second lecture Ngaio discusses the actor's search for the truth in every role:

The actor in Shakespeare, then, must, like his author, create in depth. He must command an exacting technique. He must submit himself to the discipline of the theatre, know himself to be fellow in a sort of players. More than all that, he must recognise that he is working in a medium that transcends naturalism or literal representation, that he is speaking a language which for all its startling reality is not, nor does it purport to give the illusion of, everyday conversation. That he cannot reduce his part to terms of contemporary dialogue and hope to realise its full value. He must feel the character grow within himself and out of his own personality and he must make it known, boldly and widely, to however many persons may be waiting on the other side of the curtain.

To demonstrate how the actor may be confronted with the utmost simplicity distilled from the height of tragedy, Ngaio quotes from the recognition scene in *King Lear*, the scene that so moved her as a little girl when introduced to this play by her governess.

The third lecture, 'The Audience', reveals Ngaio's considerable experience as actor, producer and member of an audience. She finds an audience 'a strange and wonderful thing', and that 'each audience has a character of its own'. She describes the experienced actor who 'angles for his catch and plays it with dexterity'. Her lecture looks at audiences at the Globe, and goes on to Pepys; she ranges from eighteenth-century theatre to contemporary films. The audience is seen as the justification for the entire theatrical process:

Shakespeare's act of creation, the actor's changing attitudes over three hundred and sixty odd years, every advance in stage-me-chanics, every interpretative discovery: the whole accumulation of theatrical history that has gathered round the production of one of these plays, has been for one final purpose only: to bring them to life before an audience.

Or, more vividly, she sees her audience as 'a great fat, cat, waiting to be fed'. The lecture series ends with a plea for more support for professional theatre in New Zealand, reminding her listeners of the success of Shakespeare in their own theatres in Christchurch, and the recognition overseas of the fine actors who emerged from these productions. The country's most talented artists can return to New Zealand only if there is work for them to do.

The Macmillan Brown lectures were given in April 1962. In complete contrast, a few weeks earlier, *Woman's Journal* had begun to serialise her new novel *Hand in Glove*. Collins followed this with publication in May. But it was as a defender of the theatre that she addressed more than 800 lunchtime guests at the opening of the Auckland Festival of the Arts on 26 May, announcing firmly that 'we come from a race which has never segregated the arts and it is high time we looked on them not as the inessential pansy trimmings of the beardies and weirdies but as a vital, integrated part of our growth'. She deplored the fact that there was only one play in the Festival programme, and left the audience with the unsettling thought that the real value of an arts festival as 'the degree to which New Zealanders were reminded of the absolute necessity of the things of the mind'. This may have been unexpectedly robust material for the Festival organisers, who probably expected a white-haired sixty-seven-year-old to deliver a less aggressive speech.

Back in Christchurch, Ngaio was in the initial stages of her next novel, *Dead Water*, with its echoes of her trips to Devon and Cornwall, and beginning to plan rehearsals for *Macbeth*. This was scheduled for winter 1962 to open the Shakespeare Festival run by Canterbury Repertory Society. She wrote apologetically to David Farquhar in July about delay in writing words for songs, saying that 'rehearsals for *Macbeth* are starting at 8 in the morning and finishing quite often at 2 the following morning. We open tomorrow. After that, what is left of me will attempt to concoct some rhymes on the lines you indicate. Sorry for the delay'.

Ngaio had last staged *Macbeth* in 1946 and now she was fortunate to have the young history student James Laurenson as the thane and Helen Holmes as Lady Macbeth. Worried that her thanes might look effete, she sent down to the country for sheepskins and bound them round the actors with leather thongs. She played these powerful figures against a harsh metallic set. The actors were gripped by the experience. Ngaio held strong views on *Macbeth*'s contemporary reference: 'the savagery, the terrors and the beauties of the language, although they are set in a remote barbaric period, are expressions of the very elements that disturb the modern world.

Macbeth's ambition has the same sick quality as that of any contemporary dictator: he is corrupted by power and disintegrates as inevitably as Hitler'. Her engagement with the most powerful elements of the play astonished James Laurenson. He acted opposite her at one rehearsal when Helen was unable to attend, and during the temptation scene experienced a sexual charge that was nothing to do with a sixty-seven-year-old woman and a twenty-one-year-old man. As Ngaio the novelist makes her director say about Lady Macbeth in her last novel, *Light Thickens*, 'She's as sexy as hell . . . she uses it. Up to the hilt'.

And it was time for Ngaio to receive the thanks of the University of Canterbury for all she had done for student theatre; time to revel in academic robes rather than Shakespearean costume. On 31 October, 1962 the University of Canterbury, which had become an independent institution the previous year, awarded its first honorary degrees, and Ngaio Marsh received the award of Doctor of Literature. The Chancellor, Mr C. H. Perkins, said that, 'the university wished to honour those who brought honour to it', and, wearing robes of scarlet with a grey hood, Ngaio joined a distinguished Professor of Chemistry and the Chairman of the New Zealand University Grants Committee to receive her degree. A member of the academic staff still remembers the flourish with which she wore her gown: 'no one had ever worn academic dress quite like Ngaio Marsh'. The University Public Orator praised her contribution to New Zealand culture, her 'diligent application, her craftsmanship and the inventiveness which enabled her to publish one book a year'. She was especially thanked for her work with the University Drama Society. At last she was recognised within her own country as a writer as well as a woman of the theatre, and she was deeply grateful for this honour.

Although Ngaio was still struggling with *Dead Water* in November ('I'm still in the throes with the final stages of a book that refuses to come clean', she wrote to David Farquhar), she was already making plans to attend the dress rehearsal of *A Unicorn for Christmas* on 2 December and to entertain the director and leading singers to dinner at the Waterloo Hotel in Wellington. The guest list included her old friends Fred and Evelyn Page, Douglas Lilburn the composer, and the diplomat, Sir Alister Mcintosh and his wife, Doris. Although not actively involved in any aspect of the production, Ngaio knew that she would be called on to make a speech from the stage after the first performance, and did so, making a striking impression with her pure white hair and her tall figure in a full-length black gown cut low on the shoulders.

A Unicorn for Christmas brought Ngaio into national prominence as a theatrical figure. Since the Dan O'Connor tours of the late 1940s and the Commonwealth Players' tour in 1951, her work had been largely restricted to Christchurch, and New Zealand cities tended to remain local in their interests. This type of Christmas entertainment was exactly the sort of 'high culture' that Ngaio found particularly satisfying, and the prestigious backing of the New Zealand Arts Advisory Council ensured extensive publicity for the venture.

The libretto was certainly not one to frighten the Christchurch gentry, with its portrayal of the aristocratic but impoverished House of Lacey and an evident nostalgia for 'home' with all its outdated social values. The setting changed from Victorian times in Acts I and III to Tudor England in Act II and the designer, Desmond Digby, costumed the piece lavishly. The change of historical period also appealed to the composer, who found that it allowed him to write in a variety of musical styles.

Reviews of the Wellington first night varied considerably. The reviewer from the New Zealand *Listener*, Roger Savage, praised Farquhar's music but had serious reservations about the play:

> As for the *Unicorn* being the 'first New Zealand opera'—well yes, in the sense that the first New Zealand things had a way of being fiercely Colonial. The *Unicorn* is a loving homage to Home eleven thousand miles away, more English than the English if not more Brittenish than Britten.

Not everyone was so scathing, and many newspapers agreed with the Auckland *Star* that 'it turned out to be a theatrical occasion of the first magnitude for New Zealand, an exciting event that had the audience stamping with enthusiasm at the final curtain'.

The Wellington *Dominion* pinpointed the positive nature of the achievement: 'the six-night season of *A Unicorn for Christmas* has proved beyond doubt that New Zealanders can conceive, bring to birth and then to the full maturity of public presentation that most complex of musical entertainments, an opera'. This reviewer also praised the music at the expense of the plot—'a flimsy foundation on which to build a Christmas opera'—reinforcing Roger Savage's tart comment that 'Farquhar has had to bite off rather less than he can chew'. But the public loved it, and popular interest was reflected by two newspaper cartoons featuring unicorns after the opening night.

Controversy surrounding the opera grew as arrangements were announced for a Royal Gala Performance before Her Majesty the Queen on 7 February 1963. Prime Minister Holyoake had announced on 26 December that the Queen and Prince Philip did not wish any personal gifts during their visit to New Zealand, but that instead the Queen wished to see the establishment of a national arts fund. The government had decided that as an impetus in this direction, all the profits from the gala performance of *A Unicorn for Christmas* should be donated to such a fund. This meant that ticket prices would be high, and the newspapers complained bitterly at the charge of over £15 for a seat in the stalls. Public criticism had to be countered a week later by Sir Robert Kerridge, who defended the arrangements and pointed out that the organisers hoped to raise £10,000-12,000 for the Arts Trust. In the end only £7,000 was raised from the gala performance, and a total of £9,000 was donated to the Trust after the three-day season.

The company and the librettist had only two months to polish the performance, and Ngaio was not at all happy with the staging. She wrote to Jonathan Elsom that 'the acting in the few passages of dialogue was so bad that I made no bones about saying so'. In a detailed letter to Farquhar on 14 January, Ngaio hoped 'in Auckland, to be able to bring the spoken performances at least within hailing distance of the singing. In Wellington, through nobody's fault, the acting techniques were at a dismal level but this need not be so. You may—and very understandably—look upon the dialogue merely as unavoidable little lumps of story material but I'm sure that as such it should be competently handled and with some degree of professional technique and I'm equally sure the company is capable of doing it'. Not only was Ngaio dissatisfied with the action; her old *bête noire*, the nasal sound of New Zealand vowels, was haunting her again:

One other point. The 'Boo' sounded pretty dreadful to me. For one thing the Wyvern makes it 'Beeyew' or as near as dammit and so does the audience. I visualise the Duke of Edinburgh sticking his head around the Queen's door and saying 'Beeyew' to the merriment of all concerned. Do you think we could change this unfortunate vowel trap?[3]

When she did appear at rehearsals, the effect was immediate. Honor McKellar, who played Lady Lacey, rehearsed the dialogue of one scene with Ngaio 'till it had shape, variety of pace and form, with a real climax, like musical composition'.[4] Paul Person, who played Michael, acknowledges that 'She taught me more about dialogue in half an hour than anything I had previously learned and this has stood me in good stead ever since'.[5] Ngaio was at the dress rehearsal in the St James Theatre, Auckland, when proverbially many things went wrong, including a light bulb falling from the proscenium arch into the orchestra pit, narrowly missing a cellist, and bursting with an explosive bang. Heat and humidity were intense and the performers suffered in their heavy costumes.

The gala performance, 7 February 1963, was reported as 'not only a glittery social occasion but also one of the greatest milestones in this country's history'. Ngaio, dressed in pink and grey chiffon, was seated behind the royal party and was introduced during the interval. After the performance, the Queen and Prince Philip went on stage to speak to the cast. When Mary O'Brien, playing the *Unicorn*, apologised for being unable to shake hands with the Duke, he quipped 'I just couldn't shake hoofs with you, could I?'

Having indicated their enjoyment of the evening, despite the heat, the royal visitors departed, the short Auckland season closed, and it was time for assessment. Ngaio could not have been unaware of the widespread criticism of the libretto as 'awkward' and 'a literary farrago', and that it was constantly being compared adversely to the music. The standard of acting by opera singers, especially in the non–musical scenes, disappointed her. The problem of the libretto was more serious, but even so, the quality of opera librettos is often ludicrous when exposed to the cold light of day.

The criticism of its thoroughly English atmosphere was more serious for a country which was trying to establish a distinctive national culture in the 1960s. Yet locally based theatre and ballet

181

was being allowed to starve for lack of funds, exposing the fallacy that New Zealanders wanted indigenous themes. *Children of the Mist*, a ballet based on a Maori legend choreographed by Leigh Brewer with music by Christopher Small, was first performed in 1960 by the Wellington Ballet Group, but their funds were too limited to mount a tour, and no one offered to assist with costs. Bruce Mason's Maori plays received only occasional studio performances, and his most famous play, *The Pohutukawa Tree*, first produced in Wellington in 1957, was not seen in Auckland until 1978. The poet Allen Curnow pleaded in 1971 for 'a New Zealander's play that New Zealand audiences will go to, will want to see again, in more places, or another by the same author, simply because they like it . . . a play about themselves and for themselves by one of themselves—a play performed in the spirit of the theatre, not that of a cultural fertility rite . . .'.[6] But where were the plays, and where was the audience?

A Unicorn for Christmas satisfies few of Curnow's requirements, but it did achieve many important things, and if some responses were negative, they are none the less valid because of that. In practical terms, attention had been focused on the Queen Elizabeth II Arts Council and why money needed to be found to support the arts. New Zealand actors, singers, dancers and stage designers had worked together on a lavishly supported production which had received the ultimate sanction of royal approval. And much thinking had risen to the surface about the nature of genuine New Zealand theatre, music and ballet. If a pastiche English pantomime was considered unsatisfactory, and if David Farquhar was considered a composer who deserved better material for his next opera, what should the subject matter be? Who was going to write it? And, most crucial of all, would the New Zealand audience support it? Although it was easy to criticise *A Unicorn for Christmas* and to ask that Farquhar should have 'an opera of Dominion status for him, one which will call on more than facility and charm', was there, even in 1963, sufficient commitment to New Zealand writers and artists to make them feel that they were speaking for a culture and not for an elite? In 1972 Australia was galvanised by a Prime Minister who not only valued cultural nationalism but was willing to provide funds to make it flourish. Australian writers, film-makers, painters and musicians all benefited from those heady days of the Gough Whitlam era, and their effects are still being felt. Unfortunately New Zealand has never backed its artists in this way, and it is hard to see the gala performance as much more than a one-off occasion in the mind of the government, having no real connection with what Ngaio had called for in her Arts Festival speech: culture as 'a vital, integrated part of our growth'.

Over twenty-five years later it is possible to take a wider view. The almost complete neglect of *A Unicorn for Christmas* since its gala performance was certainly compounded by bad luck, when a fire in the New Zealand Opera Company's warehouse destroyed all the magnificent costumes only six weeks after the royal visit. Plans to take the production to Christchurch were dropped and since then the only revival has been a studio recording before an invited audience at Radio New Zealand in Wellington in 1974. David Farquhar, the composer, still values the opera, and, far from being alienated by the fairy-tale element of the story, went on to write another opera with a fairy-tale theme. The critic William Dart writing recently in *Music in New Zealand* concludes:

> It seems to me that *A Unicorn for Christmas* stands as an important work and event in our country's operatic history. It is not without its problems, although the wit and dash of the score more than makes up for a few troublesome spots; it is unabashedly Eurocentric, but it is a period piece true to its period.[7]

Perhaps a new production of *A Unicorn for Christmas* would allow a revaluation of its merits, and establish it not in the ponderous role of the first New Zealand opera, but simply as entertainment for Christmas, with excellent music and a fairy-tale plot to delight all ages. That was, after all, what Ngaio had originally intended it to be.

After the excitement of the royal performance, Ngaio had little time to reflect on the lasting significance of the opera. She went back to Christchurch to plod on with work on a school textbook about New Zealand for American children: 'a difficult assignment for an American publication I've been dotty enough to take on'. And there was *Henry IV Part I* coming up in July, with auditions at the end of April and only four weeks for her to prepare the production script, devoting her usual scrupulous care to the language and the staging. When there was a spare moment she worked on the autobiography that was being urged on her by Billy Collins. She was very diffident about the whole idea, adding a post-script to a letter to Billy Collins in August 1963: 'how touched I am that you should think an autobiography worth doing: believe me I am—never would such a notion have occurred to me of itself.'

Perhaps the absence of a sustained period to work on this and a natural disinclination to write about herself led to the rather scrappy nature of the text, with its many inaccuracies as to dates and places. None of this detracts from its warmth and charm, but one can see that writing *Black Beech and Honeydew* (published in 1966) had to fit in with the next detective novel, which was hard work, and the next Shakespearean production, which was equally tough but infinitely more pleasurable. Not surprisingly, she was unhappy with the final text: 'it's not what I hoped it would be', she told John Dacres-Mannings. In a letter to Denys Rhodes she admitted to a great reluctance to write about her own life, saying, 'I'm sure you're right about the autobiog. It should have been called "Other People" only, unluckily the title has only just occurred to me. Dear Edmund says I'm too much of an introvert for the job and I've a notion he's dead right'. For once Ngaio's judgement on her writing was absolutely correct. When the question of a reprint arose in 1980 even her own publishers were lacking in enthusiasm: 'the original book was pretty dull,' said Elizabeth Walter, then Editor of Collins Crime Club, 'largely because of her reticence. I have every sympathy with this, but if you are going to write an auto-biography, you have got to be prepared to let your hair down a little, and this she didn't do'. In America, only 4,100 copies were sold and Little, Brown lost money on the issue.

Black Beech and Honeydew may have been a mistake from various points of view, but Ngaio's position as the best-known contemporary New Zealand writer was firmly established. Further recognition had come from *The Times* of London, which invited her to contribute a major feature on the arts in New Zealand to a special supplement to be published on 6 February 1963. The Queen's recent tour had focused attention on the Commonwealth, and *The Times* selected a popular writer rather than an academic or a journalist for this commission. The article is wide-ranging and comprehensive, stressing the New Zealanders' British roots but also their desire for an indigenous culture: 'an isolated country that has, in the course of one century, two years and rapid expansion, never lost sight of things of the mind'. Ngaio discusses the pitfalls of mere local colour in painting and the novel, and looks back to the response of the earliest settlers, who had 'no Victorian formulae to encompass the violent landscape, the uncompromising clarity where blue screams blueness and vegetation lies in clots of wicked green on knife-edged mountains; where the Maori people had their own involuted, secret culture and where they themselves were interlopers'.[8] Praising Katherine Mansfield, the short-story writer, and Frances Hodgkins, the painter, as 'rarities', Ngaio considers Janet Frame to be 'our most distinguished living novelist'. The composers Douglas Lilburn and David Farquhar are mentioned, together with Allen Curnow, the poet. But she was still concerned that New Zealand continued to lose her best talent overseas: 'talent constantly emerges and the opportunities presented in other countries are often irresistible'. And those in control 'are on the whole, less sympathetic to the arts and to pure scholarship than to industrial expansion'. In 1949, while discussing an art exhibition in London, Ngaio had displayed a similar worry, but she was more confident then that New Zealand would shape itself into a land fit for artists not only to live in but to make a living in.

The year 1963 was turning into a very hectic one. In a letter to Jonathan Elsom written in June she admitted that 'as I grow older I seem to grow busier. These past twelve months have been, I think, the most demanding I have ever tackled. A series of lectures, the libretto for David Farquhar's opera, two books, one on New Zealand for American children which has been and continues to be hell, the other the usual 'tec and now the play. What a life!' The play was *Henry IV Part I*, and it was scheduled for the usual winter opening in July. Rehearsal premises as always were impossible to find and this time the company ended up in the unheated dog-show arena at the Show Grounds. The director was pleased with her new muster of freshmen, but the comic scenes were giving trouble and she found herself 'engaged with the distressing symptoms of people with no rudiments of technique trying desperately to be funny'. *Henry IV* opened as scheduled on 19 July and somehow the 'tec writer had also managed to complete *Dead Water* and read the proofs ready for publication in the US early in October. After correcting the proofs (Ngaio never failed to marvel at how copy-editors and proof-readers for her English and her American publishers always found completely different things to grumble about and sometimes wondered if they should be introduced), she was at last able to allow herself some time to attend to the garden. When Joyce Grenfell arrived in Christchurch that month as part of an Australian and New Zealand tour, she came to Valley Road for Sunday lunch and strolled among flowerbeds filled with spring blossom.

The pressure of the past year certainly shows in the writing of *Dead Water*, with caricature taking the place of characterisation and a ludicrous plot about a magic well and a cure for warts. The gap of nearly three years before her next novel, *Death at the Dolphin* (*Killer Dolphin* in the US) was undoubtedly beneficial. This book was firmly rooted in the theatrical world, and shows a successful return to her best form.

Her next production, *Julius Caesar*, in 1964 was particularly interesting. In many ways Ngaio replicated the production of 1953 that had taken place in the Great Hall of the University, but the change of venue to the inflexible Civic Theatre in Christchurch meant that much audience involvement was lost. What she did strengthen was the power of the mob, maintaining that it domi-nated the play. In fact this is not so; the mob appears in only a few scenes, but Ngaio enhanced its power by writing extra dialogue and by placing tremendous emphasis on the mob's role in bringing down Brutus and supporting Mark Antony. She appealed to the students for a crowd of a hundred, but had to make do with only eighty:

> This play might be subtitled 'The Mob'. To a very great extent it depends upon a concerted, eloquent and organised crowd so articu-lated that each individual is given an opportunity to develop and project a clearly defined personality. I want our crowd to populate the theatre . . .

Every word of those tense scenes in the Capitol was recut and freshly polished so that the audience wondered if they were hearing a new play. Even the change from the accustomed emphasis when Mark Antony says 'Lend *me* your ears' set up a new level of tension between him and Brutus.

The production was full of high drama and menace. Costumes were based on Fascist uniforms, and the death of Cinna the Poet was made electrifying by the simultaneous opening of flick knives. Battles were depicted by swirling banners illuminated by ultraviolet lights and heightened by vivid sound effects. No one would have claimed that it was a subtle production, but it was great theatre.

Black Beech and Honeydew was finally completed and sent off to her agents, full of incorrect dates and vague attributions, indicating, untypically for her, a lack of interest in the whole project. Dorothy Olding was keen for her to come to the US for a publication launch in September 1965, but Ngaio felt that she couldn't stand the ballyhoo. The almost complete absence of reference to her detective fiction in the autobiography must have disappointed her American fans, although New Zealanders appreciated the descriptions of her early days in Christchurch.

Recognition as a writer had always come first from overseas, so it was not surprising that the first approach from a library interested in preserving her manuscripts as an archive should have come from the United States. Howard Gottlieb from Boston University asked her for contributions to an archive he was establishing as a centre of study and research in contemporary literature. For several years Ngaio generously passed on her manuscripts to Boston, until the National Library of New Zealand made a plea to have the material placed in their collection, and most of her papers are now in the Alexander Turnbull Library, Wellington. Correspondence was meticulously destroyed every year.

Now nearly seventy, public demands from all sides, including many letters from readers that had to be answered, were contriving to make Ngaio feel her age. The production of *Julius Caesar* had left her exhausted, and she was set back by an unexpected bout of illness. First of all she caught flu, and her friends the McIntoshes encouraged her to visit them in Wellington to recuperate. Ngaio liked to have a short break after her Shakespeare productions, so she went. On this visit she first met the Governor-General, Sir Bernard Fergusson and his wife, Laura, and they remained good friends for many years. Unfortunately in Wellington she caught measles, quite a serious illness for someone of her age, and was ill for several weeks. But she had to be back in Christchurch for the Christmas

Tree, with all its precious associations for her. As usual, Christmas Day was spent alone.

Ngaio may have regretted the fact that there was no student production in 1965 but the extra time was profitably devoted to her latest novel, *Death at the Dolphin*, which was developing well. The plot unfolded easily and for once there was no pressure on the work as it progressed. There was time for some public speaking, usually on topics related to theatre. The most daunting was a lecture on 'The Theatre in Australasia', which she delivered in Christchurch Cathedral on 1 March 1965 as part of the Pan Pacific Arts Festival. Her wide-ranging and scholarly address defends the player's rightful place in a church, reminding the audience of the medieval Mystery plays and Miracle plays, in which ordinary tradespeople annually acted out Bible stories on the feast of Corpus Christi. In the early days of New Zealand theatre and in her own experience of the turbulent life of the pit in the Theatre Royal, Christchurch, she finds a parallel with the energetic and forthright crowd that surrounded the pageant wagons in the market places of medieval England. She ends with a familiar message, a plea for living theatre in New Zealand, and for encouragement to talented youngsters to bring their expertise back home.

Another formal event later that year was her speech at the Katherine Mansfield Memorial Award luncheon in Wellington. In a fairly abrasive short talk about Katherine Mansfield she makes it quite clear that, in her view, few New Zealand writers have even begun to approach her achievement. Janet Frame and James Courage are singled out as exceptions. She mourns the decay of the spoken word in her native country and the fact that many contemporary writers seem unaware of the debased currency they trade in. Mansfield represents 'style' for Ngaio Marsh, and in a final moment of her speech she reveals a startling intuitive understanding of another practitioner in prose:

> I think, solitary figure that she is, in our short history of letters, it is salutary for us to return to her every now and again. In doing so we may be led, even to wonder, after all, why 'style' should be a dirty word among our advanced contemporaries; to observe with a writer like Katherine Mansfield how a short story may be ripened and nursed before it is plucked, and how in writing, a nuance may echo

an emotion and a cadence faithfully give out the inward breath of an idea.[9]

The Katherine Mansfield award was made to novelist and short-story writer Frank Sargeson, whom Ngaio had described as 'a writer of great distinction'. Although his idiomatic, proletarian language was very far from the ideal she favoured, she did recognise that Sargeson showed a rare artistry in the way it was used.

There was no Shakespeare production in 1965, but the arrival of Jonathan Elsom on a visit to Christchurch was too good an opportunity to waste. An entertaining two-hander, *Two's Company*, enabled Jonathan and Brian Bell to play a variety of short scenes in a production for Canterbury Rep, directed by Ngaio in the unpromising venue of the Provincial Council Chamber. Clearly the absence of a modern small theatre suitable for amateur productions was becoming a serious problem, but moves were finally under way to build a new university theatre to replace the burnt-out Shelley Theatre. The University of Canterbury was now established on a new campus on the outskirts of the city, and at last the opportunity existed to provide a venue for the performing arts. In addition to new university theatres, small, well-equipped theatres with professional or semi-professional companies were established in all major New Zealand cities during the next ten years, including Downstage (Wellington, 1964), Mercury (Auckland, 1968) and the Court Theatre in the centre of Christchurch which opened in 1971. Professional theatre was expanding throughout the country, creating the opportunities for young, talented people that Ngaio had called for many times.

CHAPTER 9

A Damery: 1966–71

By the end of 1965 Ngaio was making firm plans for her next visit to England. She knew that new tax laws would prevent her from staying more than six months and she was determined to extract the most from her holiday. She frequently planned excursions with a view to finding a plot, and she wrote to Denys Rhodes 'I think of doing a canal-cruise as it might make a bit of plottery and anyway sounds interesting in a dozy, pottering kind of way'. She had also arranged for another Aegean cruise in August. The closed community of shipboard life provided exactly the right ambience for an observer of character, notebook in hand, tucked away in a quiet corner of the upper deck.

Early in 1966 the manuscript of *Death at the Dolphin* was sent off, and after a brief visit from John Dacres-Mannings, now a successful financier based in Sydney, Ngaio said farewell to her beloved cats Smokey Joe, an aristocratic grey, and Nekko San ('Cat Esq.' in Japanese) who was a plump and inscrutable black and white. Her garden was now at the height of summer fragrance, and had recently been extensively featured in *Vogue New Zealand*.

By mid-April she was staying in the Hyde Park Hotel, trying to recover from the stomach ailment that seemed an invariable part of travel by ship for her. As she grew older she became more and more susceptible to stomach upsets when she travelled. Generally she recovered quickly, but if any illness was 'in the air' Ngaio was likely to succumb. The 'family' from Kent descended in quantity to cheer her up, and Eileen, the practical joker *par excellence*, put Ngaio in a fluster by having the porter announce the arrival of Mrs Roderick Alleyn. When this had been sorted out the company caused additional confusion by ordering iced coffee, as it was a hot day: 'a bewildered foreign waiter brought first of all an enormous po full of ice and then after a long, long, long wait boiling hot coffee and jugs of scalding milk, which, when poured over the ice created a sort of thermal resort through which we all peered at one another'. Despite unexpected callers and a string of interviews with the BBC and various newspapers—'for the first fortnight I have scarcely known whether I am on my topsy or my turvey',[1] she wrote to her friend, the dramatist, Bruce Mason—Ngaio managed to see *You Never Can Tell, The Killing of Sister George, Trelawny of the Wells* and *The Voysey Inheritance.* She also secured the lease on a flat in Pont Street. By the end of the month she already felt at home, and the diary was filling up with professional and social engagements. As well as seeing her friends the Rhodes family, she was invited to stay with Billy Collins in Kent, who liked to submit his guests to watching cricket on the village green. In London there were meetings with publishers and her agent, Edmund Cork, an awards dinner with the Crime Writers' Association, and plans for a week in Stratford in June. June, however, was to be a month of rare excitement.

The award to Ngaio Marsh of DBE (Dame Commander of the British Empire, the female equivalent of a knighthood) in the Birthday Honours List of 11 June 1966 brought satisfaction to many people throughout the world. Letters and telegrams poured in to Ngaio in London and to Rosemary Greene, who was handling her correspondence in Christchurch. Former New Zealand Prime Minister Sir Walter Nash wrote particularly warmly to offer his congratulations:

In my opinion there is no one in New Zealand who is more worthy of the honour than you. Thank you for all you have done for drama, for literature and in general for the stage and those associated with it who with your help have made excellent progress through the years.

The Wellington newspaper the *Dominion* headed its first leader on 11 June with the words:

In a country where women play much less than their due part in public life, it is refreshing to find a woman's name heading the Queen's Birthday Honours list. It is pleasing, too, to find the top honour being awarded because of its recipient's prominence in cultural activities.

The Australian Prime Minister Sir Robert Menzies cabled as 'one of your most devoted readers', but most welcome of all, perhaps, was the cable from Canterbury University Drama Society saying, 'No man here but honours you and doth wish you had but that opinion of yourself which every member of the Canterbury University Drama Society bears of you'.

Scores of letters and telegrams had to be acknowledged, and requests for interviews organised. Nothing prevented the trip to Stratford, however, and the promise to open the village fête at Birling on 2 July was kept. But by the time for the canal cruise in the middle of July, Ngaio was indeed ready for what she had described as a little 'dozy pottering'.

A five-day cruise on the Trent was sufficient to provide all the gruesome detail necessary for *Clutch of Constables* which was started later that year. Ngaio told an interviewer from *The Times* when the book was published that 'it was fun setting violence in such a tranquil scene'. In this novel Troy would look idly over the side of the boat into Ramsdyke Lock and see there 'Hazel Rickerby-Carrick's face, idiotically bloated . . . her mouth, drawn into an outlandish rictus. She bobbed and bumped against the starboard side. And what terrible disasters had corrupted her river-weed hair and distended her blown cheeks?'

But more pressing problems than the next novel were emerging with regard to the date of the Investiture for her Decoration on 15 November 1966. Tax laws required visitors to stay no more than six months before becoming liable for British income tax on all their earnings. By planning to extend her stay until November Ngaio was in difficulties, but she had already intended to help the situation by being out of the UK in August on her Aegean cruise with Joan Pullen, her secretary during the past year in London. The passengers on this cruise must have been disappointing material in terms of 'plottery', since no novel with a Greek setting emerged, although she wrote to Edmund Cork that she had been hoping for a suitable shipboard conspiracy. Unlike Agatha Christie, for whom travel and a variety of contacts were part of everyday life as the wife of a distinguished archaeologist, Ngaio had to work much more deliberately to establish unusual settings and characters. Although the cruise did not provide her with a good murder, she did not waste her time; instead she worked on an article about Stratford-upon-Avon for the *Atlantic Monthly*, which was published in February the following year. Back in England she made arrangements to stay for several weeks in the Republic of Ireland with her old friend Gwendoline Jellett, daughter of the doctor with whom, many years previously, she had collaborated in *The Nursing Home Murder* and the play which was based on this novel. The visit to rural Ireland may have stretched even Ngaio's taste for old-world eccentricity as she stayed in a decaying and rather cold country house in County Cork. But she survived it, and was back in London at the beginning of November to make preparations for the reception at Buckingham Palace and her party afterwards. This included the final fitting for the wool suit and smart mink hat that she wore for the event.

The story of the investiture of Ngaio Marsh at Buckingham Palace in November 1966 would be brushed aside as a piece of outrageously overdone comedy had it occurred within the pages of her own fiction. At that time one of the Rhodes family was part of the Royal Household, and 'the Lampreys' were notorious for practical jokes. In a letter to John Dacres-Mannings Ngaio described what happened:

> The Investiture was pure magic. You will not be surprised to hear that Denys, who had been staying at Balmoral, had told the Monarch that I preferred to be called Dame Edith and that I was a cripple and unable to curtsey. With the result that a wheelchair was thoughtfully provided at Buck House! Isn't he a devil? The Queen was smiling so broadly that I'm quite sure she knew from the outset it was all my eye. I don't have to add, I hope, that I did not occupy the wheelchair although it would have served Denys right if I had.

The thoughts going through her head as she found that her limousine did not join the line of elegant cars waiting at the main gates, but was directed round to the back, must have been frantic indeed, and she described it vividly many years later to visiting American writer, John Ball:

I entirely missed my opportunity to make a suitable entrance into the Palace and to be announced. Instead my car was stopped at a small side door. When I got out, there was a perfectly groomed footman waiting for me—with a wheelchair.[2]

Little wonder that a few years later, in writing to the architect of this elaborate hoax about an invitation to a dinner party given by royal visitors aboard the royal yacht *Britannia* in Lyttelton Harbour, Ngaio firmly ordered, 'I'll thank you not to send any silly messages to anybody about bathchairs', and seems to have retained her dignity on that occasion.

Two days later there was a glittering party in Eileen Mackay's flat in Knightsbridge, where many friends from the world of theatre and books gathered in her honour. Especially welcome was the presence of her young second cousin, Flight Lieutenant 'Bear' Mannings, who had also received a decoration on the same List, the Queen's Commendation for Valuable Service in the Air.

Then, on 25 November, she was again at sea, heading south for the antipodean summer aboard the *Gothic*, and arriving in New Zealand on Boxing Day, 'of all sub-human days of the year'. This time the food poisoning she contracted on board took several weeks to clear and she was anxiously looked after by friends and by Mrs Crawford, who had managed the house in her absence.

Death at the Dolphin had been published under the title of *Killer Dolphin* in August by Little, Brown in the United States, but Collins did not bring it out in Britain until the spring of 1967, by which time it had already been serialised in *Woman's Journal*. It is dedicated to Edmund Cork, Ngaio's agent, a gesture he greatly valued. This novel, which is one of the most successful of her theatre-based mysteries, deals with the restoration of a bombed-out theatre in London, and the theft of a glove reputed to have belonged to Hamnet, Shakespeare's son. Ngaio is at her wittiest and best in dealing with theatrical people, revelling in their gossip, their jealousies and the practical problems of getting a production together. Even the tone of the newspaper reviews of the play is caught exactly. In keeping with her ability to devise violent death by unexpected means, the victim is battered to death by one of the ornamental bronze dolphins which are the emblems of the re-stored theatre. Roderick Alleyn is already at the theatre advising on security relating to Hamnet's glove, and when he takes over the murder investigation, a mesh of conspiracy must be carefully unwound. The whole novel is dramatic from the near-fatal accident in the opening pages, and the reader feels that the writer was living the production along with her imaginary cast. This impression is strengthened by the sketches which illustrate her manuscript, depicting several of the events within the story. Among these is a full-page sketch of Alleyn, looking handsome but surprisingly feminine.

The inspiration for *Death at the Dolphin* must have lain dormant for many years before the author decided how to use it. During her extended stay in London in 1949–51, Ngaio was whisked off down the River Thames in a launch with Tyrone Guthrie, his wife Judy and Bob Stead to look at a bomb-damaged theatre on the banks of the river—'the idea was that, if it could be made usable, a Shakespeare season should be held there during the Festival of Britain. Audiences would be invited to take water to the play, going downstream by barge from Westminster Pier'. But although their trip down the Thames was fun, with the Guthries singing from his current production, *The Barber of Seville*, the theatre was a write-off. 'No good, dear', said Guthrie after one glance at it. 'What a pity'.[3] The party of theatre-hunters could not have suspected that the ruined Dolphin Theatre would come back to life, sixteen years later, through the imagination of the crime fiction writer. In the novel the theatre is rebuilt by a mysterious and wealthy Greek financier, and no money is spared to make the building beautiful and full of Victorian charm:

> The foyer was alive. It was being painted, gilded, polished and furbished. There were men on scaffolds, on long ladders, on pendant platforms. A great chandelier lay in a sparkling heap on the floor. The two fat cherubim, washed and garnished, beamed upside-down into the resuscitated box office.

This loving description of a ruined theatre being brought back to life also has its roots in the many decayed theatres that the British Commonwealth Players visited on their New Zealand tour in 1951, where rats infested the dressing-rooms, tattered curtains stirred in the draughts and rain dripped through neglected roofs. *Death at the*

A sketch of the actors in the bar at the Dolphin Theatre which appears in the manuscript of *Death at the Dolphin*, together with this drawing of a cat which probably kept Ngaio company while she wrote chapter 3.

Dolphin deserved the praise it received from reviewers, and it marks the beginning of a series of detective novels which show Ngaio at the top of her form, combining a strong plot with well-developed characters and a variety of unexpected detail.

Back in New Zealand, Ngaio was soon to be genuinely involved with raising a new theatre from its foundations. The University of Canterbury had finally undertaken the building of a theatre to replace the Shelley Theatre that had been destroyed by fire in 1953. Located in the Students' Union, a modern concrete building, the theatre was being financed partly by the University, partly by a public appeal, and partly by a levy imposed on all students by the Union. It was virtually complete by the time Ngaio returned to Christchurch although the stage was not equipped or curtained. Her first view of the theatre must have been very disappointing for someone with such clear ideas, born of experience, of what actors and audience really needed; the story is told that when she first saw inside the building, she wept.

The auditorium is more like a lecture hall than the cosy and intimate space she favoured, and the architect must have been remarkably ill advised about the practicalities of production, since he provided neither the means to fly scenery nor space to draw it aside. Theatres should be like icebergs, with a great deal of space beneath the surface, and this theatre had virtually no area around the stage for the actors to circulate. Amazingly, the lift dock door, through which heavy scenery could be brought straight on to the stage, was one storey up and could not be used until an expensive hydraulic lift was installed two years later. Even with a steeply raked auditorium the sightlines were poor and necessitated the extensive use of rostra. Nothing could be done to alter the fact that audience access was from the second floor, and there was no lift. In later years this idiosyncratic feature was to prevent her from attending productions by her student players.

Always one to make the best of things, Ngaio was soon busy giving what practical advice she could to help the students get the new theatre functioning. The long room at Valley Road filled up on many occasions with students and staff making plans for using the new building. She was able to influence some remaining purchases of equipment and fittings and insisted on the provision of black

197

velvet for the 'legs' or back curtains; no cheaper substitute would do and her advice proved to be sound. Her own collection of books about the stage was drawn on heavily by students involved with the new theatre, and Ngaio's supply of coloured masking for lights was used when no other source could be found. She also bought the students a new cyclorama, always one of her favourite theatrical devices. It is still there and still known as Ngaio's cyc.

The first play to be mounted in the new theatre was *Twelfth Night*, with Ngaio in charge of production. This commemorated the inaugural production by the University Drama Society back in 1935, and a tribute to Dame Ngaio Marsh was printed in the programme: 'it is appropriate that for our first production in our new home, Dame Ngaio, a trail-blazer for Shakespearean production in New Zealand, should direct that play which Professor Pocock chose for our audiences in a cold mid-winter, 32 years ago'. The history of the society since that time was largely a history of Ngaio's efforts, and the tribute ended with a hope for future development. The inauguration of the theatre in June 1967 was loyally seen as recognition of 'that remarkable, exacting, modest woman, who lifted us from the doldrums, made the good times for us and carried us through the bad'. As a concrete expression of its regard, the University of Canterbury named the new theatre after her, and the students made her a life member of the Students' Association.

The Dame Ngaio Marsh Theatre is still much in use. A portrait of its founding figure painted by Vy Elsom, Jonathan Elsom's mother, hangs in the lobby, and two large landscape paintings by Ngaio are displayed at the back of the auditorium. The metal sculpture commissioned by Ngaio from Tom Taylor, designer of the student productions for many years, has disappeared.

Having a theatre named after her, even one with so many flaws in its design, was still very satisfying and she wrote to tell Pamela Mann the news: 'Very touchingly the University of Canterbury has called its terrifically posh new theatre after your old Mum who opened it with a production of "Twelfth Night". We ran for 3 weeks to capacity houses and have made a net profit of almost 1,000 pounds. Crikey'. Even now she retained the custom of signing all the first-night programmes, a tradition she had maintained since the first Shakespeare production with students in 1943. Clearly this version of *Twelfth Night* had gone extremely well, and one of her student players who was at that time a Lecturer in Drama, Mervyn Thompson, wrote to her that it had been 'wonderfully imaginative and illuminating, but in the grain of the play, never in the least gimmicky'. Ngaio interpreted the play as having 'a character that is, I believe, unique in English comedy, a particular tinge of sadness that is the complementary colour of aesthetic pleasure. One listens to it with the half sigh that accompanies an experience of perfect beauty. This is an element that has much to do with music and nothing at all to do either with sentiment or with tragedy and it is the quintessence of *Twelfth Night*'.[4] The only piece of Shakespearean criticism that she ever published was on this play, in the prestigious annual journal *Shakespeare Survey* in 1955, after the British Commonwealth Players' tour.

By September she had recovered from the strenuous efforts of knocking a new theatre into shape and her thoughts were turning back towards her next detective novel, which she had been sketching out during the past six months. This was to be *Clutch of Constables*, a complex piece of work combining art forgeries and thefts with murder aboard a canal cruiser. There is some anxiety about Mrs Roderick Alleyn, who happens to be on board, seeking a little relaxation after a busy period, and who finds herself being passionately kissed by the murderer. Ambitiously for Ngaio, who generally took few radical steps regarding structure, the main action of the novel is filtered through flashbacks arising from Alleyn's lecture on the case to a Police College. His regular assessments of the investigation, and his scarcely concealed concern for Troy, adds an interesting texture to the narrative. The convoluted plot must have seriously exercised even Ngaio's nimble intelligence, and it is hardly surprising that she wrote to Denys, 'I'm trying to finish a beast of a book and am in despair: a not unusual condition, I may say'.

A welcome break came with an invitation to visit Government House in Wellington to say farewell to the Governor-General, Sir Bernard Fergusson (later Lord Ballantrae) and his wife Laura, who were leaving New Zealand in 1967 after a successful five years in office. Ngaio admired him, and was impressed with his 'strong and completely genuine affinity with the Maori people'. This was obviously reciprocal; part of the farewell ceremonies for Sir

Bernard and his wife involved a day-long ceremony in a Maori village where many tribes gathered to honour them. Ngaio attended the ceremony along with the Fergusson family. Sir Bernard and Ngaio kept up a sprightly correspondence until his death in 1980. Their letters are full of amusing anecdotes, including a long-running joke about publisher Billy Collins' habit of using 'isn't it' at the end of sentences. Among the exchange of compliments is this Gilbert and Sullivan parody written by Ngaio in praise of the Governor-General after his departure:

> He was the very model of a Kiwi Governor-General
> In matters ceremonial, portentous or ephemeral.
> In protocol perfection, in diplomacy immaculate
> Proconsular in dignity and in assessment accurate.
> Well up in Maoritanga too, he spoke it with the best of 'em
> At home with politicians, intellectuals and the rest of 'em
> At laying stones or cutting tapes or launching a Centennial
> He was the very model of a Kiwi Governor-General.
>
> Remarkable amalgam of a soldier and a Solomon
> He verifies delectably: – astonishing phenomenon!
> As master of the mot juste he is never at a loss and he
> Displays in light fantastic vein the utmost virtuosity.
> In rhyming far excelling mere purveyors of the jingle he
> Can rival in dexterity a Gilbert or an Ingoldsby.
> In short, since I cannot compete
> It must suffice to tender all
> My most respectful thank you to our former Governor-General.

Laura Fergusson also made a lasting contribution to New Zealand society by establishing a Trust which led to the provision of residential homes for the disabled.

At the turn of the year Ngaio was tempted by an invitation she found hard to refuse. The New Zealand Ambassador to Italy, His Excellency Alister Mcintosh and his wife Doris, who were friends of long standing, invited her to stay with them in the New Zealand Embassy which then occupied a Renaissance building in the centre of Rome. Although Ngaio was writing to Dorothy Olding early in 1968, 'I wish I could say we'd meet in London in the spring but, darling Dorothy, I have only just got home and can't bounce around again so soon', the idea of a trip to Rome was clearly becoming irresistible. Within a few weeks she was gleefully telling Denys that 'I'm going over to Rome. Ha-ha, sucks. I mean literally on 30 March to stay at our Embassy'.

This unexpected invitation threw her into a frenzy of activity; finishing off *Clutch of Constables* before she left was obviously essential. She worked furiously on the novel, halted only by the sad news in February that her old friend Nelly Rhodes had died at the age of seventy-two. In writing to Denys about his mother, Ngaio spoke of 'all the gaiety and love that she gave us' and found some comfort in the fact that she had died suddenly after a happy family gathering. The hasty completion of *Clutch of Constables* did not seem to affect its quality, and both Edmund Cork and Dorothy Olding were very satisfied. Dorothy wrote, 'I truly do love this book, I think it is one of her very best'. By now, Dilys Wynn of the *New York Magazine* was claiming that 'It's time to compare Christie to Marsh instead of the other way around'. Billy Collins was elated by the initial sales and wrote to Ngaio disclosing that a special fan of hers, Viscount Montgomery, had been sent an advance copy of the book and confessed himself delighted.

En route to Rome, Ngaio spent a few days in London, where she hastily contacted friends and had the unusual experience of lunching at the Special Services Club. This discreet establishment is run for members of the British Intelligence Service and Ngaio was brought there by two ex-spies. But the highlight of this trip was not to be England, but Italy, and by 10 May she was in Rome.

Ngaio was entranced by the city, finding the ambassador's apartment in the Via di San Pantaleo 'beautiful beyond words'. The McIntoshes were sensitive and intelligent hosts who did not overburden her with sightseeing, for which she was grateful: 'I have rather a low saturation point for Sights. Like Macbeth, you may remember ('No more sights') but greatly enjoying them when so tactfully introduced'. Members of the Ambassador's staff at that time remember Doris McIntosh and Ngaio Marsh returning down Via Capo le Case from some outing on a very hot day, in floppy summer hats and looking rather heat-worn and very Anglo-Saxon against the local background.

The tapestry of Roman life, with Etruscan statues and floodlit ruins from the past mingling with a street riot in the present (this was, after all, the summer of 1968, when most European cities experienced civic unrest), was just what the writer's imagination needed. *When in Rome*, her next novel, published in 1970, is filled with the sounds and sights of this fascinating city, and its themes are topical and direct. For once the questioning detective is kept very much in the background, and the English upper classes are seen as thoroughly corrupt. Perhaps the heady politics of 1968 were reaching through, and the riot, described so lightly in the second edition of *Black Beech and Honeydew*, disturbed her more than she wanted to admit. Certainly in an otherwise high-spirited letter to Denys she asked, 'Do you think that before long people will begin banging and rioting and killing each other without bothering to put a label on why they are doing it?'

But the treasures of Rome, and the joys of sitting in small cafés beside ornate fountains in ancient squares or in fragrant; flower-bedecked roof gardens gave Ngaio great happiness, and she stored away every detail for future use. She particularly responded to Etruscan sculpture, finding the faces 'strangely smirking, enigmatic and startlingly lively'. The Etruscan theme is brought into *When in Rome* very ingeniously, when the Dutch couple, the Van der Veghels, are revealed as having Italian origins which explain their unusual facial features. Ngaio did not find the Renaissance painters to her taste, however—'have decided I am unresponsive to Renaissance flamboyants (Titian and Bellini) with all those rowdy saints galumphing about the heavens'.

Pamela Mann was invited to join Ngaio to complete the Italian holiday with a drive through northern Italy, visiting several cities including Perugia, Assisi and Florence. After a whirlwind of sightseeing crammed into two days, Pamela bravely took the wheel of a small car and drove out of Rome, preceded by the Ambassador's car as a pilot. Ngaio, always a fast and impatient driver, urged Pamela on to greater speed, but she wisely resisted and they arrived safely on the outskirts of the city, where they said farewell to the McIntoshes.

The tour was a great success, but by now Italy was getting very hot for sightseeing. Ngaio was limping and relying on a walking stick because of a severe attack of gout, so she took the opportunity whenever possible to stretch out full-length on a church pew to survey the scene in comfort. 'Besides', she remarked to Pamela, 'this is what they must expect if they decorate the ceilings'. Evening excursions in horse-drawn carriages along the Arno in Florence were especially memorable for them both, and as they strolled around the Michelangelo sculptures Ngaio remembered her art classes at the School of Art in Christchurch and how the figures of David and the statues of Night and Morning from the Medici Tomb had been drawn and redrawn. They went one evening to the hill village of Fiesole, where an outdoor festival of Antonioni films was being held in the ruins of the Teatro Romano. Dining beneath the stars, they found themselves at the next table to this internationally renowned film director.

They were staying at the Pensione Hermitage in Florence. Its carefully tended roof garden, full of the scent of jasmine and the sound of canaries, provided the setting for Barnaby Grant to sit mourning his lost manuscript in *When in Rome*. (Edmund Cork constantly lectured Ngaio about the danger of losing her drafts when she was travelling about; fortunately this never happened to her.) After a week in Florence they escaped to the fresher air of the hills, and stayed a few days with friends of the Mulings who lived near Lucca. The trip ended with a rail journey from Viareggio to Genoa where they were to spend the night before catching the express train to Paris. The train pulled into Genoa for a brief stop only, there was a lot of luggage, Ngaio's leg was giving her trouble and in the confusion her walking stick was left behind. But a night in a good hotel with breakfast in bed ('The Time of London I bring you, Madam') restored them both sufficiently to face the overnight sleeper to Paris next day.

Paris in July 1968 was extremely volatile, and Douglas MacDiarmid, whom they had planned to visit, advised them to spend no more than a few hours in the city. His view was shared by Mr McIntosh in Rome, who had been concerned about the planned stay in Paris for some time. So Ngaio, Pamela and Douglas MacDiarmid strolled around only for a morning, with frequent pauses in street cafes where, according to Pamela, 'he and Ngaio talked as though they were starved of conversation'. MacDiarmid acted in the early productions of *Hamlet* and *Othello* in Christchurch, and he realises that the experience opened up a world of the imagination for him that he did not appreciate until later. Now a successful artist his affection for her is still as warm as ever seeing in

Ngaio 'true success if ever there were—the fine human being beyond all creative, professional acclaim'.

After this strenuous journey back to England, Ngaio did nothing to slacken the pace. There was no point in renting a flat for the short time that remained so she based herself at the comfortable and old-fashioned Basil Street Hotel in Knightsbridge. At the end of July she had the cosy and very British recognition of her status as a public figure when she was invited to inhabit Roy Plomley's desert island, on the BBC radio programme, *Desert Island Discs*. She wrote to Pamela Mann in August that 'truly your old Mumsie has been madly rushed about and such spare time as I've had I've used up in taking little cat-naps and looking at my papers. I've had proof correcting, interviews, radio, publishers, company calls and nips into the country'. As well as going to Stratford with Eileen, Ngaio was swept off to *Eugène Onegin* at Glyndebourne by Elric Hooper, who was then working in London, and to *Hadrian* by her other protégé, Jonathan Elsom.

But the trip was coming to an end, and at the end of August she was bound for New Zealand. Again the journey was made unpleasant because of food poisoning, which was widespread among the passengers. For the first time ever she longed for the voyage to end, and it took several weeks at home to recover. The after-effects dragged on until October when her friend Betty Cotterill wrote to Pamela that she was still under the weather, 'but picking up and cheerful as ever'.

Ngaio recovered in time to narrate the dialogue for Prokofiev's entertainment for children, *Peter and the Wolf*, for the Christchurch Civic Orchestra's Christmas concert. The orchestra was conducted by the American Dobbs Franks, and Ngaio contributed her deep and beautifully modulated voice to the occasion. She found the experience 'terrifying but fun' and thoroughly enjoyed portraying the different characters and animals. Regrettably the performance and this unique reading were not recorded.

An attack of fibrositis was shrugged off, so she could make her usual elaborate preparations for The Christmas Tree, and again she was pleased to have members of the Rhodes family present. The year had been eventful, and at the end of 1968 Ngaio's zest for life was still strong. Now, at the age of seventy-three, she settled down to work on her latest novel, knowing that she had already promised to produce *A Midsummer Night's Dream* for the students in 1969. It was just as well that the writing of *When in Rome* started off with unusual facility, because she was interrupted for some time in March with auditions. Aspiring actors were summoned to her home in the Cashmere Hills. Many felt as Mervyn Thompson had done ten years earlier:

> Vividly I remember those first auditions. Climbing up to the great lady's house in Cashmere for a preliminary try-out. Being conceited enough to think I might try for the part of Antony. Reading the part gruesomely while all the time trying to banish the thought that I was really playing Pip to a time-resistant Miss Havisham.[5]

Ngaio described the students coming for audition in a letter to Denys in March 1969:

> Among them was a huge creature with shoulder-length hair, filthy bare feet, unspeakable jeans and sweater and an enormous gruff voice. When I asked him what part he was considering he said in the thickest of New Zealand accents, 'Yeah, well, I'm not setting me sights on a fairee'. He turned out in subsequent conversation to be charming and highly intelligent with an extremely nice sense of humour. Why they elect to make such scarecrows of themselves is puzzling but at that age we were all rebels of one sort or another, of course.

Miss Havisham and Pip were not so far apart after all.

The cast of *A Midsummer Night's Dream* was strengthened by the return of Elric Hooper from London to take the part of Puck and to be Associate Director. 'She wanted me to do it before arthritis set in', quipped Elric, and he found himself in the company of several 'old hands' from earlier productions, with Mervyn Glue as Bottom and David Hindin as Quince. Sam Neill (now an international film star) played Theseus and Annette Facer helped with production. Elric's considerable and varied overseas experience, with Joan Littlewood in London, the Berliner Ensemble in East Germany, the Royal Swedish Theatre and the Old Vic in London, brought a new sophistication to the University Drama Society. Elric found working with student players and amateurs both rewarding and unpredictable. Bottom was fond of nipping off to the pub, with a raincoat over his costume, and once he just managed to get back on stage in time, galloping through the wings and tossing his coat behind him as he ran. Across the stage Ngaio's eyes glinted in fury, enough to bring any enchanted weaver to his senses very quickly.

Few people realised that Ngaio had paid Elric's fare out of her own pocket, and she did her best to secure him acting engagements in New Zealand. She wrote to Bruce Mason asking him to use his influence in Wellington, stressing that 'I'm resigned now to taking the full punishment for sticking my neck out and don't in the least regret it. I would, however, very much like to see full advantage being taken of Elric's visit. He is, I promise you, a dynamic force in the theatre and his work with us here is electrifying'.[6] In bringing Elric out to Christchurch Ngaio made a major contribution to New Zealand theatre in the 1960s. His subsequent work with the Court Theatre there was ample reward.

With another successful Shakespearean production behind her, Ngaio was under pressure to complete *When in Rome*, which, not surprisingly, was beginning to run into difficulties regarding Italian police procedure. She wrote distractedly to Denys in November, 'When does Il Deputi take over from il Signor Questore and when do the Agenti yield place to the Carabinieri? And who is the real boss of the Squadra Omicidi and how far is il Ministero dell'Interno likely to muck in on Alleyn's job? Mama mia'. She consulted legal authorities in Rome, and the book was packed off with much relief just before Christmas. By now her confidence in the novel was at a low ebb, and she had only two copies typed because she was expecting her agents to demand substantial rewrites.

The Christmas Tree party took her mind off this troublesome manuscript, and the entertainment went with its usual style. This year Ngaio had engaged three staff to assist, and according to Simon Acland, son of Sir John and Lady Acland, it was the only private house in New Zealand he ever visited where servants waited at table. Ngaio worked hard to create an English country house atmosphere, enhanced in later years by antique furniture, chintz curtains and lavish floral arrangements.

After Christmas the news from London and New York was very encouraging. Edmund Cork wrote on 8 January 1970, 'I have no doubt at all that this is the best detective novel you have ever written. It has everything, and will go very far'. And Dorothy

Olding was 'tremendously excited' by the book. Then followed a sustained and serious exchange of letters regarding the stage at which a corpse dropped down a well would begin to smell. The author was worried about the lapse of time before Sebastian Mailer's body was discovered, and told Edmund, 'I looked up all the disgusting information in books on medical jurisprudence and the facts seem to be that facts, to an extreme extent, alter circumstances. The circumstance of the cold running water would undoubtedly delay the onset. On the other hand, Mr. Mailer's full and unhealthy habits and his recent large meal would accelerate it . . . Perhaps I could slip in an intervening day?' They eventually got round it with a heat wave and the passage of an extra day.

There is no doubt that the novels, despite the mental anguish that accompanied their parturition, were emerging with great facility. By May the next one was under way, although Ngaio wrote to Denys of 'that awful opening phase of writing as if through a load of treacle and lead: fifteen words a day and cross them all out next morning is my form for the first fortnight and am I an artist at dreaming up excuses not to begin!' She soon needed expert advice on police organisation in England, and wrote to Edmund Cork about the appointment of Chief Constable of the County. Edmund passed her request on to Collins, who made the necessary enquiries but got a fairly dusty answer, along the lines that the author must be living in the past. A carefully worded version of this reply was sent to Ngaio, who was by now always shielded from criticism by her agents. The edited reply solved her immediate problem with the plot, and she was able to keep plodding on. Further difficulties emerged when the manuscript was submitted in July 1971, and these were crisply dealt with by Elizabeth Walter, who was now handling the Marsh books at Collins.

Tied Up in Tinsel (1972) is set at Christmas in an English country house and the mistakes in the manuscript reveal Ngaio's fantasy view of this festival. She had never spent Christmas in an ordinary English household, and her view of the practical side of preparing traditional dishes was very hazy. In the first draft of this novel the characters go into the kitchen on Christmas Eve to stir the pudding and make a wish. Miss Walter quite correctly pointed out that Christmas puddings are made weeks before the event, and sit maturing darkly in their bowls ready for lengthy boiling on the day. She suggested that the characters view the decorated Christmas cake instead, but Ngaio remembered that the first bite of a mince pie also allowed one a wish, so the manuscript was altered accordingly. She manages to incorporate the giving of presents around the tree in manorial fashion, while village children, on their best behaviour, gaze about them, properly impressed. Even Troy, who is there to paint a portrait, is in love with the Christmas tree:

> And really, thought Troy, it was an enchantment. It was breathtaking. At the far end of this long room, suspended in darkness, blazed the golden Christmas Tree alive with its flames, stars and a company of angels. It quivered with its own brilliance and was the most beautiful tree in all the world.

The theatrical Christmas described in the novel, with its recorded sounds of sleigh bells and a gilded sleigh laden with huge decorated Christmas boxes for each family, is an elaborate version of Ngaio's own Christmas parties, held in a hot Christchurch summer.

This novel is very dated, and hopelessly old-fashioned when compared with *When in Rome*; a return to the classic thirties style with very little to recommend it. No wonder Dorothy Olding remarked that she didn't care for it very much. Little, Brown were happy to publish, however, and American readers enjoyed its quaint atmosphere. The difference between the fiction arising from direct and recent experience such as *Clutch of Constables* and *When in Rome* and those that depended on out-of-date memories was becoming very apparent.

During 1969 Ngaio also found time to assist Susan Acland with the private publication of the reminiscences of her mother-in-law, Evelyn Acland. The book, published by the Caxton Press, contains a prefatory note by Ngaio, who had valued the friendship of Evelyn and her family for many years, and used to enjoy Evelyn's tales of hospital work in the early days of the settlement.

Other memories flooded back in January 1970 with news of the death of Allan Wilkie at the age of nearly ninety-two. In an obituary in the Christchurch Press Ngaio paid tribute to his long career as an actor-manager of the old style, who had brought good theatre wherever he went.

The remainder of 1970 was a mixture of hard work in the theatre, where she was engaged with a production of Pinero's *The Magistrate*, and public appearances on radio and television. In September 1970 lovers of crime fiction throughout the world joined in celebrating Agatha Christie's eightieth birthday. Edmund Cork wrote to Ngaio about a luncheon party held at St James' Place, and Ngaio was interviewed direct by BBC via satellite. The reality of what went on behind the scenes happily bears no relation to the broadcast interview, because even Ngaio's ability to sustain an amused tolerance in the face of amazing ineptitude wore a little thin. The interview was scheduled to take place at midnight, which was not a problem for a writer who habitually worked until the small hours. The link with Britain was finally established at 2 a.m., but the interviewer had not yet arrived. A junior member of the crew thought he had better do something as precious satellite time was ticking away, so he started the interview off by asking Ngaio what she thought of Agatha Christie's leading character, Lord Peter Wimsey. According to the hapless victim in the interviewee's chair, the event ended in total confusion.

Tax problems continued to take her by surprise and she was quite incapable of dealing with them. Ngaio found it impossible to believe that her earnings, most of which went direct to her company, Ngaio Marsh Ltd, which then paid her an annual salary, were being so heavily taxed when she herself received only a modest income. As usual Edmund Cork wrote comfortingly: 'Don't worry too much, dear Ngaio, about the tax matter—I am sure it can be dealt with without too much upset'. And so it was, leaving Ngaio mystified, but reassured. As she often said, she had no interest in money apart from its spending power, and as long as she could afford to be generous to her friends and to afford her trips back to England, she was quite content. Certainly her tax portfolio was less complicated than that of Edmund Cork's other Queen of Crime, Agatha Christie, but by the 1960s serials of the Marsh novels were running in many countries, and together with options for TV and foreign translations, quite an intricate financial situation had developed. Agents on both sides of the Atlantic did their best to keep this in order, while Ngaio's secretary, Rosemary Greene, looked after the household and personal expenses in Christchurch. Ngaio, herself, just kept on writing.

The year was saddened by the deaths of two people to whom she had been particularly attached. The first was the actress Brigid ('Bid') Lenihan, 'our bright star'. Bid's sudden death at the age of only forty-one came as a great shock. Ngaio wrote an affectionate tribute for a special edition of *Act*, the theatre magazine edited by Bruce Mason in Wellington. She ended her tribute:

> When I think of Biddy, she is singing. Sometimes it is Douglas Lilburn's heartrending setting of the Willow Song, sometimes the bawdy snatch she flung at her audience in 'Characters' and some-times 'I attempt from Love's Sickness to Fly' with which she opened the Bridie play [The Anatomist]. She was a brilliant and most lovable creature.[7]

Then in early December, when Ngaio was doing an arduous promotional tour of bookshops in the North Island ('an odious sort of publisher's shop-crawl'), came news of the death of Eileen Mackay, Nelly Rhodes' eldest daughter. Although they had not corresponded regularly for sometime, Ngaio still had fond memories of their collaboration on books and plays, their trips to Stratford, and a shared love of Shakespeare. It is typical of Ngaio's strength and her ability to maintain a public face in spite of private grief that although she was writing, deeply shocked, to Eileen's sister Maureen Balfour on 5 December to acknowledge the cable, she did not seek to escape from her promise to open Evelyn Page's major retrospective exhibition two days later at the National Art Gallery in Wellington.

Evelyn Page was now beginning to feel the crippling effects of arthritis, but she continued to paint with more exuberance than ever. Her husband Frederick had recently retired as Professor of Music at the Victoria University of Wellington, and he now de-voted himself to making life easier for his wife so that she could continue to paint as much as possible. Like Ngaio, she seemed to have received an unexpected creative boost in old age, and her late nudes are remarkable for their honest celebration of the female body. All her life she had struggled to capture the effect of dappled sunlight on human flesh, and several nudes painted in the 1960s reveal her mastery of colour and texture. Her biographer, Janet

Paul, describes the paintings of this period as 'an enchantment of the senses . . . faces and skin glowed or greened in leaf-broken sunlight; roses and daffodils bloomed and light flooded through open French doors over her serene thickly fleshed nudes seated sewing, washing or lying beside bowls of fruit and swathes of opalescent cloth . . .'[8]

Eve remembered Ngaio once looking at one of these sumptuous paintings of a generously displayed female nude who had been painted in the Pages' garden. The house was flanked by rows of lime trees, which provided a background for the painting that Ngaio promptly dubbed 'Fanny by Limelight'. Evelyn talked about painting Ngaio's portrait, but Ngaio had a passage booked to England in 1971 and regrettably the right moment never arrived when they both had time and energy available.

By 3 April 1971 Ngaio was again bound for Britain, having surmounted the problems of letting the house and making arrangements for her much-loved cats. She wrote to Denys about her travel plans, revealing that domestic ties were becoming more and more of a deterrent, but that the itch for London was still strong. She was travelling aboard the P&O liner *Orsova*, an elderly ship that she described as 'trembling like a great apprehensive blancmange'. She arrived in London on 13 May, planning to stay for six months. The schedule appeared arduous for a woman of seventy-six, including a trip to Denmark at the invitation of her Danish publishers, followed by an autumn cruise in the Mediterranean. No wonder Bruce Mason described her as 'indestructible'.

A radio version of *Death at the Dolphin* had recently been broadcast by the BBC, and Ngaio went to hear the tape with Peter Howell, who had played Alleyn in this version by Alison Plowden. Ngaio had established a good relationship with the BBC since her first broadcasts in the early 1950s and by now several of her novels had been adapted as radio plays. Radio drama in the United Kingdom was a popular genre and she was well served by her scriptwriters: Giles Cooper, who was widely respected for his distinguished work for radio, adapted *Artists in Crime* in 1953 and Cedric Messina dramatised *Final Curtain* in 1964. John Tydeman, now head of BBC Radio Drama, adapted *Death in Ecstasy* in 1969 and this was followed by radio versions of *Black as He's Painted* in

1976 and *Death and the Dancing Footman* in 1986. These plays were broadcast on the entertainment channels of BBC, first on the Light Programme and Home Service and later on Radio 4. Even after television was established in Britain, the audience for radio drama remained high, and in the 1970s *Saturday Night Theatre*, which broadcast many 'whodunits', had an average audience of 1.5 million.

John Tydeman found the Marsh dramatisations great fun to do, with actors particularly enjoying the more raffish and eccentric roles. With her well-defined, colourful characters and sharp, humorous dialogue, the plays adapted well and were popular with the audience. Roderick Alleyn was usually portrayed as a bastion of sanity in an abnormal world, with Inspector Fox bringing his comfortable support to every situation. Ngaio liked the new play, and was delighted that her friendship with Peter Howell was being maintained through his work for radio.

By the time Dorothy Olding arrived on her annual business trip to London in late May, Ngaio was about to move into a small basement flat in Montpelier Square. The meeting with Dorothy, necessarily compressed into a few days, was bitter-sweet. In a touching letter written after Dorothy had returned to New York, Ngaio disclosed how valuable this friendship had become:

> I so much hated you going that I suddenly jibbed at walking out on the pavement and then thought how damned silly and made after you, only to be called back to the telephone as I got to the steps . . . when I came out of the telephone box you had gone. It was lovely having even that brief bit of you, sweetie, but frustrating too.[9]

Ngaio was well used to saying goodbye to people of whom she was fond, but this vignette suggests a loneliness that was seldom revealed. Neither of them depended too much on the proposed plan to meet on board ship during Ngaio's return voyage because of the difficulties of booking a passage for Dorothy at this late stage. To their mutual satisfaction however, Dorothy was able to secure a berth on the ship from Nassau to San Francisco, enabling them to spend a relaxing few weeks together. Dorothy called in July: 'Have cabin on Oronsay. Nassau to San Francisco. Yo ho ho and a bottle of rum', which brought the reply: 'Extravagant rejoicing. Love Ngaio'.[10]

On the two-week visit to Denmark as the guest of her Danish publisher, Samleren, Ngaio made a memorable trip to Elsinore. Although there is no evidence that Shakespeare ever visited Kronborg Castle, it may have been described to him by other travellers. Pacing the battlements that had confined her favourite Shakespearean hero, Hamlet, Ngaio found a unique opportunity to blend reality with the illusion of a play that had fascinated her for many years and was inextricably bound up with her own life in the theatre. Ngaio enjoyed the trip but found it exhausting. In press interviews she joked about bringing Roderick Alleyn to Copenhagen to have an excuse to return to fairy-tale Denmark: 'perhaps my next book should be "Alleyn in Copenhagen" '. But Ngaio was now seventy-six and foreign travel was beginning to seem more of an effort than it ever had before. The possibility of a mystery set at Kronborg was no doubt in her mind, but the practical problems of researching it were beyond her. Even writing the country house novel, *Tied Up in Tinsel*, had created far more problems than ever before, as she discovered when the proofs arrived on her return from Denmark.

The proofs of *Tied Up in Tinsel* were delivered just before she was to set off on her Mediterranean cruise and although she was battling with a dose of flu at the time there was nothing to be done but cope with them. At this late stage she discovered that she had made Halberds Manor face north, a perfectly logical way for an antipodean house to face, but distinctly odd for Britain, where country houses usually face south so that public rooms at the front get the sun. This mistake meant a lot of fussy changes and, together with Elizabeth Walter's earlier list of objections to the Christmas rituals, must have made Ngaio feel thoroughly fed up with the entire book. She returned the proofs in two days with a crisp and businesslike letter, devoid of her usual friendly flourishes.

On 13 October she embarked with Joan Pullen, her secretary, on the *Oronsay* for a Mediterranean cruise. By now she had given up the notion of wintering somewhere warm like Corsica, and was resigned to her scheduled departure for New Zealand in December. On the cruise Ngaio worked on a stage version of *When in Rome* that Hughes Massie was anxious to market. Her idea was to have a modern, stylised set like a cross-section of the catacombs, with action on different layers. Producer David Kirk, who two years later ran two successful tours of *Murder Sails at Midnight*, a play based on *Singing in the Shrouds*, was not happy with the production she envisaged. He felt strongly that the staging would be very difficult to handle, and the fascinating descriptive detail of the novel, which is certainly part of its appeal, would be completely lost. *When in Rome* never reached the stage, although Ngaio continued to tinker with it off and on for over a year. As a film, however, the novel would have worked well, especially if the atmosphere of Rome, which had gripped the author so positively, could have been captured as the mystery unfolds.

Back in London, Ngaio was confronted with another set of proofs from Little, Brown in America, and after meetings with friends to say farewell, and a few interviews, the visit was coming to an end. Perhaps for the first time she was beginning to feel less in tune with London life, as she revealed to Graham Lord in a *Sunday Express* interview just before she left in December. The streets at night were frightening in a way they had never been before:

> I love London and I find it all very stimulating. In fact I get more of an emotional feeling coming back to London than I do when I go back to New Zealand—a real turnover of the heart. But it's changed very much in feeling. I do a lot of writing at night and I like to go out and walk around the block to freshen up. But this trip, for the first time, I felt uneasy. I left off doing it. I felt someone might knock me on the head.

Dorothy joined the ship in Nassau as planned, and found Ngaio laid low with the bronchitis which was widespread among the passengers. She too shared this ailment by the time they had gone through the Panama Canal and were steaming up the California coast. But it was a relaxing time, even though Dorothy found her friend now 'really quite frail and more than a little deaf'. At leisure, without the glossy public image that was part of her London persona, Ngaio was indeed beginning to look, and feel, her age.

CHAPTER 10

Her Greatest Hour: 1972–75

The Ngaio Marsh who was called upon to produce a play for the opening of the James Hay Theatre in the new civic centre in Christchurch in 1972 is revealed in photographs as careworn and tired. Originally Tyrone Guthrie had been expected to open the theatre with a production of the medieval drama *Everyman*, but his health was failing, and he died in 1971. Ngaio was invited to take over this prestigious, but demanding, task. She chose *Henry V* for the occasion, not because it was one of her favourites, but because it was a chance to exult in spectacle and to use Shakespearean theatre as a source of direct public experience. Ngaio saw *Henry V* as a play about the interaction between the audience, standing and jostling in the pit in Elizabethan England, and the players, struggling to sweep the audience away to the shores of France and to battles in foreign fields. She wrote perceptively about this aspect of the play:

> Like many another dramatist who was to follow him, Shakespeare was irked and frustrated by the theatre's limitations and excited by its potential. So he created 'Chorus' to explode upon the opening scene with his 'O, for a Muse of fire', to lament and apologise and exult and light a flame in the hearts of his unruly audiences. Again and again he came before them at that opening performance, four centuries ago in The Globe, to woo, to beckon, to reach out over the physical and emotional gulf that every actor must bridge. It is in the thoughts of the audience, he insists, that the reality of a play is born . . .[1]

The 1972 production of *Henry V* was the nearest thing to community theatre that Christchurch had ever seen. The cast of

215

nearly 100 was backed up by a production staff of the same size, with many more helpers from the student body and from the city. Jonathan Elsom was invited from England to play the part of Chorus, and many of Ngaio's reliable and experienced actors were cast. Helen Holmes was invaluable as Ngaio's right hand, calling for her in her car and briefing her on what needed to be done. Often Ngaio was so fatigued that she could hardly remember which scene they were about to rehearse, but once on stage the old charisma returned and her power as a director seemed enhanced, not diminished, by age. As preliminary rehearsals were going ahead, Ngaio quietly celebrated her seventy-seventh birthday.

This was to be Ngaio's final production of a Shakespeare play, and it was also the most challenging for her. The James Hay Theatre seated an audience of nearly 1,000 in a fan-shaped auditorium with an open stage. The acoustics were untried, workmen were still busy up to the last minute, and, worst of all, the sophisticated new lighting system was held up by a dock strike in England. The lights failed to arrive in time, and desperate temporary measures were taken to hire lights from suppliers all over New Zealand and Australia. Although promised rehearsal time in the theatre for five weeks before opening night, the cast were in fact allowed access to the stage only two days before the opening performance, and those 48 hours had to include the dress rehearsal as well as mechanical and lighting rehearsals. Helen Holmes and others worked throughout the final night to prepare the stage.

Even in the midst of such chaos, Ngaio had arranged a proverbial 'touch of magic'. Her perception of Chorus as speaking for Shakespeare himself had been at the back of her mind for some time, and she wrote to Jonathan, then still in England, to obtain a Shakespeare wig, modelled on the Shakespeare Monument in the parish church at Stratford-upon-Avon. (This bust was probably based on the Droeshout engraving that prefaces the First Folio edition of Shakespeare.) Her idea was that Jonathan, dressed as Shakespeare, should emerge from a mysterious mist at the back of the stage, walking down towards the audience and begging them to give him 'a Muse of Fire; that would ascend/The brightest heaven of invention'. They had kept this a secret from the rest of the cast, and Jonathan still remembers their amazement at the dress rehearsal when, against a blue cyclorama, dry ice quietly fizzing in the background, he emerged from the mists of time. The device also captivated the audience, and Bruce Mason, who was there as reviewer for the New Zealand *Listener*, wrote to Ngaio: 'I was lost in admiration of much of it; the Droeshout idea was inspired, and brilliantly executed by Jonathan . . . The opening was quite unforgettable: a brilliant idea, and astonishing and dazzling'.[2] The device became a legend and even Ngaio's actors who went on to work overseas remember it as a 'marvellous imaginative insight'.

Ngaio replied to Bruce with some feeling about the teething troubles of the new theatre: 'all I can say is . . . the James Hay Theatre must have the jaws and dental equipment of a dinosaur'. The safety curtain gave trouble all the way through, delaying even the opening performance, and on one occasion kept the audience waiting for an hour while someone clambered about in the flies trying to free it.

The first performance was on Sunday, 1 October 1972, and the season ran for ten days. Every night was sold out. Ngaio avoided the obvious jingoism of the play, presenting Henry as 'a complex, faulty, lonely and troubled young man', but still dazzling in his royalty. Whether it was a wise decision to have two actors sharing the role is hard to say, as each offered a different interpretation. One was experienced in Shakespearean roles, the other was a young newcomer, but the decision indicated yet again how the director liked to give youth a chance to shine. She knew it was 'a bold and hazardous step' but, having made the decision, she stuck to it. Her sense of poetic rhythm and her ability to orchestrate crowds was shown to full advantage, and Bruce Mason admired above all 'the heraldic ebb and flow of it, and the sense of space and distance, so that one seemed many times not to be in a theatre at all but in the midst of some endless unfolding panorama of life and history'.[3]

Ngaio had confided to Denys Rhodes in a letter written in August that 'I am lost in wonder that an old girl like your Ish can stay the course', and retired into 'a sort of not unpleasant haze of exhaustion for several weeks'. Perhaps because of extreme fatigue, Ngaio fell on the steep path to her house, but although badly bruised and severely shaken, suffered no serious injury. It was well after Christmas before she could force herself to start work on a new novel, conscious that in 1972 she had done nothing to boost her income. The notion that she was driven by financial necessity to keep writing was completely false, as the new novels were selling well, serials were running on radio, and Ngaio Marsh Ltd. was flush with funds. Nevertheless, Ngaio was terrified of not having enough money to live on, and Elric Hooper remembers with sympathetic amusement once finding her in tears over a large tax bill, saying 'But Elric, what shall I do for my old age?' She would have been in her eighties at that time.

The preoccupation with *Henry V* had given Ngaio little chance to think about a production of one of her own plays, *Murder Sails at Midnight* which was touring in Britain in 1972 and 1973. Valentine Dyall played Roderick Alleyn, with Richard Scott as Mr Merryman, the murderer who obsessively strangles his victims and then sprinkles them with flower petals. The play was well received in theatres from Croydon to Aberdeen, and it was sold out on many occasions. Although the producer David Kirk considered Mr Merryman the most interesting part for an actor, he felt that his star had to play Alleyn in order not to offend 'whodunit' etiquette.

Meanwhile in New York Dorothy Olding had been making attempts to place a children's novel, *The Faraway Boy*, with a New York publisher, without success. This novel, written several years earlier, remains unpublished. It is a fairy-tale set in Scotland, and although no worse than many vaguely charming stories of its type, it is certainly no better. The reader for Little, Brown, who reluctantly rejected it, thought it lacked a sense of place or character, like a pastel sketch rather than an oil painting. He makes the shrewd suggestion that Ngaio could use a New Zealand legend or background and write 'a unique and fascinating children's book'. Given the use of Maori culture in *Colour Scheme* this idea was very creative, but by now Ngaio was probably too old to embark on a new direction of this kind. Thirty years earlier, perhaps, at a time when Shakespeare was not such a dominating force in her life, she might have felt the confidence to use Maori legend in this way, as several recent Australian writers have done with Aboriginal myths. Certainly Ngaio's response to New Zealand landscape and the natural world is always vividly expressed in the rare snatches of description she allows herself in her detective novels, and her fondness for children would appear an obvious incentive to write for them. Of course the problem, as always for Ngaio, with her strong bias towards Europe, would have been the temptation to use misty, ethereal tales from the northern hemisphere rather than forging a new store of legends and tales from her own country.

By the beginning of 1973 Ngaio was beginning to regain her strength, and she wrote to Denys in March:

> I've gone into purdah with a new book. It's always a huge effort to get back into harness after an interval in the theatre and this time it's been uphill all the way. Any excuse not to sit down and grind out words, a long opening period when anything one does seems to stink to high Heaven and at last, with any luck, the trembling hope that perhaps, after all, it's not quite ghastly. I've saddled myself this time with a complicated and hideously exacting *mise-en-scène* and am just crossing the half-way mark, full of black forebodings laced with pale streaks of hope.

March was made memorable by the visit to New Zealand of J. B. Priestley and his wife, Jacquetta Hawkes. Ngaio had been acquainted with them for several years, and had stayed with them at their elegant country house, Kissing Tree, in Warwickshire. Priestley's trip to New Zealand was set up by his publishers, Heinemann, and sponsored by the New Zealand government. If they had hoped for a glossy travel book about beautiful New Zealand, they must have been disappointed. Although there are some interesting and perceptive comments about the country and its people in *A Visit to New Zealand* (1974), the narrative often reveals a rather crusty and tired old man, who at the age of seventy-nine, dozing in the car as he was driven through New Zealand's magnificent scenery, lacked the energy to deal with the public demands made of him.

But his visit to Christchurch was almost entirely successful, and included dinner with Ngaio and her friends. The story of how the Priestleys' flight from Dunedin was cancelled because of a strike, and how they had to charter a small private plane to make the journey to Christchurch, is well told in Priestley's book. He found that to his surprise 'this was the only occasion in which I really enjoyed flying',[4] and the comfortable and spacious modern hotel in Christchurch, in its pleasant setting beside the River Avon, put the Priestleys in an excellent mood for Ngaio's dinner party that night. Despite the many problems of the last few months, Ngaio took exquisite care with the arrangements, and this did not go unnoticed. Priestley recorded that

> it was altogether an exceptionally good dinner party. Our hostess had brought to it her considerable social experience and her drama director's eye for decor and detail. We tried to match the excellent food and wine with our talk, sitting at a round table in a panelled dining-room, looking across the flames from the great silver candelabra. It was almost like the first act of a high comedy at the Josef Stadt, Vienna. We were a mixed but civilised lot, with some ballast of legal folk and academics, but with the Theatre never far away. [5]

Present at the dinner were Ngaio's long-standing theatre colleagues, Gerald Lascelles, Helen Holmes, David Hindin and Mervyn Thompson, who was now beginning to find his feet as a producer and dramatist.

Priestley and Jacquetta commented to each other later on the sense of going into an old family home, which is of course the impression that Ngaio strived very hard to create. To Jacquetta it was 'so good, too, to see an old-fashioned family house of gentlefolk', an accolade that would have given Ngaio much satisfaction. Mrs Priestley also remembered that 'evidently I had been talking rather too assertively about the flight and our determination not to fail her (or something of the kind) when with a mischievous look she said, "We would have had dinner without you, you know" '. To which Jacquetta generously commented, 'I was evidently touché since I remembered this passage when much good talk is forgotten'.

Their visit to Christchurch included a tour around the new Civic Centre, which impressed them both: 'the best short description of this Christchurch Town Hall is that it's a knock-out'.[6] Ngaio and Helen Holmes showed them around, and Mrs Priestley was surprised to realise just how important the theatre was to her friend; infinitely more so than her novels: 'she made it plain that her greatest hour was to have directed the opening play—*Henry V*'. In Christchurch J. B. Priestley found all the Anglo-Saxon virtues with a refreshing sense of achievement. The visit ended with a successful picnic in the hills, which were bright with autumn colours and fresh with the scent of winter blowing from the Alps. Jacquetta went for a walk, J. B. painted pictures, and Ngaio sat and brooded on her latest plot. Judging by Priestley's book, this was probably the happiest part of their visit to New Zealand, and they left Christchurch with regret for the thermal resort of Rotorua.

The novel Ngaio was thinking about as she sat on a tussock eating sandwiches with the Priestleys was *Black as He's Painted*, and on 5 June 1973 she wrote exultantly to Pamela Mann that she had just written the last word. The title was not settled at that stage, and Ngaio wrote to Dorothy Olding in New York, about the possibility of using 'What's Horrible', a favourite phrase used by her editor at Little, Brown, Ned Bradford. Ned liked to begin his letters and memos in this way, assuming that in the maelstrom of publishing there was bound to be a crisis somewhere. Indeed, a cable sent to the *Oronsay* in December 1971, when Dorothy and Ngaio were somewhere in the Panama Canal, began like this, and the subject was lost proofs. The title went through a number of changes—'Unfinished Portrait', 'Skin Deep', 'Black Mark', 'Black Background', 'Black As He Is Painted', and finally Black as He's Painted. Both Dorothy Olding and Edmund Cork were full of praise for the novel, and her editor Robert Knittel wrote enthusiastically from Collins on 12 September:

> I have just finished reading your latest novel and I think it is splendid. A real vintage Ngaio Marsh. The Boomer is a terrific character, he really dominates the story as he was meant to and all the other people in the book are also extremely credible, including Lucy the cat.

The flurry of supportive letters about the manuscript arrived as Ngaio was again recovering from a fall on her slippery garden path, this time serious enough to send her to Wellington for treatment. With her deep desire for personal privacy, and, perhaps, to keep her public image inviolable, Ngaio was always very reluctant to let people know when she was unwell. She was very secretive about the whole affair, and in July her secretary Rosemary Greene wrote to Dorothy Olding, saying simply that Ngaio was away in Wellington but without giving the reason. Not until September did Ngaio confess that she had been less than hale and hearty, and by this delay she unwittingly created problems for Dorothy in New York.

Esquire magazine had commissioned a number of short stories from different authors, including one from Ngaio, but she was not enthusiastic and the deadline passed. Then they cabled to her, extending the deadline to August, by which time Ngaio was convalescing in Wellington. Eventually they reached her by telephone, offering her a dollar a word. Instead of admitting that she was unwell, Ngaio decided to try to produce a story, although she confided to Dorothy that 'as you know I'm not much of a short story writer'. What Ngaio managed to produce was a version of a story she had drafted many years ago, 'A Fool About Money', about two ladies suspecting each other of rifling their purses in a railway compartment. Ngaio dispatched the story on time, but with considerable misgivings. Then the problems began.

Esquire decided not to publish any of the commissioned stories after all, and Dorothy insisted that they pay the $1,000 as promised. The subsequent correspondence between the doughty agent and the editor of *Esquire* is a masterly joust of conflicting prose styles. From Gordon Lish at *Esquire*:

> Would you like to hear me tell you that things are tough for me? That I'm crazy for you? That it's very difficult keeping my shoes shined? Myself sober?

Dorothy thundered by return of post:

> I cannot agree that 'Esquire' is not obligated to pay $1,000 for the Ngaio Marsh story even though you do not intend to publish it . . .

Dorothy won. Gordon Lish capitulated the following day:

> Okay, okay, okay. You matter to us more than the grand does. Heaps more. Check coming . . . Friends?[7]

Meanwhile Ngaio was feeling guilty about pursuing *Esquire* over a story with which she herself had not been happy, but Dorothy reassured her: 'if "Esquire" pays us for the piece you did for them so willingly and under difficulty, and I hope they will, I think we should accept it. They made the terms and should adhere to them; besides they have plenty of money and can afford it'. So that was that; Ngaio got her payment, Dorothy's status was enhanced, and the story was eventually published in *Ellery Queen Mystery Magazine* in December 1974.

Dorothy's other efforts on behalf of Ngaio, to secure serial publication of *Black as He's Painted* in such American magazines as *Good Housekeeping* and *Redbook* were not successful, but *Woman's Journal* in London accepted it for serial publication from 1 January 1974.

Christmas 1973 was a mixture of proof-correcting under pressure for Little, Brown, and the Christmas Tree party, this time for thirty-seven visitors, the usual mixture of adults and children. Ngaio wrote to Maureen Balfour early in November saying that she was already busy decorating the boxes—'they seem to take ages to prepare and get more elaborate every year, I can't think why'. She had also been entertaining her old friends Lord Ballantrae and his wife, Laura, who had returned to New Zealand for a holiday.

By the end of the year Ngaio had firmly decided to make a booking for another trip 'home' in 1974. The choice of passenger liners travelling to England was now very limited, but she managed to secure a passage on the P&O liner *Oriana*, which was leaving on 4 March for England via the Pacific Ocean and the Panama Canal, and calling at various ports around the United States. Ngaio had hoped that Dorothy might be able to join her for this part of the trip, perhaps between San Francisco and Miami, but Dorothy was too busy and Ngaio was reluctant to leave the ship and travel overland to New York. Eventually they planned to meet in London in May, a simpler solution for them both. Ngaio also wrote enthusiastically to Maureen in Kent: 'I can't wait to begin painting funny faces on hard-boiled eggs for Easter'. The New Zealand press was painting an alarming view of an England suffering from strikes and terrorism, and Ngaio wondered if she would be 'groping about in the dark, shuddering with cold and dodging bombs'. In referring to Walnut Tree Farm as a refuge from all this she was joking, yet the Balfours did provide a very necessary refuge for her later that year, when a serious operation for cancer brought her closer than ever before to a realisation that her life might soon be over. This was to be Ngaio's last trip back to England, and although a triumph in many ways it made her aware of her own vulnerability and how dependent she was on her many friends, who were to offer unstinting support through her final years.

The journey to England this time was pleasant and uneventful. Ngaio enjoyed shipboard life without any illness. Sailing into San Francisco harbour at dawn was unforgettable: Ngaio was among the small group of passengers invited to join the captain on the bridge as they sailed under the Golden Gate Bridge. This visit must have sparked off the idea for another shipboard mystery; her papers contain a sketch of a ship's bridge in her own hand and a drawing of the same area in a very neat hand, obviously prepared by an officer, and dated 27 March 1974. Extensive notes for a novel called 'Seascape' accompany this, involving passengers who are first encountered on the ship's bridge at dawn. The list of characters gives an interesting indication of how Ngaio planned her mature fiction, beginning, as always, with the interaction of characters:

1. The Victim – a Philandering Officer (PhO)
2. The Guilty – a Woman Doctor (WDr)
3. The Other Woman – (OW)
4. First Suspect – Another passenger in love with OW (OP)
5. Possible Intended Victim – Naval Officer? (NavO)
6. Suspect if Nav. O was intended victim - Seaman who has it in for him
7. OW's husband – Rich Business Man (RBM) like Mr. R.
8. Captain Eros

The voyage was to involve Troy, sailing out of Honolulu after painting an altarpiece, and Alleyn, who would join the ship at Nassau after investigating an illicit drugs case. In a fragment of the novel Troy muses about Captain Eros: 'If he were a fruit, Troy thought, he would be a black-currant. Not that apart from his scant hair and smallish eyes, he was particularly dark. He inclined to be rosy. His mouth was small and in repose looked as if it was buttoned up against an inclination to giggle'. But Ngaio went on to give Captain Eros 'immense authority, the more impressive for being unstressed'.[8] He was obviously intended to be a stronger character than the hard-drinking captain who had failed to support Alleyn in *Singing in the Shrouds*.

Sixteen pages of notes, including a sketch of Troy sunbathing, form a tantalising embryo novel which would probably have grown to full term if Ngaio had not been so frantically busy on arrival in England, and unexpectedly taken ill after four months. The sketch contains all the typical Marsh detective novel features, starting with a group of interesting characters, most of whom she would have closely observed during a sustained period aboard ship, and involving precise detail on ships, their officers, cabins and commands that she had gathered on many lengthy sea voyages. These sketches make an intriguing comparison to the notebook jottings of Agatha Christie, which are invariably concerned with incidents and dramatic events. 'Seascape' looks promising, but prevented from developing it by her exceptionally heavy schedule Ngaio must have lost interest in the plot and turned instead to other possibilities.

At the beginning of April 1974 Ngaio was again settled in the Basil Street Hotel, which she affectionately called 'the pub'. *Black as He's Painted* had just come out in Britain, and there were several press and radio interviews, together with the pleasant bustle of seeing old friends.

Even more strenuous were the literary lunches in the north of England arranged by her publishers. At the first, given by the *Birmingham Post* on 24 April, Ngaio shared the top table with novelist Henry Cecil and biographer Margaret Laing. After a couple of days back in London Ngaio was off again, this time to a *Yorkshire Post* literary lunch on 7 May. Here she was in the company of Julian Symons and H. R. F. Keating, and they solved the *Times* crossword puzzle on the train on the way to Yorkshire. Although Harry Keating is now a well-known writer and President of the elite Detection Club, having taken over from Julian Symons, he was then a very young arrival on the literary scene, and his detective, Inspector Ghote, had not yet become a favourite. Keating remembers the book-signing sessions after lunch, with huge crowds for Ngaio, a respectable number for Symons, and for himself a handful of people who had got bored waiting in the other queues. But as a young writer he was grateful for the serious interest that Ngaio took in his work, and for her view that he was doing something worthwhile. He was aware of that sense of receiving Ngaio's full attention that so many of her friends have referred to, and found it 'very flattering'. On the train back to London the three writers talked shop, and Julian Symons revealed that he was searching for a title suitable for his new novel based on Sherlock Holmes. After listening to his description of the plot, Ngaio suggested without hesitation 'A Three Pipe Problem', and Symons was delighted. The book, published in 1975, was dedicated to Ngaio Marsh, 'who gave me the title'. Later that year Ngaio was finally made a member of the Detection Club, along with John le Carré, Peter Lovesey and Gwendoline Butler, but she was too ill to attend the ceremony.

Back in London, Ngaio made plans to meet Dorothy Olding in June, something she looked forward to very much. Before Dorothy's arrival, Ngaio had again been north, this time to stay in Holyrood House in Edinburgh as a guest of Lord Ballantrae, who was then Lord High Commissioner of the General Assembly of the Church of Scotland. *Black as He's Painted* was still on the *Sunday Times* bestseller list, and Ngaio continued to be much in demand for talks and interviews. Eventually she managed to escape for a few quiet weeks in Kent before visiting the Priestleys at Kissing Tree House, and joining Bob and Mizzy Stead for a canal cruise in Warwickshire.

On her return from Warwickshire, even the indomitable Ngaio had to admit that she was seriously ill. Within a few weeks she was undergoing major surgery for cancer (a hysterectomy) in King's College Hospital, London. On the dates when she had hoped to be visiting Dorothy in New York, Ngaio was slowly re-covering from her operation. Although she had written to Maureen that she expected to be 'in cracking form' after the operation, the close friends who gathered round knew that she was very much afraid she was going to die. This did not, however, prevent a group of Ngaio's actors entertaining her until the small hours the night before the operation, and eventually being thrown out by the hospital staff at 3 a.m. for being too rowdy.

Ngaio had a high opinion of her surgeon, Mr Brudenell, whose ancestors had been in the Charge of the Light Brigade, and she confided to James Laurenson that her pre-med hallucination included a vision of Mr Brudenell advancing down the ward towards her swinging a scimitar. James Laurenson, who had been a powerful Macbeth in Christchurch and was then acting with the

Royal Shakespeare Company, visited Ngaio a few days after the operation. His scurrilous theatrical tales so entertained her that the stitches in her incision began to give way, and wiping tears of laughter from her eyes, she had to summon help. As James crept away he wondered guiltily if Ngaio's recovery had been seriously set back by his extravagant accounts of current production disasters at the RSC, but concluded philosophically that helpless laughter at theatrical confusion was probably the ideal way for Ngaio to go, if go she must.

Fortunately the stitches were swiftly repaired and Ngaio made an excellent, though slow, recovery. She left hospital on 2 October to convalesce with the 'kindest and dearest of friends' in Kent, Maureen and John Balfour. By the end of the month, but in a quavering hand, she was able to write to Dorothy in New York. Already she was talking business, referring to a new deal concluded for *Black as He's Painted* and suggesting that 'after glancing in horror at hospital bills I think in a panic that I ought to get cracking on a book but will wait until I'm a bit more nippy on my pins—and in my top storey if it comes to that'. She apologises for being 'the woman who never stops talking about her operations, which is just about the deadliest form of woman it can be one's misfortune to meet'.

After a series of medical checks early in 1975, Ngaio was allowed to travel to Jersey for a holiday at the end of February. Again she was accompanied by Joan Pullen, who helped with the travel arrangements. The change of scene, even with the inevitable bout of stomach trouble, cheered her up enormously, and, looking out over empty beaches and sparkling sea from her bedroom window, she began to write another novel. This was to be *Last Ditch*, which is set on an unidentified Channel Island, and gives a large role to the Alleyns' son Ricky, now an Oxford graduate. Notes exist for another Channel Island novel which gives a prominent place to Alleyn's valued associate Inspector Fox who, supposedly on holiday, begins to uncover a drug ring. As with 'Seascape' the details are ingenious and the plot full of promise, but nothing exists beyond a few handwritten pages.

Ngaio's confidence in herself was gradually returning. This was helped not only by the start of her new novel, but also by a commission from Granada Television to write a play for their popular 'Crown Court' series. These courtroom dramas always ended on a cliffhanger, with the audience as jury being invited to decide the outcome of the case. Prosecuting Counsel in the series was Ngaio's protégé Jonathan Elsom, and Joan Hickson, later to become much loved for her flawless portrayal of Miss Marple on television, also had a part. The script is not one of Ngaio's most powerful pieces, but it has an attractive quirky humour. Ngaio researched it by accompanying Maureen, who was a Justice of the Peace, to the local Magistrate's Court and to the Crown Court in Maidstone.

'Evil Liver' begins with a squabble between neighbours over a dog chasing (and catching) a cat, an apparently trivial episode, but to use one of Ngaio's favourite metaphors, the ball of wool starts to unwind and all the knots give way. Eventually a murder is uncovered, centring on poisoned liver, hence the punning title for the play. Rehearsals took place during July, and Ngaio was well enough to travel to Manchester to see them in the studio. The three episodes were complete before she had to leave for New Zealand in August. Joan Hickson, who showed Ngaio around the Granada studios, noticed her interest in all the practical details of lighting and cameras. Gazing up at the dark galleries and gantries overhead, she remarked feelingly, 'Oh, I *do* think that this would be a marvellous place for a murder!'

The prospect of returning to New Zealand via New York had eventually been shelved when Ngaio decided that she could not afford it, but she may not have been able to face the effort involved. Eventually Dorothy agreed to fly to San Francisco when the ship called there before striking off across the Pacific. Ngaio wrote to Dorothy about her regret at leaving England: 'everything here is now astronomically expensive and there are awful anxieties and prophecies of doom but in my book it's still the England I love and I'm leaving it with sorrow'.

She spent the last few days in London, saying goodbye to friends and doing some shopping. Ngaio had ordered some clothes at Hardy Amies, and she wrote amusingly to Maureen about the manageress being 'in smashing form and running about the shop—literally running—which is in itself a comic phenomenon, as she was trying to serve several ladies all at the same time and her ecstasies were shrill indeed and could be heard up and down the fitting room: "Fabulous. It's fabulous. Aren't you delighted? Don't you look fantastic?" She was so busy that her hair began to fall down—probably for the first time in history. I will allow and must admit that the black dress is really very good indeed and will live, I should think, quite as long as I do . . .'

On 4 August 1975 Ngaio and Joan Pullen sailed on the *Oronsay*, a ship she had sailed on before, and which was now making her final voyage before being broken up. Did Ngaio suspect that she was never to see her beloved London again? She must have known that, with increasingly fragile health, the likelihood of another visit was remote, but even after several heart attacks during the last years of her life, she never lost the hope of another trip back until very near the end. 'That London feeling', the zest for life that always came to her when she first arrived, released from the confinement of provincial New Zealand life, was very hard to see as something that could no longer be realised.

The voyage did not go well, and Ngaio longed for it to be over. She contracted food poisoning almost immediately, along with most of the other passengers. This was followed by severe bronchitis, and her hopes of making progress on *Last Ditch* during the long weeks at sea came to nothing. She had already written about 40,000 words of the first draft while staying at Walnut Tree Farm, so she was able to show half the book, then called 'Deep Cove', to Dorothy Olding when they met in San Francisco as arranged.

Ngaio was feeling very unwell, and the reunion was far from the joyous occasion it might have been. She described herself to Dorothy as 'a feeble creature', unworthy of Dorothy's kindness in crossing America to see her. Since this was to be their last meeting Dorothy was later very glad that she had made the effort, but Ngaio's ill health was a matter for concern. Dorothy was also worried about 'Deep Cove', which she had skimmed through while sitting in Ngaio's cabin on board the *Oronsay*. Back in New York she wrote to Edmund Cork's daughter, Pat, in London, who had taken over most of the work of the agency from her father: 'had only time to read seventy odd pages of her new book which I thought very slow and wandering but didn't tell her'. Substantial cuts in the opening sections were eventually agreed, and Dorothy was able to write her usual enthusiastic letters to Ngaio. Both

Dorothy Olding and Pat Cork were well aware of how vulnerable Ngaio felt about her fiction, and they treated her with great sensitivity at this time.

The *Oronsay*, sailed on across the Pacific, and was described by Ngaio as a hospital ship as more and more people became ill. Ngaio said nothing about this to her good friends in Kent, instead dispatching a series of amusing letters describing the adventures of her companion Joan Pullen in her tiny cabin piled up with luggage and peering out above it, 'the general effect being like Pyramus and Thisbe'. There was also the ongoing saga of strange items smuggled into her luggage; this time it was not a set of false teeth (these had been sent to New Zealand in a hollowed-out copy of a Japanese edition of one of Ngaio's novels and caused quite a start to a casual browser among the bookshelves one day) but a scarlet altar-cloth which Ngaio had been carrying back and forth across the Pacific for years. Despite all her attempts to leave it at Walnut Tree Farm in a carefully selected hiding place, Maureen always managed to arrange for it to be found in Ngaio's suitcase when she opened it at sea.

By the end of September 1975 she was very relieved to be back in her own house in the Cashmere Hills, enjoying the spring flowers in her garden—'it's a mass of fruit blossom, wattle, camellias, daphne and all the good smellers and lookers'. Lady McIntosh had met her at Auckland and escorted her to Wellington, and she was met at dawn in Lyttelton Harbour by her secretary Rosemary Greene and 'three of my young theatre chaps'. They arranged for her favourite homecoming, driving her up over the hills to look over the light-filled Canterbury Plains. Other friends had tidied up her garden and Ngaio was deeply touched by the warm welcome she received from many people who had been concerned about her illness during the past year. Even her favourite cat, Lt Pinkerton (RN Rtd), gave her such an ecstatic welcome that he raced around, jumped up on the grand piano and broke two T'ang dynasty ceramics. His high spirits must have continued as did Ngaio's own pleasure at his company, because in her next letter to Maureen she apologises for the peculiar writing caused by Lt Pinkerton jumping on her lap and playing with her pen.

As soon as house and garden were restored to Ngaio's high standards after an absence of a year and a half, and the after-effects of the food poisoning from the *Oronsay* had been treated, Ngaio had to force herself to finish off 'Deep Cove', which had made little progress during the past few months. As usual, the final stages were a dreadful grind, and she wrote to Maureen in November about 'this wretched book' and how she would be 'thankful indeed when it's behind me'. It was not published until 1977, after extensive revisions. Ngaio joked about the eventual title, *Last Ditch*, warning her friends that this should not be taken as an indication that she was giving up for good. But neither *Last Ditch* nor the subsequent novel, *Grave Mistake*, published in 1978, can be considered vintage Marsh. Real creative stimulus was to come from a return to the New Zealand landscapes that she loved, the Southern Alps that are the setting for her penultimate novel, *Photo-Finish*. After all, Roderick Alleyn had promised to show his wife this spectacular country when he wrote to her from Mount Moon station in *Died in the Wool*, and by using an invitation to Troy to paint a portrait, Ngaio added a touch of exoticism that had been sadly wanting in her previous two novels.

CHAPTER 11

A Final Flourish: 1976–82

The year 1975 ended with Ngaio directing a play, writing a book and holding a Christmas party as though nothing had changed. The Christmas Tree was, as always, a treasured opportunity to invite old friends and their families to the house, and perhaps to pretend that she was in better health than was really the case. Her friends were so pleased to have her back that they made a particular effort with the entertainment for the Christmas Tree that year, and they had an elaborate programme printed, which offered an 'Incredible Extravaganza' presented by 'Theatrical Families Inc'. The play was called 'Red Riding Hood Incarnadine' or 'All Swell that Eat Well' or 'The Battered Bard', and its starry cast consisted of Pyramus and Thisbe, Pistol and Bardolph, Red Riding Hood, Herne the Hunter, Grandma and a TV Announcer.

But nothing could be guaranteed to revive her more than a medicinal dose of Shakespeare, especially when it was administered by her old friend Jonathan Elsom. Jonathan had returned to New Zealand on a visit with plans to devise a one-man show called 'Sweet Mr. Shakespeare', and wanted Ngaio both to direct him and to help to write the script. Ngaio threw herself into the project with enthusiasm, causing her to abandon *Last Ditch* for several weeks. Between them they crafted an elegant script, a mixture of biography, anecdotes, sonnets and speeches. The show was well received at the Court Theatre in Christchurch, and moved to Downstage in Wellington for a short season in March 1976. Ngaio accompanied Jonathan to Wellington where Bruce Mason, reviewing the performance for the daily paper the *Dominion*, found it 'a patrician entertainment, a grave and moving nocturnal meditation of the highest accomplishment'.

Ngaio was determined that Jonathan should get more recognition for the piece, and tried hard through Dorothy Olding in New York to set up a tour of American campuses. But Jonathan was not well known, and a success in New Zealand was light years away from success in the United States. American agents were unimpressed. Meanwhile Jonathan had returned to England and secured a good part in Tom Stoppard's West End hit *Dirty Linen*. Ngaio wrote rather frostily to NewYork, pointing out that Jonathan would soon be playing on Broadway when the Stoppard play transferred, and implying that the opportunity to sign up a fine actor and an original piece of theatre had been missed. Eleven years later the famous Shakespearean actor Ian McKellen was very successful with a similar one-man show in London, *Acting Shakespeare*, but the Marsh/Elsom collaboration must have been either ahead of its time or behind it; the piece was never staged outside New Zealand, although it was filmed for Norwegian Television in 1985.

As well as being heavily involved with 'Sweet Mr. Shakespeare', Ngaio found time to make a short *Encounter* programme for Television New Zealand, which began with her sweeping up the Cashmere Hills at the wheel of her Jaguar XK150. The image of the indestructible, glamorous woman was still there for the cameras, but failing eyesight due to cataracts would soon mean that her driving days were numbered, and the steep path up to the house was an increasing trial. Nevertheless she went out driving with Jonathan to practise for her driving test which needed renewal, not because she really expected to drive much in the future, but to prove to herself that she could still do it. She passed the test.

By Easter 1976 *Last Ditch* had finally taken shape, after an unprecedented number of cuts and alterations. Ngaio, never bursting with confidence about any of her manuscripts, had been seriously worried about this one because the writing had been so interrupted that she never managed to achieve the sustained period of composition she preferred. Writing to Lord Ballantrae she admitted, 'I despaired of this one; to such an extent indeed that I jolly nearly scrapped the brute'.[1] She was far from happy with even the much corrected manuscript—'I privately thought it stank', she told Maureen, 'all those stops and starts, you know'—but in May Billy Collins wrote personally to tell her it was 'marvellous' and that he 'enjoyed it as much as any book of yours I have read'. As was often the case, the agents discussed the script fairly frankly among themselves but concealed their reservations from the author. Dorothy Olding wrote to Pat Cork in London: 'I enjoyed it though I did think it petered out a bit at the end (which of course I won't tell her) . . .'[2] The same day she wrote enthusiastically to Ngaio, saying how much she had enjoyed it.

This tactful approach was obviously the right one. Ngaio was sufficiently encouraged by their praise to start work on another novel, Grave Mistake, which was set in a village very like Birling near Walnut Tree Farm. While coping with the proofs of Last Ditch she also wrote a short piece, 'Birth of a Sleuth', for well-known American publisher and bookseller Otto Penzler, describing how she started to write detective fiction, and how Roderick Alleyn got his name. This short essay was published the following year in a journal called The Writer. Ngaio wrote it swiftly and found it 'regrettably twee' but readers were delighted by it. At last she had been persuaded to write something serious about her fiction. It was matched shortly afterwards by 'Portrait of Troy', which was published in Murderess Ink: The Better Half of the Mystery (1979), edited by Dilys Wynn.

By now her eyesight was becoming seriously impaired and she was increasingly affected by deafness, working her way through a series of hearing aids, none of which were satisfactory. After-effects of her operation needed further attention, and she wrote to Pamela Mann about being prodded and X-rayed: 'I am thought to perhaps "have fluid" . . . though what they propose to do about it if it's there I don't know. Put in a kitchen tap, perhaps, that I can turn on and off at will'. But she wrote cheerfully to Maureen that she was 'keeping well, as if one was a pot of jam', and was leading a quiet and uneventful life. Cold weather kept her close to home. The winter months of July and August 1976 were particularly harsh, with thousands of sheep lost in snowdrifts in the Southern Alps. The mountains were deep in snow, creating a vivid picture from Ngaio's bedroom window at first light: 'rose red and shining with only a sea of mist between us'. It was a view she never tired of, a view that made her understand why she always returned to her house on the Cashmere Hills.

The retirement of Ngaio's housekeeper, Mrs Crawford, who

had been with her for over thirty years, was a great blow. She had been with the Marsh family since before Ngaio's father died and was fiercely devoted to her. Not only was she an excellent plain cook but she was happy to keep up the high standards in the house that Ngaio expected. She had been overwhelmed by Ngaio's 'damery' in 1966 but was a little hazy about the exact nature of the award and how Ngaio should be addressed. She started to refer to her as 'our lady', and friends used to delight in phoning up to hear her announce that 'our lady is in the garden but I shall fetch her to the telephone'. Although Mrs Crawford had never lived in, it soon became apparent to Ngaio's friends that before long she would require constant and reliable attention, and this meant substantial alterations to the house to convert Ngaio's study into a housekeeper's flat. For the remaining years of her life, Ngaio became increasingly dependent on the many good friends in Christchurch who were able to offer friendship and practical help. Not only did people like Sylvia Fox, Helen Holmes and Rosemary Greene help Ngaio with everyday problems, both domestic and literary, they also drove her to the theatre so that she could keep in touch. When Bruce Mason had a season at the Court Theatre in September 1976 Ngaio was driven down to see two of his plays. She also managed to travel down to the Acland station at Mount Peel to help out her friend Simon Acland and his wife with a small Arts Festival organised by the Acland family. She gave a reading from *David Copperfield* at the first festival, and used her influence to secure guest performers for future festivals.

Many of those involved in theatre in Christchurch found their way up to Valley Road to consult Ngaio about new developments and, from her vantage point above all the usual theatre rumours and gossip, Ngaio could offer advice and, occasionally, consolation. Mervyn Thompson, now well established as a dramatist and producer, found that on these visits to Ngaio he began to get close to her at last: 'in a one to one relationship Dame Ngaio could be the most sympathetic and loving of people. It was here rather than in her role of theatrical genius that I felt her real greatness. And her essential loneliness . . . Ngaio was all the time helping me to define something in myself and in my work'.[3]

Rumours were beginning to circulate about a New Zealand television production of the three Marsh novels set in New Zealand— *Vintage Murder, Colour Scheme, Died in the Wool*—and *Opening Night*

235

which although it takes place in London theatre, has a New Zealand actress as chief character. Ngaio was concerned about the choice of actor to play Roderick Alleyn. At an early stage, and rather predictably, she suggested Jonathan Elsom or Bruce Mason from New Zealand, but the producers preferred to bring a well-known actor out from England for the role. Ngaio was not displeased with the choice of George Baker—'in looks and ability it's a good choice (I rather reluctantly must concede)'—but she would have been more satisfied to see a friend in the role. Some filming for *Vintage Murder* took place in the old Theatre Royal in Christchurch, and Ngaio was in the audience. The plays were shown on New Zealand television during 1978. The broadcasts brought a great deal of publicity for Ngaio including a caricature of her, mischievously smiling, and holding a cocktail glass on the cover of the wide-circulation New Zealand *Listener*. Although satisfied with George Baker's performance, she felt, with some justification, that the productions lacked pace: 'there was no team element in those television performances—none'. She wrote to Jonathan with a detailed evaluation of all aspects of the plays, concluding: 'The net result was thoroughly professional but the direction was often mistaken, I thought, especially when it came to humour. The director was entirely concentrated on mechanics and seemed to miss the comedy . . . Still, they might have been a lot worse, by and large'.

The year 1976 was marked by the unexpected deaths of two old friends. Bob Stead, the tour manager for the early Australian tour and for the British Commonwealth Players, threw himself from a window. Ngaio wrote to Pamela Mann that she was 'terribly shocked about poor Bobby Stead's death and still can't believe it happened'. Then in September came news of the death, at the age of seventy-six, of Sir William Collins, Chairman of her British publishers. Ngaio had always been flattered by invitations to stay at the Collins' country house, and was perhaps over-deferential to Billy Collins, as she was to many people she considered to be in positions of authority. Ngaio had no difficulty in speaking her mind in New Zealand, as when she tackled Finance Minister Sir Walter Nash personally at a formal dinner party about her swingeing income tax bill, but her engrained acceptance of the British Establishment was hard to shake. And although Billy Collins wrote to her cosily in 1965 about a tax problem, saying 'I would like to help you just like one of the family', Ngaio never seemed to appreciate the fact that as one of the company's bestselling authors she was a valuable commodity, and richly deserved their attention. Ngaio Marsh and her agent belonged to a less financially voracious publishing world than that of today, and she would never ask for more than the publisher offered. Collins were generous with royalties to give her the income she needed, but their advances were low to compensate for this: even her last novel, *Light Thickens*, received an advance of only £1,000 in 1982. Little, Brown, in the US, were more generous with advances but offered less attractive royalties. Although the outsider may feel that there was an element of financial exploitation in Collins' dealing with Ngaio, there is no doubt that she felt secure with them, and the death of Sir William was the loss of a valued friend. The death of Agatha Christie in the same year was also a matter for regret, even though they had met infrequently and only on formal occasions. Ngaio gave a brief interview on New Zealand Radio with some recollections of her fellow crime writer, praising her magnificent ability to create complex and fascinating plots that never failed to engage the reader. Of the four 'Queens of Crime' of the Golden Age of the 1930s, Ngaio was now the only one left.

During much of 1976 attempts had continued in London to mount stage productions of some of Ngaio's novels. A version of *Final Curtain* prepared by Kurt Ganzl was sent out to New Zealand at the end of the year, and Ngaio set about 'an elaborate rejoinery' which involved her in a great deal of effort. Unfortunately, like *When in Rome*, this dramatisation never reached the stage, although the restricted setting of Final Curtain, in an English country house, would have made it much more practical to stage.

At the beginning of 1977 Ngaio was still sitting in her easy chair at Valley Road trying to make progress with *Grave Mistake*, but as with her heroine Verity, who was tinkering with the last act of a play, she faced constant interruptions. In fact the writing did not go much more smoothly than *Last Ditch*. She wrote thoughtfully to Lord Ballantrae, who was becoming more and more of a literary confidant, 'I wish I could set them up in an orderly well-planned fashion as I'm sure my brothers and sisters in crime do. But no. However much I try to discipline myself as to plot and general whodunnitry, I always find myself writing about a set of people in a milieu that, for one reason or another, attracts me. And then, bad cess to it, I have to involve them in some crime or other. Does this mean one is a straight novelist manquée?'[4] In her portrayal of Verity Preston, the self-sufficient middle-aged playwright who finds the intriguing foreigner Nikolas Markos to be the only person in the village with whom she can discuss her work, Ngaio may be writing in a little more of herself than she knew, thinking back to the days when Val Muling would share in the problems of plot and character as her novels developed. Curiously enough Elizabeth Walter at Collins shrewdly spotted this relationship and, in writing to Ngaio about the manuscript when it was finally completed, observed, 'I enjoyed the book enormously, in particular the characters of Verity and Nikolas Markos. I felt you were resisting the temptation to let their mutual attraction develop and indeed I am not at all sure that they were right for each other, but they linger in my mind in the way that the best characters in a book so often do'.

Naturally the novel had been set aside for the Christmas Tree party. For Christmas 1976 there were nearly fifty guests. Although Ngaio was still reasonably healthy for a woman of nearly eighty-two, as well as gout and cataract she was suffering from a hernia that gave her constant discomfort and fatigue. She felt awkward about the 'deafening rumbles' that this condition produced, but pointed out philosophically to Maureen that she could only hear them when she wore her hearing aid, and so was spared embarrassment much of the time.

Several public appearances early in 1977 caused her to take time and trouble for other people, yet Ngaio still loved ceremonial, even though she now moved more slowly and was increasingly unsteady on her feet. Early in March she was invited to introduce a charity performance of Heinrich Schütz's *The Passion According to St Matthew*, to be performed in the Roman Catholic Cathedral in Christchurch. She researched this unfamiliar topic carefully, and produced a graceful and humane introduction, perfectly suited to the audience who were there as much for the charity (the Laura Fergusson Trust for the Disabled, set up by the wife of her old friend) as for the music. Ngaio reminded her audience of the timelessness of great art, comparing the piece to *Hamlet* as a masterpiece of the Renaissance. With great understanding she referred to Schütz's 'lonely old age' and to the fact that he composed the piece in his eightieth year. Ngaio herself was in her eighties when she delivered this address, and was working on her thirtieth novel. The cathedral was packed and Ngaio found the experience moving, even if she did consider herself a very 'wobbly C of E'.

Another public event was a service in the Anglican Cathedral in Christchurch for those holding decorations from the Crown. Ngaio's sense of humour seemed to get the better of her on this occasion:

> We all assembled in Cathedral Square, clanking with ironmongery, to get our marching orders from the Dean. In order to make himself heard he mounted a wooden bench and raised his hands for silence. At this moment, as if on cue, the Cathedral bells, all thirteen of them, burst into a deafening clamour of Treble Bob Majors or Grandsire Triples or whatever. Bootlessly the Dean continued to give out his utterly inaudible instructions, pointing this way and that, while all of us milled about asking each other what was meant. It was most alarming to find the Very Reverend Forefinger singling one out for one knew not what exercise. We formed up in some sort of disorder and entered the Cathedral in a mêlée of distracted banners and puzzled clergy.[5]

With these occasions behind her, Ngaio tried again to concentrate on *Grave Mistake*. By the end of March she was still at Chapter 4, bogged down in a slow-moving plot about a valuable postage stamp, and a murdered body that is added to a newly dug and already occupied grave. The novel is set in an English village and Ngaio admitted that 'Birling has a strong tendency to pop up when least expected'. The narrative lacks the rich, evocative detail of the last novel set here, *Off with His Head*, and the plotting was a struggle that required much rewriting towards the end. Ngaio always hated being interrupted in the middle of a detective novel. She worried about making mistakes that readers would unfailingly pick up, and she was extremely self-critical. *Last Ditch* had suffered from a patchy period of composition, and now *Grave Mistake* was to be held up for several months because of a serious deterioration in her health.

In May 1977 she was admitted to hospital in Christchurch suffering from angina and a thrombosis in her right leg. She wrote to Maureen from the coronary unit apologising for 'a doleful sort of letter' but asking her not to give it another thought: 'the last book is doing well and you've all been picking primroses in Ryarsh Woods so what the Hell'. She wrote jokingly to Bruce Mason from her 'bedder sickness' saying that there was 'life in the old girl yet. I wonder if there was a Victorian Music Hall number of that title? Should have been, surely'.[6] The first of her premature obituaries appeared in England at this time. It caused great consternation to her friends throughout the world, but afforded Ngaio a little amusement: 'I'm told on the whole it was favourable'.

Home at last after three weeks in hospital, Ngaio had to accept, with great reluctance, that a live-in housekeeper was now essential. The need became even more pressing when Ngaio again fell on her garden path and broke a rib. Helen Holmes made most of the arrangements for this. Every time Ngaio took up the much-abandoned manuscript of *Grave Mistake* it became harder to force herself on and she lost all confidence in what she had already written. Finally she sent it off saying, 'heaven knows what it's like; I'm sure I don't'. The novel had completely lost its focus, and when Collins eventually received it early in 1978, the Crime Club editor Robert Knittel wrote tactfully that 'we look forward to publishing this autumn with great success', but that there were 'one or two little revisions that seem to be called for'. Uncharacteristically for an author who normally took such care with initial character and plotting, the whole motive for the murder of Sybil Foster was unclear and Ngaio had to make substantial alterations, agreeing with Knittel that 'you are right about apparent absence of motive and think the trouble came about through the book having been interrupted so often by illness'. Problems continued, even to mistakes in the dust-jacket blurb, and Ngaio despaired of ever seeing the book in print. She wrote to Edmund Cork that it was hanging round her neck like the Ancient Mariner's albatross. But eventually it was published in September 1978, and was particularly successful in the United States, where her English village mysteries were always popular. Lord Ballantrae wrote in September assuring her that he had read the novel with delight, and added some revealing thoughts about his perception of gentlemen detectives:

> As a failed novelist, I never know which I admire most, your ambience, your characters, your plots or your dialogue. I think one

of the most enviable things about your dialogue is that you know when to introduce an irrelevance which entertains without distracting. I like most of Dorothy Sayers' books but have always thought Peter Wimsey a consummate bounder—the sort of chap I meet in Whites! . . . but your Alleyn is a real chum—more like a member of Brooks's!'[7]

The relief at finally completing *Grave Mistake* and her 'utter incredulity and complete flabbergastation' at its warm reception cheered Ngaio up considerably and she even began to think about another trip to England. But she was still being closely monitored by her doctors, and by the nurses (nicknamed the 'Daughters of Dracula') who came regularly to do blood tests: 'making whoopee twice a week on my coagulated gore'. Although Ngaio began every letter to the Balfours with the wish that she was waking up in her little room at Walnut Tree Farm, or picking wild flowers in the woods, the general medical advice was against a long air journey. The days of leisurely sea passages were now over, and Ngaio hated aeroplanes.

Despite her aversion to flying, slightly surprising in someone who was so fond of fast cars, she did make the effort to fly to Sydney that year to see John Dacres-Mannings and his family and, true to form, the malevolent Fates arranged for a violent storm on her return flight. Ngaio, suffering the after-effects of a stomach upset, found that china was smashing, doors and drawers in the plane were opening and closing with a crash, and 'everything was bouncy-bouncy until we landed in a torrential gale at Christchurch'. Ngaio seemed to be unlucky with air travel: when she made the short trip to Auckland the following year to collect an award from the New Zealand Publishers' Association and to take part in a television quiz on Shakespeare there was another violent storm. She wrote to Maureen, 'I have only got to sit in one of those horrid things for blue skies to at once turn plug-ugly and for tornadoes to hurry up from the South Pole and bounce us about like a yo-yo'. Advised by the stewardess to hold on to anything handy as they struggled from plane to terminal, Ngaio found that 'a couple of large gentlemen were handiest for me so I clung to them and we all three did a sort of tango across the tarmac'. Consequently Maureen's suggestion that Ngaio fly back on Concorde for part of the journey was not very tempting. Nevertheless, it was not until 1981 that Ngaio finally wrote to her English solicitor, John Balfour, requesting that nearly all her funds in banks be transferred from England to New Zealand. She now knew that she would never be able to return to England again.

The possibility of travelling to Los Angeles in 1978 at the invitation of the Mystery Writers of America also had to be reluctantly refused. Ngaio, along with Daphne du Maurier and Dorothy B. Hughes, was being awarded their highest accolade, the Grand Master Award for 1977. John Ball, the well-known American mystery writer, had visited Ngaio in Christchurch earlier in the year, and tried to persuade her to make the effort to attend the ceremony, but while greatly appreciating the honour, she was now too frail for such an exhausting trip. In an introduction to the American edition of *Death in a White Tie* that he was preparing, John Ball describes her as elegant in a white trouser suit in a room that 'suggested perfect taste exercised over a number of years: a rich patina of family tradition infused every corner'.[8] The award, a little ceramic statuette of Edgar Allen Poe, was posted to New Zealand, with a covering letter from Awards Chairman Hillary Waugh describing the Congress and the Dinner. 'Edgar' still stands on a glass shelf in her sunny living-room. Ngaio wrote enthusiastically to all her friends, with many variations on a joke about grand masters and grand mistresses—'a bit equivocal', she thought.

A further honour, but rather harder work, was an invitation from Julian Symons, then still President of the Detection Club, to contribute a short story to a volume being produced by Faber and Faber with most of the royalties going to boost the funds of the Detection Club. Ngaio had often admitted that she was 'no dab at the short story', but as she had always admired Julian Symons she wrote to Edmund Cork that 'it would be curmudgeonly if I said I wouldn't try to oblige'. Although Symons had suggested that all the stories should involve a jury and a verdict, Ngaio produced an ingenious and unusual piece of work which initially seems totally distanced from trial by jury. It is certainly the best short story she ever wrote.

'Morepork' is set in a camp site in the mountain forests of the South Island of New Zealand, and the sounds, sights and aroma of the bush were as vivid here as they had been in her school essay on

Glentui nearly seventy years before. The story is about a murder made to look like an accident. Caley Bridgeman, a fanatical bird-watcher and recorder of bird song, falls to his death into a flooded mountain gorge when his wife's lover, a solicitor, loosens the makeshift bridge made by the campers. The murder plot is exposed by Caley's tape-recording equipment, high in a tree above the gorge, which has captured not only the sound of the elusive mountain owl, the 'morepork', but the voices of the adulterous couple planning his death. The trial aspect comes in when the campers are joined by a party of deer-stalkers which includes a doctor and an English barrister, and knowing that they will be cut off by the floods for several days, they decide to establish an *al fresco* inquest. So the campers gather in a tent, sitting on greenwood benches and dry fern, an acetylene lamp hissing on a rough plank table, and an unlikely inquest takes place. It ends with the exposure of the murderer. As the dead man's voice is heard over the tape introducing the recording of the 'morepork', he adds the macabre detail that among the Maori people the bird is regarded as a harbinger of death.

The idea of using a tape-recorder to expose a crime is not new, and indeed Patrick White wrote a not-dissimilar story, 'Willy Wagtails By Moonlight', where a recording of a bird also includes illicit couplings in the undergrowth. What is interesting about 'Morepork' is that after such a dispiriting struggle with *Grave Mistake* Ngaio was able to produce an excellent story so quickly and seemingly without great effort. The story was printed in *Verdict of Thirteen: a Detection Club Anthology*, published by Faber and Faber in 1978, and in the following year by Harper and Row in the US. Ngaio found herself in distinguished company in this anthology, and the story is still much admired.

Apart from writing 'Morepork', Ngaio found that for much of the early part of 1978 she was taken up with domestic affairs. She had many visitors, including Stella and her other relatives from the North Island. Extensive alterations to the house were planned, to allow for a new suite of rooms for Ngaio on a lower level but connected to the upper storey by a lift. This new room, finally completed in 1980, gave her a wonderful view over her garden and across the city to the mountains. She regretted not having made this improvement long before, even though the cost was high. Now

Ngaio could enjoy her garden from her window; her weak heart had made it impossible for her to climb the steep terraces among her rose beds. Yet in the last few years of her life Ngaio bought and had planted hundreds of new roses for the garden, as if determined that her much-loved landscape would thrive and grow even after she had gone.

Proofs of *Grave Mistake* started to arrive in June 1978, and amazingly, Ngaio was again beginning to think about a new book. Perhaps using the spectacular scenery of the South Island as a background to 'Morepork' was the necessary stimulus, because by October she was working hard on the preliminary stages of what was to become *Photo-Finish*. She was also writing to Jonathan Elsom about devising a one-man show based on the life of Pepys: 'perhaps a script based on his domestic and his public lives would be best. One would of course "discover him" at work on the diary and leave him cautiously locking it away in the desk after using one of the extraordinary contraptions designed to help his failing sight'. But by the next year she was less certain; her letters admit that although this was a tempting idea, a great deal of work would have to go into the script.

Now in her eighty-third year, Ngaio's letters show that her amused and self-deprecating view of life was in no way diminished. Even a fairly formal letter to Bruce Mason, accepting a further term as President of the New Zealand branch of the international writers association PEN (she was President of Honour in 1978 and 1979), incorporates her comic approach to everyday life:

This note has been twice interrupted by my eldest cat, Ernest, (neé Eartha Kitt but on expert examination the importance of a name change became evident). He has developed halitosis. I have arranged with 'Pet Transport' for him to visit a vet and—
Later still: He has bolted, a visitor having opened the door. A frenzied search is now in progress. 'Pet Transport' postponed.
Ernest Recovered: 'Pet Transport' re-engaged but huffy. Ernest deeply suspicious. Whew![9]

Even more comic, despite its serious result, is her description of how a local dog stole a joint of meat from her kitchen table, spilling the marinade and causing Ngaio to slip on the oily liquid:

I bustled into the kitchen, did a complicated figure in ice-skating, flung my feet at the ceiling and crashed down on the back of my head and end of my spine. Concussion ensued but I swarmed up the leg of the table to a semi-upright position . . . In due course I recovered.

Ngaio seemed to have had a burst of energy in the second part of 1978. She found time to write indignantly to her English solicitor about the pirating of twenty-seven of her books in the United States, and the publicity which accompanied the transmission of the television versions of her New Zealand novels gave her the opportunity to speak out several times about her favourite *bête noire*, New Zealand speech. These querulous pieces printed in the *Listener* reveal a sad absence of recognition of the positive qualities of New Zealand at that time. While we may sympathise with Ngaio's pleas in 'It's Not What We Say' for the enlightened use of speech, 'the elegant, sophisticated instrument with which each of us has been provided: an instrument capable of sounds as subtle, varied, delicate or dynamic as those of a violin or organ',[10] it is harder to go along with her harsh view that 'in the dialect we have developed and are rapidly consolidating, we may be said to use these facilities in the manner of a pianist wearing clown's gloves, keeping his foot on the soft pedal and, on the whole, despising the instrument he plays'. Ngaio's attacks on 'New Zillan' speech went deep and even those who admired her achievements found them offensive. They caused her friend Mervyn Thompson to write in his poem 'On the Death of Ngaio Marsh', printed in the New Zealand literary magazine *Landfall* in 1982:

Why was it we dreamed your dream
Not our own?
Aimed to speak like English gentry
Twelve thousand miles from home?
So detested the sound of our own voices
We strangled them in the cradle of your desire?
Stood like costumed leaden sentries,
Affecting nobility, fearing your ire
If once we wore our own bodies instead?
Why to fulfil your living vision
Did *we* have to be pompous, stiff and dead?[11]

What was not printed at the time, and might have softened the impression that her vitriolic attacks on New Zealand speech were creating, was Ngaio's own comic poem, found among her papers, beginning,

Dear Sir: referring to the way
We speak our native tongue today
May I inquire why as a nation
We wade in mispronunciation?
Sir, is this habit a display
Of arrogance or just the chance
Of Can't-care-less
Or Ignorance?

Fortunately Ngaio was soon again engrossed in *Photo-Finish* and laid aside her polemical journalism. The plot was complex, and required more than eight months' solid work to bring it to a satisfactory conclusion. Most of 1979 was devoted to it, but at the same time Ngaio was also revising and extending her autobiography, *Black Beech and Honeydew*. This was in response to a request made by Billy Collins before he died, and Ngaio had been thinking about it for some time. Collins (New Zealand) were particularly keen because the book had recently been read on New Zealand Radio, which created a demand in bookshops for a book that was out of print.

In the new chapters of *Black Beech and Honeydew* Ngaio at last acknowledges her work as a detective fiction writer, and talks about the background to some of her novels, particularly *When in Rome*. She also writes about old age and death, acknowledging reluctantly that:

Old age has caught me completely by surprise. It was the sudden onset of uncertain health that did the trick and the realisation that the activity one most valued and passionately enjoyed was no longer possible, it must be packed up and put away with theatrical photographs and old programmes: a tidying up process before a journey on which one will be obliged to travel very light indeed.[12]

Further thoughts would have crowded in about the death a few months earlier of her friend Ned Bradford, her editor for many years at Little, Brown, and the unexpected and unwelcome news that Bruce Mason had recently undergone extensive treatment for cancer. In a moving letter to him, Ngaio said that his courage and optimism had 'brought my heart into my mouth'. Wishing him well, she comments on the new generation of actors and directors that she and Bruce had helped along the way. Elric Hooper had taken over as Director of the Court Theatre in Christchurch, producing theatre 'streets ahead of anything that has been seen in this benighted city for many and many a day'. And James Laurenson and Jonathan Elsom were both drawing splendid notices for their work in London. She ends on an elegiac note: 'so all this old bird's chicks prosper, thank the Lord'.[13] Bruce Mason did not win his battle with cancer, and died shortly after Ngaio in 1982.

The two books that Ngaio was working on late in 1979, the novel and the revision of her autobiography, nurtured each other in an unexpected way. In rereading *Black Beech* before making her additions, Ngaio was reminded very powerfully of her holidays as a young painter on the west coast of the South Island with its dramatic scenery, its unique aroma of ferns and damp moss distilled in air of intense purity, and the poignant sound of bell birds and tuis. She would have remembered the mountain lakes with their sudden, dangerous storms, and the skies that 'would make sails for Cleopatra's barge'. In the early pages of the first edition of *Black Beech* Ngaio had described the wild beauty of Lake Brunner, and this becomes the setting for Montague Reece's magnificent lake palace in *Photo-Finish*. As Alleyn and Troy descend the notorious zig-zag road into the Otira Gorge, Ngaio must have thought of her own first descent of this precipitous route, on the box seat of a Cobb and Co. coach, plunging 'into a chasm where tree-tops were no bigger than green fungi and the great Otira River, a cold shimmer'.

Direct comparisons can be made between the two works. For instance, in the autobiography, Ngaio says at this point, 'I am badly affected with height vertigo', and in *Photo-Finish* Troy 'suffered horridly' from the same condition at the same spot. Troy also looks down 'as if from a gallery in a theatre on an audience of treetops, and saw the river'. Instead of whipping up the horses as they reached the plain, the Alleyns' driver changes into top gear. And Lake Brunner, named Lake Waihoe in the novel, does not disappoint the artist, who gazes, astonished, at sunset reflections in unruffled water. Alleyn and Troy share Ngaio's faith in the touch of magic that can transform everyday life, when, as they wait for the launch to take them out to the island in the middle of the lake, Alleyn remarks, 'Do you know, in a cockeyed sort of way it reminds me of one of those Victorian romances by George Macdonald where the characters find a looking glass and walk out of this world into another one inhabited by strange beings and unaccountable ongoings', to which Troy replies, 'Perhaps . . . the entrance to that great house will turn out to be our own front door and we'll be back in London'.

The mysterious storms that affect Lake Brunner in the novel are deliberately associated with *pakeha* (white) intrusion on a *tapu* (sacred and forbidden) Maori burial site. The Maori opera singer Eru Johnstone admits to Alleyn that had he known the location of the great singer's house, he would not have come. Further echoes of Ngaio's own experience come from her memory of the three young men who were drowned in Lake Brunner while she was painting there, caught in a sudden storm, and who were found 'quite close in-shore, under a few feet of clear water'. Powerful memories indeed, and they infuse *Photo-Finish* with some of the sense of mystery that still exists in this unspoiled wilderness, a landscape that makes Troy say as they leave the island, 'this landscape belongs to birds: not to men, not to animals: huge birds that have gone now, stalked about in it. Except for birds, it's empty'. She echoes Ngaio's words in *Black Beech and Honeydew*, when she found on one of her earliest camping trips into the mountains that 'for all our adoptive gestures, our presence here was no more than a cobweb across the hide of a monster, that in spite of our familiarity with its surface we had made no mark upon our country and were still newcomers . . . it is a feeling that deepens rather than modifies one's attachment to New Zealand'.[14]

Photo-Finish, with its small group of people confined to an island in the middle of a lake, satisfies the standard detective novel requirement of a closed community with a variety of suspects. The famous opera singer Isabella Sommita is murdered by asphyxiation and then stabbed through the heart with a photograph lanced on to the dagger. The Maori theme is sustained by the use of a Maori artefact for the deed.

The author develops a number of variations of the revenge

theme, almost in the manner of a Jacobean tragedy. Mafia revenge is there in the presence of Maria and Reece, and Maori revenge, harder to quantify, adds a distinctive flavour to the narrative. The description of the private first performance of a lamely written opera, with socialites and opera lovers being transplanted to the island from all over New Zealand, is handled with relish. There is a skilful mixture of sympathy for the young composer who realises how poor his work is but finds himself trapped in the situation, and irony at the pretensions of the diva with her startling note of A above high C.

The first draft of *Photo-Finish* was completed in October 1979 and Ngaio wrote to Maureen that she had finished 'a book that from start to finish has given me pink Hell to write—partly I think because it's set in New Zealand which, for me, presents its own acute difficulties. About two hours ago I finished it after eight months' difficult "pregnancy". There's still a lot of revision to be done and I'm heartily sick of the whole job and will be glad to put it—good, bad or stinking—behind me'. Before sending the manuscript off, Ngaio consulted musical friends, Fred and Eve Page in Wellington, to make sure that there were no musical gaffes. The book was dedicated to the Pages, 'Fredaneve', in recognition of an enduring friendship. (Ngaio had a habit of running together the names of her married friends, such as 'Fredaneve' Page or 'Valanita' Muling.) The few weeks' respite between sending off the manuscript and starting on revisions was filled with Christmas and 'the unavoidable but exacting fuss arising out of even modified jollity'. An unexpected luncheon guest, but one who was always welcome, was the pianist André Tchaikovsky, whom she had met several times before on his international tours.

Ngaio admitted to Maureen that she was having some problems with her heart, more specifically attacks of angina, but the letters she wrote to Collins after Christmas are as clear and businesslike as ever. Elizabeth Walter wrote from Collins in February with the encouraging news that in her view *Photo-Finish* was one of Ngaio's best books, adding that 'if my other authors can write as well as that in celebration of their 80th birthday, the Crime Club list will be assured for a very long time to come'. Collins was still printing Ngaio's date of birth as 1899 on all their dust jackets, instead of 1895, and Elizabeth genuinely did not know that on 23 April 1980

Ngaio would reach the age of eighty-five. The Collins reader's report was full of praise: 'the story is an astonishing achievement by a woman of 80 and it shows her to have kept her vitality and control much longer than Agatha did. It is witty, the setting is impressive, the plot is tidily organised and the solution is dramatic. What more?'

Elizabeth Walter asked for some minor revisions, but the American copy-editor had a more serious objection regarding the number of keys to the murdered woman's room—a crucial point in the plot. Three keys or four? Collins eventually agreed with the American editor, and Elizabeth wrote to Ngaio saying, 'we have to do something about this point if *Photo-Finish* is not to become *The Mystery of the Multiplying Keys*'. Ngaio had to rewrite the relevant pages during April. By May the various points had been cleared up ('I'd arrived at the state where I myself was becoming addled by those bloody keys', wrote Ngaio), and Elizabeth Walter, whose letters became much more chatty during the last few years of correspondence with Ngaio, was writing to her about the Collins Crime Club fiftieth anniversary celebrations which were held at New Scotland Yard. She reported with a slight tinge of regret that 'no untoward criminal incidents took place during the party—the cake was not poisoned, the gold-wrapped parcel for the Commissioner didn't explode, nobody used the sword for any purpose other than cake-cutting, and no shot rang out at a suitably dramatic moment in the proceedings'. She promised to post Ngaio a piece of the cake, and Ngaio wrote back to assure her that 'fossilised or not, I shall give my piece of cake a hearty, nostalgic munch'.

The Director of the Concert Programme, New Zealand's equivalent to BBC Radio Three, was fortunate in securing a lengthy autobiographical interview with Ngaio at this time. Elizabeth Alley conducted it personally, and with great tact and perceptiveness. The interview was broadcast on 21 May 1980, just days before Ngaio was, to use her own words to Bruce Mason, 'took crook in a big way'. A major heart attack in early June weakened her considerably, and this time she was not quite so amused by the premature obituaries on BBC and in the *Guardian*. Neither were her friends in England. Jonathan Elsom read the news in the *London Evening Standard* on the top of a bus going to the the-atre where he had a part in *A Flea in Her Ear*, and he acted like an automaton that night. Interviewed by New Zealand Radio about her response to her obituaries, Ngaio was cavalier as usual, saying that all she wanted was for someone with good taste to allow that she wrote with style. She also revealed that there was one more book to go, and when asked, 'Does it come easily?' she replied forthrightly, 'It had better'.

With indomitable will, Ngaio tried to re-establish a pattern of writing on her return home from hospital in July. Her pleasure at the new room that had been created for her, and the long-awaited installation of the lift (delayed for many months by a dock strike) seemed to provide the stimulus for what was to be the last novel. She was still slowly revising *Black Beech and Honeydew* for Collins (New Zealand) and eventually the book was issued in 1981.

Photo-Finish, published in September 1980, received warm praise from reviewers. By now Ngaio was almost completely confined to her house, and invitations to meet members of the royal family on tour were reluctantly declined because she was very unsteady on her feet. Letters from her surviving friends became more and more important and Ngaio always did her best to reply promptly, apologising profusely if her letters were late. To her valued friend Doris McIntosh in Wellington she sent books and discussed contemporary fiction, finding a shared admiration for Maurice Gee: 'I've read Gee's *Plumb* and was very much impressed: the writing—at first seeming a bit sub-fusc, perhaps, holds up most securely, I think, and develops with a kind of mastery that doesn't appear in any of the other New Zealand contemporaries that have come my way'. Until his death in November 1980, she discussed biographies and memoirs in her correspondence with Lord Ballantrae, always including a joke in her letters. She was still reading and enjoying Dickens, Trollope and the Brontës, although Thackeray never appealed—'he's a bit of a prig', and she returned to E. F. Benson's Lucia stories throughout her life. *The Moonstone* by Wilkie Collins remained her favourite detective novel, but she read very little crime fiction unless specifically asked to do so. She still corresponded regularly with Maureen Balfour at Walnut Tree Farm, embroidering on amusing incidents from her now restricted surroundings. She was able to cope with yet another visit from New Zealand television in late 1980 for their *Kaleidoscope* programme, and had sufficient energy to make a fuss about the attack made on Bruce Mason's latest play by the interviewer who was also sent to see her.

Very slowly, the novel based on a brilliant production of *Macbeth* began to take shape. Throughout failing health and against all instructions to do less and rest more the novel continued to make progress, and much of the dialogue is as sparkling as that of any of her theatre mysteries. Elizabeth Walter, having heard that she intended to write about *Macbeth*, wrote very encouragingly, and made Ngaio and Rosemary Greene laugh heartily with a description of her school production of the play: 'one of the few occasions when *Macbeth* was rapturously greeted by its audience as comedy'. Ngaio persevered, clearly working out a situation that had been in her mind for a long time. She told Maureen that it was 'an idea I've dallied with for ages and always funked in the end'. By the end of June she had completed Chapter 4 and had reached a happy stage of equilibrium with a devoted and competent housekeeper, Mrs Berens.

She had been discussing the new novel with Jonathan too, and he sent her a book about superstitions connected with *Macbeth*. By the end of July she wrote to him that 'I've got to the opening night of *Macbeth* and don't know whether to let it run for a bit or to strike now. There's going to be the devil of a mess to clear up which ever I do'. Having set up a good production of the play she was reluctant to waste even an imaginary performance; clearly crime fiction and the theatre were indivisible in the mind of the author.

The next few months turned out to be unexpectedly contented in a perverse way. Ngaio's lifelong friend, Sylvia Fox, who lived in a bungalow just above 37 Valley Road, slipped and fell in her garden and broke her ankle. Rescued by Ngaio's housekeeper and packed off to hospital, she came to recuperate with Ngaio while Mrs Berens looked after them both. For Ngaio this was a period of great happiness. The two elderly ladies joked and giggled like schoolgirls about present friends and recollections of past times.

Ngaio must have needed to make a tremendous effort for her last public appearance when in September she cut the ribbon across the doorway of the newly renovated Theatre Royal in the centre of Christchurch, declaring 'God bless this ship and all who sail in her', as she did so. The refurbishment of the theatre meant a great deal. At one time it had been threatened with demolition, and for her this theatre was indissolubly connected with her early days as an actress with the Allan Wilkie Theatre Company.

By October Ngaio had finished her handwritten draft of *Light Thickens* and it was being typed. Her frail handwriting on narrow-lined foolscap sheets moves inexorably on over 168 pages, some written while sitting in an easy chair, some while she rested in bed. She was more than usually full of misgivings. To John Balfour she wrote that 'it was extremely difficult and has the form of a fugue, really, with the superstitions woven through the growth of the play and the real threat taking over in the end. It will probably appeal to theatre people rather than my usual cosy and academic readers. It was hell to write'. Ngaio had twice produced *Macbeth*, and *Light Thickens* can be considered as her third production. The novel may keep the theatrical world trapped among its pages, but the narrative is evocative with all the paraphernalia of a company in rehearsal that was so familiar to this experienced director. Since the crime does not occur until late in the narrative, the mystery elements are subsumed into a series of alarming and sinister practical jokes that haunt the rehearsals, together with the element of superstition always associated with this play. The Maori actor, Rangi, who plays one of the witches, gives hints of supernatural beliefs that link with Gaston's obsession with the latent power of the great Scottish two-handed sword, the massive claidheamh-mor. To Gaston the sword is 'alive and hot and desirous of blood', and it becomes the means of providing the actors with a real head, dripping gore, instead of a property head of Macbeth at the end of the play.

After a quiet Christmas, Ngaio sent the novel off to her agents on 7 January 1982. She was overcome with worries and wrote to Elizabeth Walter, telling her to scrap the manuscript if she found it 'really unsatisfactory'. The next day she was trying to catch up with a huge bundle of correspondence and to make arrangements to see her Christchurch friends, who had been neglected as she pressed on with the book. A letter to Jonathan was full of plans for his visit in April: 'the car is in superb order for you', and her hopes that he would come to stay at Valley Road for a while and read through his parts with her in the long room.

Stella visited for what she knew would be the last time. Although the Reverend Simon Acland had brought Ngaio much comfort since her health declined, and had been permitted to say prayers for her in hospital, Ngaio continued to find it impossible to see a meaningful direction in religious belief. Stella was deeply distressed by this and longed to leave with some sense that Ngaio was not entirely alone, as she saw it, on the journey ahead. She parted full of sadness that there seemed no possibility of an intellectual and emotional reconciliation with religion. Yet Ngaio had made her position clear in the last pages she added to the revised version of her autobiography in 1980, when she muses upon Shakespeare's unsentimental view of death, and finds no promise, anywhere in his works, of life after death: 'consolation is to be found in oblivion'. She senses not only Shakespeare's own fear of death, as seen in Claudio's emotional speech in *Measure for Measure*, but also his offering of 'comfort as well as fear in the thought of oblivion'. For Ngaio, the dirge from *Cymbeline*, 'Fear no more the heat o' the sun' is a perfect poetic expression of her own convictions.

Telex 19 January 1982 Pat Cork (British agent) to Dorothy Olding (US agent)
I have reservations about the book especially the first half but can't see how we could ask her to alter it, do you?

Reply 19 January Dorothy Olding to Pat Cork
Afraid I have reservations about the whole book but have sent to Little, Brown.

Telex 2 February Dorothy Olding to Pat Cork
Little, Brown reasonably happy with Light Thickens. I want to cable Ngaio.

Reply 3 February Pat Cork to Dorothy Olding
Most reassuring about Little, Brown and do accept. Collins have not had time yet to make decision.

Cable 3 February Dorothy Olding to Ngaio Marsh
Little, Brown very pleased with Light Thickens. Same terms as last. Congratulations and much love.

Telex 18 February 1982 Pat Cork to Dorothy Olding
Sad to say that Ngaio died yesterday of a stroke. [15]

Dorothy Olding is profoundly thankful that despite her private views of the book she was able to send her cable in time. The news brought Ngaio great pleasure: one of her old friends, actor Bill Scannell, who visited her just after the cable arrived, found that she 'looked like a young girl who had just been praised by her parents'. She had referred to this final novel in her revision of *Black Beech and Honeydew* as bringing 'the two major interests of my life together for, as it were, a final fling', and so, indeed, it proved to be.

Ngaio's death on 18 February 1982, from a brain haemorrhage, was swift and allowed her the dignity of dying in her own home, supported by her close friends. She had made arrangements for her funeral with Simon Acland and had asked him to conduct the service in Christchurch Cathedral. 'Wobbly C of E' though she may have been, there is no doubt that she felt the Cathedral to be the appropriate place for her final farewell. Everything had been planned in advance, with Simon's help, down to the names of the pall-bearers and the charity which was to receive donations from the mourners: the Laura Fergusson Fund for the Disabled in Christchurch, a gesture to a valued friendship.

The actors she had nurtured on many stages and other friends who had supported her work in the theatre bore her coffin. A single bunch of roses cut from her own garden were the only flowers she requested. Psalm 121, 'I will lift up mine eyes unto the hills' pre-saged her final resting place in the graveyard of the Church of the Holy Innocents at Mount Peel, in the foothills of the Southern Alps, where her favourite tui birds sing in the surrounding trees.

In his funeral address on 24 February, Simon Acland paid tribute to Ngaio's many talents: 'Publicly in her own right, Ngaio Marsh was a great person. Privately, I believe that she was an even greater one'. He praised her graciousness, loyalty and generosity, and noted her ability to make all who knew her feel that they were special people, receiving her unstinting attention and warmth. She shared the attributes of love or charity listed by St Paul, but added to them the important quality of humour, because she always brought with her laughter as well as understanding. As the cortège left the cathedral, the choir sang the Russian *kontakion* for the departed, a gesture to her old friends, Val and Anita Muling. Girls from her school, St Margaret's College, mounted a guard of honour on the steps. The service was broadcast by New Zealand Radio and the cathedral was full, even though fog at Christchurch airport prevented friends from other parts of New Zealand arriving on the day.

Many tributes from around the world recognised her popularity as a writer, but her New Zealand friends also praised her work in the theatre and her ability to inspire young people. In a Memorial Service held in Wellington Cathedral on 3 March, Bruce Mason spoke of 'her ability to attract and act as den-mother to a horde of the talented young for more than forty years'.

After bequests to the Court Theatre, to her housekeeper, Mrs Crawford, and to the Social Services Council of the Diocese of Christchurch, Ngaio left her estate to her two second cousins, John Dacres-Mannings and Roy Mannings, whose lives she had woven into her own since first meeting them as young children. As a childless only child she had few close relatives left to mourn her, although many members of the widely scattered Seager and Marsh families had followed her career with interest. In England her adopted family was the Rhodes family, her fictional Lampreys, and in New Zealand her children and grandchildren comprised the scores of actors and theatre-lovers who had worked with her to create those occasional flashes of magic, so rare in everyday life.

After Ngaio's death, the manuscript of *Light Thickens* underwent considerable editorial work at Collins. Their reader had suggested in early February that the manuscript be sent back to the Antipodes for 'extensive repairs', but the task now fell on Elizabeth Walter to remove repetitions, radically edit a long section on the nature of tragedy and to sharpen the clue that emerges at the end when two small boys are playing with a train set. Little, Brown were keen to see the revised edition, and Senior Editor William D. Phillips wrote to Elizabeth Walter that 'I think we all agree this is one of Ngaio's least efforts, alas, but ironically, it may be the most commercially successful, at least over here'. He proved to be correct; in 1983 and in 1984 paperback sales of *Light Thickens* substantially outstripped all other titles. It was published in September 1982, retaining Ngaio's original title against a Collins bid to retitle it 'The Scots Play', and was dedicated to James Laurenson and Helen Holmes, the thane and his wife in Ngaio's last production of this play in 1962. American reviewers loved the book, and the *Los Angeles Times* saw behind the mystery to 'a singing of memory and love, a summoning of a personal past (there are echoes of New Zealand

and Maori culture) and a recollection of the fictional past she had created, symbolised by this return to the old Victorian Theatre beside the river. No playwright could devise a better curtain'.

Shortly after the funeral service a small group of Ngaio's friends took her ashes up to Mount Peel, where they were buried near other early settlers from the district, and not far from the grave of Vladimir Muling. It is a peaceful resting place, backed by dramatic mountains and looking out over the wide Canterbury Plains. A simple stone bears her name. The scent of pine trees and tussock mingles with the fragrance of roses from the nearby garden of the Aclands' house; a blend of England and New Zealand that perfectly reflects her divided life.

ACKNOWLEDGEMENTS

The ready assistance of the following Libraries and Archives has been indispensable to the completion of this book and I am most grateful to the staff who contributed their time and expertise: Alexander Turnbull Library (National Library of New Zealand, Wellington); BBC Sound Archives, London; BBC Written Archives Centre, Caversham Park, Reading; British Library; British Theatre Association Library; *Birmingham Post*; Christchurch Public Library; Court Theatre, Christchurch; Library of New South Wales; Lit and Phil Library, Newcastle upon Tyne; Library of New Zealand House, London; Mugar Memorial Library, Boston University; National Library of Scotland; P.E.N. New Zealand; Princeton University Libraries; Radio New Zealand Sound Archives, Timaru; Television New Zealand Archives, Lower Hutt; Robert McDougall Art Gallery, Christchurch; Robinson Library, University of Newcastle upon Tyne; Royal Society of Arts; St Margaret's College, Christchurch; Trinity College Library, Dublin; *The Times* Library; *Yorkshire Post*; University of Reading Library; University of Sydney Library; Victoria University of Wellington Library; Wodehouse Library, Dulwich College.

Permission to quote from material in the following special collections is gratefully acknowledged: Lord Ballantrae Papers, National Library of Scotland; Bruce Mason Papers (reproduced by kind permission of the Estate of Bruce Mason and the Victoria University of Wellington); Harold Ober Associates Archive, Princeton University Libraries; Special Collections, Mugar Library, Boston University. Collins Publishers have kindly given permission to quote from the works of Ngaio Marsh published by them and to quote from correspondence in their files.

Very few of Dame Ngaio's letters are available in libraries or archives. I would like to give my sincere thanks to those friends and relatives who preserved her letters and generously made their private correspondence available to me. Many of her friends from around the world have shared their reminiscences with me and helped to create this story of her life. Members of the Detection Club, the Crime Writers' Association and the Mystery Writers of America have provided fascinating details about their meetings with Dame Ngaio and the reception of her novels. The Dorothy L. Sayers Society has helped to illumine a difficult point. Members of the academic staff of Canterbury University, Christchurch and Victoria University, Wellington, and the University of New South Wales have been most helpful with advice and suggestions. Financial assistance from Northern Arts and the Open University is gratefully acknowledged. Finally, I should like to thank Dame Ngaio's literary agent, Brian Stone, and my editors at Chatto and Windus for encouragement and support through several years of research. In thanking the Estate of Ngaio Marsh for inviting me to write this authorised biography, I can only say that it has been a privilege to be entrusted with the task.

NOTES

References have been made to published works mentioned in the text and to letters that have been deposited in Library Archives. Many letters from which quotations have been taken are personal documents in private hands, and the only reference to these is in the text. In the interests of simplicity, and because so many editions exist, page references to novels by Ngaio Marsh have not been included.

Much unpublished material is held in the National Library of New Zealand (Alexander Turnbull Library), Wellington, New Zealand. The abbreviation ATL refers to this location throughout the notes. After the first reference to *Black Beech and Honeydew*, it is subsequently referred to as *BB*.

CHAPTER 1

1. P. Temple, *Christchurch Yesterday* (Dunedin, 1980), p. 3.
2. Lady Barker, *Station Life in New Zealand* (London, 1984), p. 41.
3. M. Seager, *Edward William Seager: Pioneer of Mental Health* (Waikanae, 1987), p. 156.
4. S. Butler, *The Family Letters of Samuel Butler* 1841–1886, ed. A. Silver (London, 1962), p. 104.
5. Butler, *Erewhon* (London, 1924), p. 41.
6. Butler, *A First Year in Canterbury Settlement* (London, 1863), p. 51.
7. N. Marsh, *Black Beech and Honeydew* (revised edition, Auckland, 1981), p. 25.
8. *BB*, p. 23.
9. Unpublished ms in private hands.
10. Dame Ngaio Marsh Papers in Alexander Turnbull Library, National Library of New Zealand, Ref. 1397.
11. Marsh Papers, ATL.
12. *BB*, p. 28.
13. *BB*, p. 117.
14. Unpublished ms in private hands.
15. *BB*, p. 41.
16. Unpublished ms in private hands.
17. *BB*, p. 58.

CHAPTER 2

1. *BB*, p. 63.
2. *BB*, p. 86.
3. *BB*, p. 72.
4. J. Paul and N. Roberts, *Evelyn Page: Seven Decades* (Christchurch, 1986), p. 60.
5. *BB*, p. 97.
6. *BB*, pp. 89–90.
7. Unpublished ms in Robert McDougall Art Gallery, Christchurch.
8. Marsh papers, ATL.
9. *BB*, p. 120.

10. *BB*, p. 138.
11. Paul and Roberts, *Evelyn Page*, p. 61.
12. J. Shelley, 'The 1929 Group Exhibition of Paintings', *Christchurch Times*, 10 Sept. 1929, p. 14.
13. Quoted in J. A. Catchpole, 'The Group', unpublished MA thesis, University of Canterbury, 1984.
14. Paul and Roberts, *Evelyn Page*, p. 24.
15. Paul and Roberts, *Evelyn Page*, p. 69.

CHAPTER 3
1. Interview, NZ Radio, 21 May, 1980.
2. Marsh Papers, ATL.
3. *BB*, p. 29.
4. *BB*, p. 152.
5. *BB*, p. 150.
6. R. Hyde, *The Godwits Fly* (Auckland, 1980), p. xx.
7. A. Gurr, *Writers in Exile* (Brighton, 1981), p. 17.
8. Marsh's column 'A New Canterbury Pilgrim' appeared regularly in *The Press* from Sept. 1928 to Nov. 1929, and was revived in 1937.
9. *BB*, p. 155.
10. N. Marsh, 'The Background', *The Press*, 22 Dec. 1934.
11. *BB*, p. 109.

CHAPTER 4
1. N. Marsh, 'Birth of a Sleuth', *The Writer* (March, 1977), p. 23.
2. 'Birth of a Sleuth', p. 24.
3. E. Reeve, 'Ngaio Marsh Talks About "Teckery"', *Vogue* (New Zealand), Autumn, 1964, p. 85.
4. *BB*, p. 195.
5. *BB*, p. 227.
6. J. Symons, *Bloody Murder* (Harmondsworth, 1985), p. 96.
7. R. Chandler, *The Simple Art of Murder* (London, 1950), p. 328.
8. P. D. James, 'Dorothy L. Sayers: From Puzzle to Novel', in *Crime Writers*, ed. H. R. F. Keating (BBC, 1978), p. 68.
9. C. Watson, 'Mayhem Parva and Wicked Belgravia', in *Crime Writers*, p. 63.
10. C. Dexter, 'Morse and Me', *Oxford Today*, 2 (Hilary, 1990), p. 37.
11. Marsh Papers, ATL.
12. N. Marsh, 'Entertainments', *Pacific Moana Quarterly*, 3 (Jan. 1978), p. 30.
13. P. D. James, 'A Life of Crime', *Independent Magazine*, 56 (30 Sept. 1989), p. 52.
14. Marsh papers, ATL.
15. Symons, *Bloody Murder*, p. 141.
16. J. Mann, *Deadlier than the Male* (London, 1981), p. 238.
17. Mann, p. 226.
18. W. Woeller and B. Cassiday, *The Literature of Crime and Detection* (New York, 1988), p. 152.
19. Broadcast talk on NZ Radio, 1 Jan. 1957.
20. *BB*, p. 196.
21. *BB*, p. 30.
22. D. Modjeska, *Exiles at Home* (London, 1981), p. 6.

23. Interview, BBC Radio, 9 July, 1960.
24. J. A. Catchpole, 'The Group', unpublished MA thesis, University of Canterbury, 1984, p. 60.
25. Letter dated 9 March, 1990, printed in *The Press*, Christchurch.
26. Bruce Mason Papers, Victoria University of Wellington.
27. C. Acheson, 'Cultural Ambivalence: Ngaio Marsh's New Zealand Detective Fiction', *Journal of Popular Culture*, 19 (1985), p. 165.
28. Unpublished ms in St Margaret's College, Christchurch.
29. N. Marsh, 'Portrait of Troy', in *Murderess Ink*, ed. D. Wynn (New York, 1979) p. 142.
30. C. Tomalin, *Katherine Mansfield; a life* (London, 1987), p. 7.
31. *BB*, p. 307.
32. N. Marsh (with R. M. Burdon), *New Zealand* (London, 1942), p. 47.
33. Marsh Papers, ATL.

CHAPTER 5
1. B. Mason and J. Pocock, *Theatre in Danger* (Hamilton and Auckland, 1957), p. 5.
2. Mason and Pocock, p. 6.
3. N. Marsh, *A Play Toward* (Christchurch, 1946), p. 26.
4. Broadcast on New Zealand Radio, 1 Jan. 1965.
5. Marsh Papers, ATL.
6. L. Edmond, *Hot October* (Auckland, 1989), p. 219.
7. Douglas Lilburn Papers, ATL.

CHAPTER 6
1. *Oxford History of New Zealand*, ed. W. H. Oliver (Oxford, 1981), p. 430.
2. A. Curnow, *Four Plays* (Wellington, 1972), p. 7.
3. N. Marsh, 'Shakespeare in New Zealand', *Education*, 1 (1948), p. 226.
4. *BB*, pp. 76–7.
5. BBC Written Archives Centre, Caversham Park, Reading.
6. *BB*, p. 226.
7. BBC Sound Archives, London.
8. Bruce Mason Papers.
9. R. Walker, 'New Zealand', *World Theatre*, 3:1 (1952), p. 58.

CHAPTER 7
1. *BB*, pp. 241–2.
2. Marsh Papers, ATL.
3. Marsh Papers, ATL.
4. N. Marsh, 'Perspectives: the New Zealander and the Visual Arts' (Auckland, 1960), p. 16.
5. N. Marsh, 'My Poor Boy', *NZ Listener*, 16 Aug. 1957, p. 8.

CHAPTER 8
1. David Farquhar Papers, ATL.
2. Marsh Papers, ATL.
3. David Farquhar Papers, ATL.
4. 'A Unicorn Remembered', *Music in New Zealand* (Summer 1988/89), p. 16.

5. 'A Unicorn Remembered', p. 17.
6. A. Curnow, *Four Plays* (Wellington, 1972), p. 21.
7. W. Dart, 'A Unicorn for Christmas', *Music in New Zealand* (Summer 1988/ 89), p. 18.
8. N. Marsh, 'Achievement in Fine Arts', *The Times*, 6 Feb. 1963 (New Zealand Supp.), p. vi.
9. Marsh Papers, ATL.

CHAPTER 9
1. Bruce Mason Papers.
2. J. Ball, 'Introduction', in N. Marsh, *Death in a White Tie* (New York, 1984), p. xiii.
3. *BB*, p. 230.
4. N. Marsh, 'A Note on a Production of *Twelfth Night*', *Shakespeare Survey* (Cambridge, 1955), p. 71.
5. M. Thompson, *All My Lives* (Christchurch, 1980), p. 74.
6. Bruce Mason Papers.
7. N. Marsh, 'Brigid Lenihan', *Act*, 12 (Nov/Dec. 1970), p. 2.
8. J. Paul and N. Roberts, *Evelyn Page: Seven Decades* (Christchurch, 1986), p. 45.
9. Harold Ober Papers, Princeton University Libraries.
10. Harold Ober Papers.

CHAPTER 10
1. *BB*, p. 268.
2. Bruce Mason Papers.
3. Bruce Mason Papers.
4. J. B. Priestley, *A Visit to New Zealand* (London, 1974), p. 102.
5. Priestley, p. 104.
6. Priestley, p. 105.
7. Harold Ober Papers.
8. Marsh Papers, ATL.

CHAPTER 11
1. Lord Ballantrae Papers, National Library of Scotland.
2. Harold Ober Papers.
3. M. Thompson, *All My Lives* (Christchurch, 1980), p. 76.
4. Ballantrae Papers.
5. Ballantrae Papers.
6. Bruce Mason Papers.
7. Ballantrae Papers.
8. Introduction to *Death in a White Tie*, ed. John Ball (New York, 1984), p. xii.
9. Bruce Mason Papers.
10. N. Marsh, 'It's Not What We Say', *NZ Listener*, 14 Oct. 1978, 90 (2024), p. 23.
11. M. Thompson, 'On the Death of Ngaio Marsh', *Landfall*, 36:4 (Dec. 1982), pp. 442–6.
12. *BB*, pp. 265–6.
13. Bruce Mason Papers.
14. *BB*, p. 86.
15. Harold Ober Papers.

BIBLIOGRAPHY OF WORKS BY NGAIO MARSH

NOVELS

A Man Lay Dead, London, Bles, 1934; New York, Sheridan, 1942.

Enter a Murderer, London, Bles, 1935; New York, Sheridan, 1942.

The Nursing Home Murder, with Henry Jellett. London, Bles, 1935; New York, Sheridan, 1941.

Death in Ecstasy, London, Bles, 1936; New York, Sheridan, 1941.

Vintage Murder, London, Bles, 1937; New York, Sheridan, 1940.

Artists in Crime, London, Bles, and New York, Furman, 1938.

Death in a White Tie, London, Bles, and New York, Furman, 1938.

Overture to Death, London, Collins, and New York, Furman, 1939.

Death at the Bar, London, Collins, and Boston, Little, Brown, 1940.

Death of a Peer, Boston, Little, Brown, 1940; as *Surfeit of Lampreys*, London, Collins, 1941.

Death and the Dancing Footman, Boston, Little, Brown, 1941; London, Collins, 1942.

Colour Scheme, London, Collins, and Boston, Little, Brown, 1943.

Died in the Wool, London, Collins, and Boston, Little, Brown, 1945.

Final Curtain, London, Collins, and Boston, Little, Brown, 1947.

Swing, Brother, Swing, London, Collins, 1949; as *A Wreath for Rivera*, Boston Little, Brown, 1949.

Opening Night, London, Collins, 1951; as *Night at the Vulcan*, Boston, Little, Brown, 1951.

Spinsters in Jeopardy, Boston, Little, Brown, 1953; London, Collins, 1954; as *The Bride of Death*, New York, Spivak, 1955.

Scales of Justice, London, Collins, and Boston, Little, Brown, 1955.

Death of a Fool, Boston, Little, Brown, 1956; as *Off with His Head*, London, Collins, 1957.

Singing in the Shrouds, Boston, Little, Brown, 1958; London, Collins, 1959.

False Scent, London, Collins, and Boston, Little, Brown, 1960.

Hand in Glove, London, Collins, and Boston, Little, Brown, 1962.

Dead Water, Boston, Little, Brown, 1963; London, Collins, 1964.

Killer Dolphin, Boston, Little, Brown, 1966; as *Death at the Dolphin*, London, Collins, 1967.

Clutch of Constables, London, Collins, 1968; Boston, Little, Brown, 1969.

When in Rome, London, Collins, 1970; Boston, Little, Brown, 1971.

Tied Up in Tinsel, London, Collins, and Boston, Little, Brown, 1972.

Black as He's Painted, London, Collins, and Boston, Little, Brown, 1974.

Last Ditch, London, Collins, and Boston, Little, Brown, 1977.

Grave Mistake, London, Collins, and Boston, Little, Brown, 1978.

Photo-Finish, London, Collins, and Boston, Little, Brown, 1980.

Light Thickens, London, Collins, and Boston, Little, Brown, 1982.

SHORT STORIES
'Moonshine', in *Yours and Mine*, ed. W. Lawrence, New Plymouth, 1936.
The Collected Short Fiction of Ngaio Marsh, ed. Douglas G. Greene, New
York, IPL, 1989. (This volume contains seven known short stories by
Ngaio Marsh, plus other short pieces.)

NON-FICTION
New Zealand (with R. M. Burdon), London, Collins, 1942.
A Play Toward; A Note on Play Production, Christchurch, Caxton Press,
1946.
Play Production (with drawings by Sam Williams), Wellington, Post-
Primary School Bulletin, 1948; revised 1960.
Perspectives; The New Zealander and the Visual Arts, Auckland, Auckland
Gallery Associates, 1960.
New Zealand, New York, Macmillan, 1964; London, Collier Macmillan,
1965.
Black Beech and Honeydew: An Autobiography, Boston, Little, Brown, 1965;
London, Collins, 1966; revised edition, Collins, Auckland 1981;
London, 1982.

PLAYS
Published:
The Christmas Tree, London, SPCK, 1962.

Unpublished:
Little Housebound, produced 1922, New Zealand.
Exit Sir Derek (with Henry Jellett), produced 1935, New Zealand.
The Wyvern and the Unicorn, produced 1955, New Zealand. This play was
the basis for the libretto written by Marsh for the opera *A Unicorn for
Christmas*, produced 1962, New Zealand.
False Scent (with Eileen Mackay), produced 1961, UK.
Murder Sails at Midnight, produced 1972, UK.
Sweet Mr. Shakespeare (with Jonathan Elsom), produced 1976, New
Zealand; Norwegian Television 1985 as *Gentle Master Shakespeare*.

TELEVISION SCRIPT
Evil Liver, broadcast 1975, Granada, UK. (Published in *The Collected Short
Fiction of Ngaio Marsh*, ed. Douglas G. Greene, New York, 1989.)

A number of adaptations of novels by Ngaio Marsh for radio, television and
the stage, have been made by other hands and are not listed here.

ARTICLES
'Theatre: a note on the Status Quo', *Landfall*, 1 (March 1947), 37–43.
'Shakespeare in New Zealand', *Education*, 1 (1948), 226–30.
'National Theatre', *Landfall*, 3 (March 1949), 66–9.
'A Note on a Production of *Twelfth Night*', *Shakespeare Survey*, 8 (1955),
69–73.

'New Zealand: Welfare Paradise', *Holiday*, 28:5 (November 1960), 102–8.
'Achievement in Fine Arts', The Times, 6 February 1963 (New Zealand Supplement), p. vi.
'The Quick Forge', *Landfall*, 18 (1964), 32–40.
'Stratford-on-Avon', *Atlantic Monthly* (February 1967), 116–18.
'Birth of a Sleuth', *The Writer* (April 1977), 23–5.
'Entertainments', *Pacific Moana Quarterly*, 3 (January 1978), 27–32.
'Portrait of Troy', in *Murderess Ink*, ed. Dilys Winn (Workman, New York, 1979), 142–3.
'A Dialogue with Ngaio Marsh', in *Look Back Harder*, by Allen Curnow, ed. P. Simpson (Oxford University Press, Auckland, 1987), 76–82.

A full listing of shorter, journalistic pieces is available in the Periodical Index issued annually by the National Library of New Zealand.

BROADCASTS
Recordings of radio and television broadcasts by Ngaio Marsh are held in the archives of BBC London, Radio New Zealand and New Zealand Television.

INDEX

ABOUT THE AUTHOR

Margaret Lewis was invited by the Estate of Ngaio Marsh to write the biography of this Queen of Crime shortly after her death in 1982, and it was first published in England by Chatto and Windus in 1991. Dr Lewis brought to the task a love of Shakespeare and the stage, a knowledge of Australian and New Zealand writing, and a thorough background in crime fiction. Many surprising aspects of the achievements of Ngaio Marsh emerge from this account of a lifetime's work as a writer, painter and theatre producer.

Dr Lewis was born in Northern Ireland but grew up in Canada and now lives near Hadrian's Wall in northern England. A friendship with Edith Pargeter led to the publication in 1994 of *Edith Pargeter: Ellis Peters*, a book about this popular author. Her tribute to Ellis Peters was published in *AZ Murder Goes . . . Classic*, published by Poisoned Pen Press in 1997. Much thought about the nature of biography, especially of crime fiction writers, led to her essay 'Sharing the Role: the Biographer as Sleuth' being included in *The Literary Biography: Problems and Solutions* published by Macmillan in 1996.

A member of the Crime Writers' Association, Margaret Lewis has published short stories in various anthologies of crime fiction and several of these have been broadcast on radio. She has lectured extensively throughout the world and has run workshops on creative writing and biography. With her husband Peter Lewis she helps to run Flambard Press, a small publishing company which is particularly sympathetic to writers from the north of England.